Debacle

Failing to Rebuild the Twin Towers

A Collection of Essays

Joe Wright, Editor

Opinions expressed herein by individual writers of essays are theirs and theirs alone and may not reflect the opinions of other fellow writers.

Debacle — Failing to Rebuild the Twin Towers — A Collection of Essays

First Edition, September 2011

Editor: Joe Wright
Associate Editor: Alexander Butziger
Cover design: Gary Taustine

Back cover photo courtesy of Ken Gardner and Margaret Donovan.

ISBN-13: 978-0615543444
ISBN-10: 0615543448

Published in the United States of America by
Klaatu Publishing Company
P. O. Box 20198
Staten Island, New York 10302

www.klaatupublishing.com

Debacle

Failing to Rebuild
the
Twin Towers

A Collection of Essays

Make no little plans; they have no magic to stir men's blood and probably will themselves not be realized. Make big plans; aim high in hope and work, remembering that a noble, logical diagram once recorded will not die.

— Daniel H. Burnham

Contents

Foreword

By Edward Cline

When the Greeks won their independence from the repressive Ottoman Empire in 1832, they did not replace the Parthenon, damaged by war and vandalism for centuries, but still the symbol of Western civilization, with a temple of humility and a memorial to the dead. They left it standing, one supposes, in hopes of reclaiming the glory that was once ancient Greece, the memory of which the Turks were not successful in erasing.

When central London was destroyed by fire in 1666, no wooden or thatch-roofed buildings were erected in place of those that were destroyed. Among his other accomplishments, Christopher Wren designed many new permanent buildings and scores of monuments to the glory of the city and his country. And when that same city was blitzed during World War II, it was rebuilt, first with "cloud-scratchers," then with skyscrapers.

When Lisbon was leveled by an earthquake in 1755, its citizens immediately set to work to rebuild the city, allotting a scattering of memorials to the 30,000 who perished.

When Chicago was consumed by fire in 1872, it was rebuilt to become the commercial hub of the Midwest. And when San Francisco was devastated by earthquake and fire in 1906, it was rapidly rebuilt and became the premier city of commerce, finance and industry in the West.

The phenomenon was repeated in other cities, as well. Its leitmotif is reminiscent of the *Rocky* movies that were so popular and successful, especially in this country: If knocked down, you get back up again. Pride is not a defining attribute of the vanquished. The prizefighter who lay humbled on the mat never beat the one who knocked him down.

Unlike most of the cities cited above, New York City was not the subject of a disaster, but the first target of an act of war. On September 11, 2001, two planes hijacked and piloted by Islamic suicide bombers flew into the North and South Towers of the World Trade Center in lower Manhattan. Within hours, nearly 3,000 people were subsequently murdered as the towers burned and collapsed. These twin shimmering shafts of silvery metal once dominated the skyline of New York, sharing the glory once held alone by the Empire State Building far uptown.

Their collapse created a void in the sky.

The final "official" plans for what is intended to replace the World Trade Center towers called for a humble seventy-story building topped by windmills and empty space, and two gigantic pits as a memorial to the victims of the attack. What has replaced that planned "submission" to Islam is a banal collection of nondescript structures designed by men of no vision.

If those plans come to fruition, the void will remain, except that it will be accentuated by a forgettable non-entity and the "footprints" of a murdered giant.

Another void will also remain, one almost as tangible as the physical void: the void of an absence of pride and courage, the void of the conquered.

This is not the way of a great city. This is not getting back up to stand tall and fight again. This is an exercise in humility and deference to the malevolence of a creed that demands mindless obedience and abject submission. It is a concession to murderers, to the sworn enemies of this country. As Joe Wright, editor of this volume of essays, remarks, the final plans have posthumously named Mohammed Atta as the preferred chief city planner of the greatest city on earth.

Remember, dear reader: Atta, Osama bin Laden, and all their cohorts and allies in terror and destruction wanted those towers removed. They were a reproach and a contradiction to their life-hating philosophy, an intransigent refutation of it. They removed those towers, to teach us a lesson. They attacked the Pentagon, to teach us a lesson. They might have destroyed the Capitol Building in Washington, to teach us a lesson, except that their hostages would not let them.

New Yorkers were not taught a lesson, and neither was the country. As many of the contributors to this volume point out, most New Yorkers want the World Trade Center rebuilt, "as tall or taller." They were knocked down, but got back up. They expected their political and commercial leaders to get back up. They didn't.

That must be said about former Governor George E. Pataki, the Lower Manhattan Development Corporation, Mayor Michael R. Bloomberg, or any other individual or organization responsible for what is intended to replace the Twin Towers.

They were all taught a lesson by the terrorists. Beneath all the rationalizations and excuses for not rebuilding the World Trade Center, behind all the arguments for a maudlin "memorial" to the victims, are resignation, defeat and not a little self-pity — coupled in many instances with their own hatred of the towers and America. None of those attributes describes the American way of triumph.

On the morning of September 11, 2001, I was at my desk, on the job, in Newport News, Virginia, when an employee of another company in the building came into the front office and asked me if we had a television. I said, no, we didn't, and why did she ask? "There's something in the news about the World Trade Center falling down."

I froze. The employee left. I asked a colleague to turn her radio to a news station. And it was true. Two planes had plowed into the World Trade Center. Details were sketchy.

But, I knew what it meant. Two planes? What were the chances of two planes flying off-course and colliding with the tallest buildings in the western hemisphere? I knew that it was not an accident, not coincidence, not chance. It was a declaration of war against America, carried to American soil, not against a ship or an embassy or a military base, but against the proudest symbols of America: her skyscrapers. I had watched the mammoth hole being dug for those towers, even as another symbol of American capitalism, the Singer Tower on Broadway, was being demolished. It was making way for an even taller building, the Merrill-Lynch tower and plaza. During my Wall Street years, I had worked in the Twin Towers, had used the Path and city subway stations beneath them, eaten in the underground restaurants, browsed in the concourse bookshop and bought papers at its newsstands. It had been a part of my life. And now it was gone.

Killers had destroyed it. They had declared war on my country. On me. But, my first reaction was as to a personal loss. I wept. I left work. I wept as I drove home to Yorktown, where another breed of American was victorious and unashamed of being victorious. It was the most I had ever wept in my entire life, because I knew what it meant. I knew that this act of aggression would change things, and either accelerate or block the progress of my life and ambition. I got back up and fought on.

Now, I knew that the World Trade Center was government property, owned and operated by the Port Authority of New York and New Jersey, with its office and commercial space leased to mostly private businesses. Taxes had paid for its construction, together with special bond issues. I am opposed in principle to government and business "partnerships," but this is not the place to dwell on that facet of politics. The World Trade Center towers were symbols of American capitalism, for it was capitalism that made them possible, capitalism that was responsible for every rivet, beam and fixture in their structure. The towers were living monuments to reason and liberty. They complemented the upraised torch of the Statue of Liberty in New York Harbor.

I took a series of photographs of the towers from the Staten Island Ferry over the years. They record their rise from tarp-covered stumps low to the ground to their topping off. These photographs are precious to me now. It is almost as though they were photographs of the Alexandrian lighthouse on Pharos, or of the Colossus of Rhodes. Once wonders of the world. Also gone.

I will not say much about what is intended to replace those towers. Every one of the contributors to this volume says it for me. They are angry, proud, determined people who will get up again, who refuse to accept defeat. They say that it is not a new World Trade Center that is being proposed, but a shabby, disgraceful substitute whose design and theme have been the subject of politics, committees and plain venality. Virtually every design for the site that I have seen has left me gasping in disbelief; the "final" design plans call for a stooped mendicant pleading for pity and forgiveness. They have less dignity than the Rococo facades of an old-fashioned carnival house of amusement. If the victims of September 11th must be memorialized — and I believe they should be — let it be with towers that are as tall as or taller than the ones they perished in, more shimmering and blinding in the sun than their predecessors.

If the Libeskind-Pataki plan for a tower of apology and humility is implemented, then Mohammed Atta and his crew will have had the last word. They will have taught those particular Americans a lesson. They do not speak for me.

The contributors to this book do.

Edward Cline
Williamsburg, Virginia
September 2011

World trade means world peace and, consequently, the World Trade Center buildings in New York... had a bigger purpose than just to provide room for tenants. The World Trade Center is a living symbol of man's dedication to world peace. Beyond the compelling need to make this a monument to world peace, the World Trade Center should, because of its importance, become a representation of man's belief in humanity, his need for individual dignity, his beliefs in the cooperation of men, and through cooperation, his ability to find greatness.

— Minoru Yamasaki

Rebuilding the WTC: On the Fast Track to a Train Wreck

By Andrew Oliff

On September 11, 2001, three of our landmarks and national symbols were targeted for attack by terrorists. Two succeeded, while our Capitol Building was spared due to the bravery of the passengers on board United Airlines Flight 93. After the attack on the Pentagon, reconstruction proceeded without a second thought as "Project Phoenix" quickly got underway, and even the family members of the Pentagon victims took part in its restoration. As a result of the vision and patriotism of those entrusted with its rebuilding, the Pentagon has been restored to what it was on September 10, 2001, along with a significant memorial to those who were killed. Undoubtedly, the same would have been done had Flight 93 reached its intended target.

In New York City, a similar sentiment was shared in the days right after 9/11, as Mayor Rudolph Giuliani assured us, "our skyline will rise again," while many political leaders sounded determined to "…rebuild, better than ever." Developer Larry Silverstein, who in 1999 purchased a 99-year lease of the World Trade Center, proclaimed, "it would be the tragedy of tragedies not to rebuild this part of New York. The city is not dead and can't be allowed to die. We owe [rebuilding] to our children and our grandchildren." There was much support for bringing back our skyline so as to rise above the terror and not let the forces of evil have the last word in destroying our World Trade Center and killing 2,752 innocent people. As former New York City Mayor Ed Koch explained, "a suitable memorial will be erected, but the two loved and admired towers should be rebuilt."

However, in the months following the attacks, two groups emerged with the power to obstruct the rebuilding effort at a level unprecedented in the history of any city throughout the world recovering from a wartime attack.

The families of the people who died in the attack on the World Trade Center were still reeling from the loss of their loved ones without any body to claim, a loss that could have been prevented if government agencies had taken the threat of Islamic terrorism seriously. The grief-stricken families of these victims needed and deserved much support, and did get it from people throughout the nation via charitable donations, and from a fund set up by the government.

The issue of how far we would go to ease their pain was taken to new levels when certain organized groups of victims' families came to believe that the World Trade Center site was "theirs" by virtue of their family members' having died upon it. They soon became quite vocal in their demand that no rebuilding should be done anywhere on the "sacred and hallowed ground" of the sixteen-acre World Trade Center site, nor where 7 WTC had collapsed. The emotionalism of these organized victims' families groups and their grief made them beyond reproach, while anyone with a desire to rebuild, especially those wanting to see the Twin Towers restored to their former glory, was automatically labeled as greedy, insensitive or even blasphemous to the dead. It came to be, in their minds, that the Twin Towers themselves, rather than the terrorists, were responsible for the deaths.

In reality, no one in the late 1960s, when the World Trade Center was designed, could have predicted that airplanes, fully loaded with jet fuel for a transcontinental flight, would be used as guided missiles to attack the Twin Towers. No building would have been expected to absorb an attack of that magnitude, and it is even more remarkable that they remained standing as long as they did, allowing 99% of those below the sites of impact of the planes to make it out alive. The Port Authority estimated that approximately 25,000 people were in the complex the morning of 9/11, but thanks largely to the efforts of our rescue workers, 89% of them survived.

Grief is known to influence judgment and impede long-term thinking, yet those in charge of the rebuilding effort allowed short-term "feel-good" judgments unduly influenced by grief to play an inordinately large role in shaping the destiny of Lower Manhattan. The politicians, who are used to pandering without thinking to that which is politically correct, quickly abandoned their former ideas on rebuilding. Mayor Giuliani decided that only a sixteen-acre "soaring memorial" could be built on the site, something that "enshrined forever" the destruction of 9/11. He failed to comprehend that the only thing this would do for future generations is shame them into living with an open wound from 9/11 that just says "Osama was here, and we dare not reclaim this land from his act of terrorism against us." Shortly afterwards, Governor George E. Pataki, engaging in some election-year pandering in a speech to victims' families, shortsightedly decreed that "nothing will be built where those towers stood," which the activist family groups took to mean that the site was thereafter promised to them from "bedrock to infinity." This train wreck of a rebuilding process thus started off on the wrong track with an artificial wedge driven between memorialization and remembrance on one hand, and rebuilding, recovery and renewal on the other.

How is it that this city could not follow the example of Washington, D.C., where the restoration of the Pentagon and the memorial proceeded as a singular vision, where one did not eclipse the other? Instead of working together to ensure that the Twin Towers and World Trade Center could be resurrected to their former glory as a bold statement for the future and belief in our city, complemented by a memorial to the victims, rebuilding and memorialization became opposite poles in a ludicrous, unnecessary conflict, magnified by pandering politicians who were loathe to be called "insensitive."

Everyone intent on rebuilding recognized the loss and sacrifices of 9/11, and wanted an appropriate memorial to honor those who were murdered, but incomprehensibly, those who were pro-rebuilding came to be labeled, by these victims' families groups, "anti-memorial," "narrow-minded," and "insensitive to the needs of the families." Such *ad hominem* attacks prevented any dialogue between these groups, for any desire to rebuild was tantamount to trespassing on their private graveyard.

When in the history of wartime or natural disasters has there been such an obsession over square footage and volume of a memorial, so much so as to scuttle any talk of rebuilding or recovery from an attack? What other city in history in this world has ever failed to rebuild its landmarks after acts of war? It is the nature of cities to rebuild what was destroyed. In cities throughout history, rebuilding followed natural disasters and wars that killed thousands and millions. In Hiroshima and Nagasaki, the only true Ground Zeroes, 120,000 civilians died, yet they rebuilt their cities. In Europe in World War II, over 20 million civilians perished and cities were reduced to rubble, but throughout the continent, restoration of what was destroyed proceeded without a second thought. Downtown London and downtown Warsaw were restored without obsessing over footprints and bedrock, for they would not let Nazis design their cities, nor were they obsessed with turning every incinerated edifice into a memorial park! Churchill said about the leveled House of Commons, "We will rebuild it down to the last brick."

Yet we are prepared to let terrorists design downtown New York City.

In Pearl Harbor after December 7, 1941, any ship that could be put back into action was raised and repaired, despite soldiers having died in those ships during the Japanese attack. San Francisco rebuilt after the 1906 earthquake that killed over 3,000 people, Galveston, Texas rebuilt after a hurricane in 1900 took 6,000 lives, and after Hurricane Katrina, in which over 1,000 citizens of New Orleans were killed by the flooding, there is the desire to rebuild the city, not abandon it as flooded ruins. In what way are the dead dishonored by rebuilding over the place where they were killed? How is a city or people being materialistic or greedy by rebuilding after a destructive attack or a natural disaster?

This idea of not being allowed to use a site after mass fatalities occur at a site is, when stripped of its emotional connotation, absurd and a terrible precedent, particularly in light of threats of additional terrorist attacks against our landmarks. If individuals are killed in a terrorist attack on our landmarks, are we not allowed to rebuild them?

The US government is cloning our national icons and landmark buildings, so they can be resurrected if another terrorist attack destroys them. It is doubtful that many Americans want to see their national symbols destroyed by terrorists only to be turned into footprint memorials. If we were prevented from rebuilding our national landmarks in fear that in doing so we would dishonor the dead and be insensitive to the families of the victims, it would hand the terrorists a complete victory and grant them the ability to permanently mar our cities.

On a smaller scale, one can already see the consequences of such an idea in the aftermath of American Airlines Flight 587. That plane, carrying 260 people, crashed into Belle Harbor on November 12, 2001, killing all aboard and five people on the ground as well as demolishing a house. The families of the crash victims want the land where the destroyed house stood as a memorial, while the owners sold their property to a friend who intends to rebuild the home.

The issue of "sacred and hallowed ground" has been at the root of the specious argument that it is verboten to rebuild on ground stained with blood, and Lincoln's Gettysburg Address has been misused as the blueprint for deleting the World Trade Center site from urban reality. Ground Zero is sacred ground and hallowed ground, but by what twisted sense of history has that definition come to mean that it must be left as a hole in the ground or a footprint memorial?

Those who make historic analogies to Gettysburg are advised to learn their history and actually read the Gettysburg Address! The Battle of Gettysburg took place over three days. The first day's battle took place entirely within the town of Gettysburg, including over an open railroad cut that was being built at the time. The Confederate troops routed the Federal armies from the town, who regrouped at Cemetery Ridge. Over the next two days, the battle was fought in what was farmland, and nearby barns were used as both morgues and hospitals. After the war, the barns and much of the farmland were returned to their owners, and the town of Gettysburg repaired its wounds, including that railroad where so much blood was shed. This was the rail route used by Lincoln to come to the battlefield to give his Gettysburg Address. In it, he states:

> But in a larger sense, we cannot dedicate, we cannot consecrate, we cannot hallow this ground. The brave men, *living* and dead who struggled here have consecrated it far above our poor power to add or detract. The world will little note nor long remember what we say here, but it can never forget what they did here. It is for us the living rather to be dedicated here to the unfinished work which they who fought here have thus far so nobly advanced.

According to the Gettysburg Address then, we the living who survived that day, including the 20,000 or so who made it out of the World Trade Center alive and the residents of the vicinity who were on the front lines of the 9/11 attacks, have also consecrated the ground! These individuals thus have as much right to the site as do the families of the dead, Pataki's promise notwithstanding. Indeed, the residents of Lower Manhattan and survivors of 9/11 do have a moral claim as well to the site, as per Lincoln. Their determination to rebuild their lives in a scarred area and take the World Trade Center site back from bin Laden in order to reintegrate it into the urban fabric should be commended and facilitated, and not obstructed! Additionally, those who choose to dedicate themselves to the unfinished work of those in the World Trade Center should not be denied the right to do so in restored commercial Twin Towers!

The second group of obstructionists are those for whom the World Trade Center and its association with business, finance and capitalism are something to be ashamed of. They disliked the Twin Towers as representations of greed, which, in their minds, brought on the attacks of 9/11. Now, according to these individuals, we had a welcome opportunity to remake the World Trade Center into a nonprofit paradise of cultural amenities or to indulge in any urban renewal fantasy they thought they could impose on the site. For them, the destruction of the World Trade Center was taken as a signal to have an urban renewal orgy the likes of which have never been seen since the days of Robert Moses.

While the fires in the World Trade Center were still burning, and human remains still blanketed the site, these utopian urban renewal activists acted like vultures picking over the carcass of the World Trade Center. As a result of their anti-business urban planning agenda, discussion of "commerce" and "office space" was forbidden, while the newly-created Lower Manhattan Redevelopment Corporation (which, in the spirit of anti-rebuilding urban renewal, was later renamed the Lower Manhattan Development Corporation or LMDC) wasted months obsessing over "street life," "greenery," "24/7 neighborhoods," and cultural amenities. Anything and everything was considered fair game to shove onto those sixteen acres but office skyscrapers, and every aspect of the World Trade Center as it existed prior to 9/11 had to be changed or "re-imagined." Apartment buildings, a high school, a new United Nations building, an art museum, an opera house, a fish market, jazz clubs, etc., were all at one point or another being seriously considered as part of the rebuilt World Trade Center. Never mind that other areas in the city have their own identity incorporating these elements that were to be imposed on the World Trade Center site. For street life and jazz clubs, one should go to the Village. There's an opera house in Brooklyn and at Lincoln Center. Why the sudden rush to change the commercial identity of the Financial District?

The concourse-level shopping center that was one of Westfield America's most successful malls and a favorite of workers, residents and tourists to the area, was derided as a suburban shopping mall that should have no place in the city. The LMDC soon scuttled Westfield America's desire to rebuild their shopping center by forcing most of the stores onto the streets to improve "street life," forcing this company to finally sell its lease.

Additionally, issues that were never given a second thought prior to 9/11 suddenly became requirements of the rebuilding effort. Now, the LMDC wanted every street from Radio Row days sliced through the World Trade Center site, turning it from a respite from the noise and congestion of Lower Manhattan to a traffic shortcut for cars and trucks bypassing Broadway and West Street. This must be the first time in city history that development groups favored streets filled with noise pollution and exhaust over a pedestrian-only area protected from traffic that once characterized the original World Trade Center plaza. The LMDC wanted West Street buried, for it had suddenly become a barrier that it never was before 9/11. It took the vocal opposition of residents of the area to defeat this misguided plan. To make the World Trade Center site a blank slate for urban renewal agendas is to forever acknowledge bin Laden as its urban planner.

Yet, politicians jumped on this urban renewal bandwagon, with advisory groups to the LMDC such as Civic Alliance and Imagine New York leading the way in their agenda for "re-imagination" of the World Trade Center site. In doing so, these groups and politicians paid only lip service to the importance of jobs and the economy. They failed to comprehend that if we were ever to recover from 9/11, only functional buildings fully integrated in our business district would bring back the 100,000 jobs we lost as a result of the attacks on our Financial District. The urban renewal groups had an obvious bias against skyscrapers, and created the term "skyline element" to reconcile their agenda for "human-scale" buildings with the public's desire to see a skyscraper (or preferably two) replace the towers that were destroyed. In this way, they would subvert the people's desire for tall towers to a desire for a "skyline element," and sell the LMDC on replacing the height that was lost on 9/11 by adding a fifty-story pole or antenna to a sixty-story building.

When Mayor Michael R. Bloomberg came into office, it was hoped that he, as a businessman, would recognize the value in Downtown being left as a business district. Unfortunately, in that respect, he did not contribute a thing of value to the redevelopment of the World Trade Center site, but became a champion of the urban renewal vultures. He obsessed over making Downtown more residential, as he sought to pursue utopian redevelopment schemes involving parks and affordable housing. How would this help the economy of a Downtown struggling to remain economically viable? Without restoration of the jobs lost on 9/11, few people would be able to afford the rents of Downtown housing, maintain the parks, or enjoy the cultural amenities. He also became fixated on giving our airports in Queens, comprising a total of 5,610 acres of very active land generating $188.4 million a year, to the Port Authority in return for the sixteen-acre World Trade Center site so he could have a personal sandbox in which to promote his political agenda. It is fortunate that this idea and Bloomberg's urban renewal pipe dreams for the site were killed when the Port Authority's lease on the airports was renegotiated and extended.

The Twin Towers were targeted for their symbolism, their representation of our commercial enterprise, which we as Americans should be proud of, not ashamed of. They were an important part of Lower Manhattan, which has been and always should be the financial capital of the world. The World Trade Center before September 11, 2001, was an active, diverse community with 45,000 to 50,000 workers and numerous tourists most every day.

Unfortunately, the domination of the rebuilding effort by the above two groups of rebuilding obstructionists, who had great power over the politicians and the LMDC, effectively destroyed any consideration by the powers-that-be of rebuilding the World Trade Center's Twin Towers. Their arguments also contributed to the marginalization and suppression, as well as outright denigration, of the voices of those who expressed that viewpoint.

Nevertheless, there still remained that post-9/11 idealism in which we truly believed that the aspirations of the people for the World Trade Center site, whether it be restoring the Twin Towers or rebuilding a truly monumental new World Trade Center, would be taken into consideration. This is what inspired thousands of ordinary citizens to attend the July 2002 Javits Convention Center Listening to the City event, at which the Port Authority's six plans for a new World Trade Center were voted down and criticized as too bland ("looks like Albany" was the most memorable and illustrative criticism). In fact, a desire expressed by the majority of New Yorkers at that hearing was to bring awe-inspiring towers back to the Lower Manhattan skyline. As a result of the outcry against the Port Authority's six plans, the LMDC came out with its "Nine Innovative Plans" for the World Trade Center site in December of 2002. Both the LMDC and our politicians promised an open process whereby the public's input would count as the World Trade Center was rebuilt. As a result, hearings were held at Pace University, comments were elicited, and official polls were taken. We truly believed that we would have an impact on this process and that what would rise at World Trade Center site would reflect the will of the people.

Sadly and unexpectedly, the rebuilding process turned out to be a monumental fraud: Lip service was paid to the so-called transparency and participatory nature of rebuilding, while behind closed doors, only special-interest concerns and political agendas were considered. This is blatantly obvious in how the winning site plan was chosen. The two finalists selected from the nine plans were Libeskind's Gardens of the World and THINK's World Cultural Center. This was despite the public's first choice, by a clear plurality (nearly 20% of those polled), of the site plan by Foster. All subsequent polls taken at the time the finalists were chosen indicated that the public was not satisfied with either finalist, and preferred "none of the above."

Results on Imagine New York (the LMDC's official poll):

Libeskind	205 votes	26%
THINK	260 votes	33%
None of the above	323 votes	41%
Total	788 votes	

Results on NY1:
Results since February 4, 2003

Libeskind	6,853 votes	21%
THINK	4,615 votes	14%
I don't like either of these plans.	20,892 votes	64%
Total	32,360 votes	

Results on CNN:
Which of the two finalists' designs do you prefer for the World Trade Center site?

Libeskind	33,050 votes	32%
THINK	34,867 votes	34%
Neither is good.	35,747 votes	34%
Total	103,664 votes	

The above numbers also mean that 68-86% of the people voted *against* Libeskind! Even the LMDC did not favor Libeskind, as they were prepared to go with the THINK Team! So why, if the agency entrusted to listen to us in the selection of the site plan was not thrilled with Libeskind, are we stuck with this plan? The answer is that in the end, only one issue mattered: the preference of Governor George E. Pataki. This is blatantly obvious in a *Daily News* article from February 27, 2003:

> Preference for the THINK plan… contributed to a key corporation committee's decision to endorse that plan Tuesday. But it wasn't enough to sway Governor Pataki — the top decision-maker in the rebuilding process. Sources added that City Hall considered endorsing THINK up until early yesterday, but Mayor Bloomberg backed Libeskind.

Pataki single-handedly defied popular opinion, overruled his LMDC, and imposed designer Daniel Libeskind's monstrosity on our city. Ultimately, rebuilding the World Trade Center became nothing more than a vehicle by which Pataki could advance his political career. The members of the LMDC, as little more than Pataki's puppets and political cronies, found it would be more expedient to blatantly ignore the will of the people and impose Pataki's agenda on this sacred site.

Joseph Goebbels, Hitler's Minister of Propaganda, said, "If you tell a lie big enough and keep repeating it, people will eventually come to believe it." Since February 26, 2003, when Pataki overruled the LMDC and selected Libeskind, the rebuilding of the World Trade Center has become a Big Lie perpetrated by Pataki. In his speech the next day at the Winter Garden ceremony for the winning site plan, it was sickening to hear Pataki extol the virtues of this "open and democratic" rebuilding process that resulted in the selection of Libeskind as the "winner." Such Big Lie tactics and manufactured consent are tools of tyranny used by dictators and tools of obfuscation used by corrupt, pandering politicians. A sad irony is that the date on which Pataki overruled the LMDC and selected Libeskind, February 26, 2003, was the tenth anniversary of the first bombing of the World Trade Center. Pataki helped realize the terrorists' dream as he put the final nail in the coffin of the World Trade Center, replacing a monumental landmark with an ornamental, abstract architectural "vision" comprising a useless skyline element, a morbid pit symbolizing death and destruction and cluttered office buildings that resemble steel spikes and shards of broken glass. A plan that would truly make the zero-ness of Ground Zero permanent! Is this the self-image of a world-class city, not to transcend terror with boldness and resiliency, but rather to wallow in defeat and hopelessness that will be passed on for generations to come? When did this city lose its dignity and belief in itself and its future?

There were never any plans to replace the destroyed section of the Pentagon with a foundation pit to memorialize the victims along with some abstract architectural designs and "culture centers" driven by the desire for "less military space," so why is this being done for the World Trade Center? Furthermore, the destroyed sections of the Pentagon yielded ground every bit as sacred as the World Trade Center site, yet the Pentagon rebuilt on the land where all the death and destruction took place.

The rebuilding effort thus far has produced a site plan few

New Yorkers are proud of. The so-called "Freedom Tower" went through numerous permutations from its beginnings in the Libeskind plan as a hypodermic needle pointlessly filled with various flora, to a seventy-story building brought to 1776 feet with cables, windmills, cages and an offset spire, to its current version after security concerns as a tower with a concrete bunker base and seems to exude fear and cowardice. The PA has scrapped plans for a new Windows on the World restaurant. The additional office towers appear cluttered and uninspiring. The memorial to commemorate the horrors and heroism of the day, including artifacts from the destruction of 9/11, is shoved underground into catacombs and out of sight. Instead of giving those murdered proper identity as to where they worked, who they were, and how old they were, they are listed randomly as names on a wall, anonymous statistics of 9/11. At ground level there is an abstract memorial that is little more than a new-age theme park disconnected from the reality of 9/11, with water running down into voids. In the memorial, the identity of the perpetrators of the atrocity, jihadist Muslim terrorists, will be downplayed in an act of historically ignorant and cowardly political correctness.

Meanwhile, citizens have to put up a fight to get the damaged globe that once graced the WTC plaza back to where it belongs, successful businesses were driven into financial ruin by the dithering at the site, and a block away, other successful businesses were destroyed to make way for a misguided subway integration that is behind schedule and over budget. Furthermore, the congregation of St. Nicholas Greek Orthodox church that was destroyed on 9/11 has been trying for the past eight years to rebuild without success, while Mayor Bloomberg seems to be moving heaven and earth to allow a mosque to be built near Ground Zero by an imam who stated that America bears much of the responsibility for 9/11. To see a fifteen-story victory mosque near the destroyed WTC, while not even a cornerstone has been laid for a church that was once part of the fabric of the WTC site, is symbolic of the ignorance, corruption and disgracefully mixed up priorities of the politicians and other authorities involved in the entire rebuilding process.

In September of 2003, a group of Islamic jihadists met in England to celebrate 9/11 and the martyrdom of the "magnificent nineteen." They had posters displaying the burning towers and showing the hole in the ground that now remains of the World Trade Center. Indeed, this train wreck of a rebuilding process has allowed our city to become permanently violated by what will be a tribute to the achievements of Osama bin Laden and a memorial to the terror pilots Muhammad Atta and Salwan al-Sheddi as well as to the eight other hijackers who used their planes as guided missiles to destroy the World Trade Center and kill 2,752 people. There is no honor in this.

As the memory of 9/11 fades (never underestimate the waning attention span of the American people), fewer people will visit the memorial many years from now. After all, how many people alive today have ever visited Grant's Tomb or the memorial to the victims of the General Slocum disaster, where over 1,000 people, mostly women and children, died in a 1904 steamboat fire on New York City's East River?

However, the terrorists will have a symbol of their victory over us for all eternity, which will likely inspire future generations of terrorists to attack us again, and to leave empty footprints where our landmarks and national symbols stand. Indeed, our failure to properly restore the Twin Towers of the World Trade Center can only be seen as a sign of weakness and fear indicative of deference to our enemies and/or a fetish for perpetual victim status. This is the very antithesis of the bravery and defiance we should be showing at the place where we were attacked on our own soil!

We as a nation can do better than allowing the World Trade Center to become a tribute to terrorism victorious. The bottom line is, a consensus and unified vision must emerge for the rebuilding of the World Trade Center site that is free of any and all corrupting political influences and narrow-minded, shortsighted special interest demands. It must be a vision that respects the will of the people, the vitality of our city, and the sanctity of the site. Furthermore, in order to properly rebuild, the new World Trade Center should once again be an integral part of the commercial fabric of our nation and downtown business district. It should incorporate a memorial that focuses more on the lives of those we lost, rather than their violent deaths, and recognizes the sacrifices of our rescue workers and murder of the office workers and airline passengers.

And it must give us truly monumental twin skyscrapers as tall as or taller than before and safer and stronger than ever, which allow people to ascend to their apices, and in so doing reclaim the skies over Lower Manhattan.

Although marginalized by the powers-that-be as "radical ideas" far out of the mainstream, these are common-ground ideas that are closely attuned to what the people of New York City and the people of the world desire for the World Trade Center site. It is a shame and a disgrace that New York City was prevented from getting its own Project Phoenix, a way to repair the skyline in a dignified manner, with twin skyscrapers befitting a world-class city. Together with a proper memorial, we could have had a monument to the victims' lives and legacies, who died in the pursuit and defense of commerce, and a testament to our city's honor, dignity and patriotic spirit.

People and Stone

By Ilene Skeen

My great-grandmother on my mother's side was blind, but they said that to make up for that lack, she had the gift of second sight. The family lived in Romania, in a one-room wooden shack with an outhouse behind. Every Friday morning, her children would carry the table and the few sticks of furniture outside while the floor was swept, the old straw discarded and new cow manure carried in. After the boys and girls stamped around on the new floor to pack it down, new straw was thrown down and the furniture carried back in to prepare for the Sabbath.

Around 1910, when rumors of a new round of pogroms against the Jews came to her tiny village, my great-grandmother made sure to send her children to America, telling them that it wasn't going to end, it was only going to get worse. She sent her children away, one at a time as the family scraped up the money. It took years, and when the children left, they never saw their mother again.

My great-grandmother died in Romania about ninety-five years ago, unable to follow, but successful in keeping her children safe from the pogroms and also from the holocaust which followed thirty years later. Besides the gift of life itself and the prosperity and freedom her descendants enjoy here in the United States, some little remnant of her gift of foresight was passed down to me. Sometimes it's just enough to feel a vague uneasiness, a quickening of the pulse and a catch of breath on odd occasions. Unfortunately, it was not enough for me to save anyone from the tragedy of 9/11.

The Symbol of New York

Growing up in the Bronx in 1950, I absorbed the typical trappings of New York culture. Baseball at its best meant the Yankees, hustle and bustle meant Grand Central Station, and the trademark symbol of New York was the much-loved Empire State Building, then the tallest building in the world.

When the World Trade Center was being built in the early seventies, New York was a depressed and angry city. It was dangerous for anyone to walk alone even at dusk. Muggings were rampant. A young woman who dared to cut across the WTC construction site was found brutally raped and murdered. After that, women who worked in the Wall Street area were escorted to the subway or sent home by car service if their work kept them after dark. The plaza of the World Trade Center was isolating, setting the huge buildings apart from the rest of Lower Manhattan, aloof and alone. Back then, it seemed to me that nobody loved the World Trade Center. It was just a pair of buildings with an overblown name, New York's rather pedestrian answer to Chicago's Sears Tower. Briefly, they were the tallest buildings in the world.

Times changed. Even taller buildings were built elsewhere. New York introduced community policing — the mayor and police commissioner put the cops on the street. The people stopped calling them pigs and everybody realized that it wasn't us against them, but the good guys against the bad guys. New York City became one of the safest large cities in the world. As the World Trade Center slowly filled with tenants, the World Financial Center, with a far greater appreciation for public spaces, was built on the Hudson River.

Over the years, I had been to the WTC rarely. In 1989, I had a job interview there with a recruiter. I was in his office only once and the job was uptown, but his view looking north from somewhere high in the North Tower was unforgettable, spectacular. Once, on a sunny Father's Day, my son and I took my husband to dinner at Windows on the World. The concourse was quiet, empty. Disappointingly, that day in the restaurant there was no view because the tower was enshrouded in a cloud.

The final time I went to the World Trade Center was in June 2001. Emerging from the subway just at the height of the afternoon rush hour into the underground concourse, I encountered the energy of the work-day throng at its peak. The concourse did not have the awe-inspiring architectural magnificence of Grand Central Station or even of the Crystal Palace at the World Financial Center. The WTC concourse was built, not for show, like the Twin Towers, visible on the skyline from all parts of the city, but for "real," simply to allow people to get from here to there. No view, no vault, no columns or colonnade, there was only an immense stream of people —

constant movement, energy and noise, flowing and branching through the broad channels of the concourse bounded by exquisite shops with the world's most famous brands of watches, perfume, cosmetics, jewelry, clothing, accessories and eateries. The shop displays sparkled like exotic gems on the banks of a rushing river. The people were hurrying past, and some were hurrying in and out, emerging with packages. The sparkling lights of the shops were reflected in their eyes. There were thousands, most walking singly, but some together after what had apparently been a good day at work. They were laughing and smiling, walking quickly and purposefully, some talking on cell phones, most with briefcases or satchels, some with packages and other evidence of purchase. Here was a young man carrying flowers. If there were tourists, they were not in evidence. These were simply happy people going home or out to meet friends after a good day's work. The energy was palpable. If I could have bottled it, I would have called it WTC Élan, an elixir for the pessimistically depressed, a sure cure and pick-me-up for those who suffer from urban alienation. I gasped, surprised. I hadn't known. I was standing in the center of the universe and it was thrilling.

When I think back on the happy summer of 2001, there were signs and portents. I saw them, I wondered about them, but…

July 2001: My neighbors next door, in my Midtown Manhattan co-op just north of the Empire State Building, suddenly put their apartment up for sale and within two weeks were gone. The move was abrupt, even precipitous. I hardly knew them. The men were mostly out and the women kept to themselves. I did know the young brother and sister, about six and seven, growing up it seemed without any real supervision. They would be put in the hall to play, usually running back and forth with a soccer ball, screeching. I got to know the boy after a fashion as he would shoot me with his finger saying, "I kill you," whenever I came out of the elevator. A grown son had a habit of pacing the hallway talking into a cell phone in a mixture of English and another language. I thought they were from Egypt. Suddenly they were gone. I wondered about this.

August 2001: At my Midtown job not far from the UN, an up-and-coming manager quit. He had been hired as permanent staff in 2000, after working for the company for five years as a consultant. It had seemed to me that he should have been a "lifer." His wife was a pediatrician with an established practice. They had bought a big house in Westchester and she had had a baby. In April, he had gotten a big promotion to manager. Suddenly, no new job lined up, he gave two weeks notice and quit. He put his big house up for sale and moved to San Francisco. No party, no goodbye. He was from the Philippines. I wondered about this.

The night of Monday, September 10, 2001, was warm and clear. Walking on Fifth Avenue around 10 PM, I had a surprise. The Empire State Building, always a Mecca, usually bustling even at that time, was closed. That night there were no tourists or sweethearts thrilling to see the romantic lights of Manhattan below them and the stars above. There were barriers up and the street vendors, usually much in evidence selling souvenirs, pictures and rickshaw rides, were gone. About half a dozen cops were standing around, talking in small groups. I wondered about this.

The next morning, of course, the whole world knew what was going on.

A few days after, there was a story on the news that federal officials had expected an attack "on a symbol of New York."

To me, that explained everything — anyone born in New York before the 1970s would necessarily assume that "*the* symbol" of New York was, is, and always would be the Empire State Building. The World Trade Center was a symbol of much, much more.

It didn't start out that way, but by 2001, the World Trade Center had come to embody superlative achievement, the frenetic energy of commerce and the quintessential icon of Western civilization. By 2001, New York was host to the two greatest images of the dreams and hopes for the future of humankind: the UN, as a symbol of world peace — that talking in the world community is better than fighting, and the WTC, as a symbol of prosperity — that trade is better than poverty, terror, destruction and death. When the World Trade Center was destroyed, it was not New York, it was not even the US, it was 10,000 years of Western civilization that the terrorists sought *and still seek* to reduce to rubble.

To me, New York was its appropriate host, but the World

Trade Center was a symbol of the world.

Of course, a bomb had been used on the WTC in 1993, and by the very same people. It would have been reasonable to assume that the enemy had absorbed at least some of the canons of Western culture: *If at first you don't succeed...* But I couldn't fault the officials. When I heard the phrase "the symbol of New York" it was not the World Trade Center I thought of either.

Crazy Annie's Vision: People and Stone

In the 1980s my young son had a picture book about the history of Manhattan. Simple, happy, colorful illustrations accompanied each page of text. It always brought tears to my eyes, but I never knew why. I'd read it and get choked up at the end, annoying him with his boy's impatience for sentiment. That's probably why he didn't request it often, but it was one of my favorites.

The book told the story of how Peter Minuit bought Manhattan from the Indians for beads and trinkets — how the Dutch settled and began to fish, farm, trade and prosper. The featured character, maybe fact, possibly a legend, was "Crazy Annie," who talked to herself and pointed to the sky as she wandered around the village of New Amsterdam witnessing its early history. Whenever anyone questioned the future of this isolated outpost at the frontiers of the New World, Annie was there, pointing, mumbling, waving and ranting. Her mantra: The village would grow and be great.

The book introduced children to the drama of Manhattan's early times. It told how Wall Street was the northern barrier, and how the town grew quickly. The harbor was busy with trading, and the streets busy with news. It told about Peter Stuyvesant and his surrender to the British and how New Amsterdam became New York.

The book recounted the growth of New York and important moments in its history. It told about the New York publisher, John Peter Zenger, jailed for libel. It told how he was defended by Andrew Hamilton, and how the jury agreed with Hamilton's contention that if the story in the newspaper was true, there was no libel. Zenger's acquittal had far reaching effects. It established the precedent of freedom of the press in the colonies.

The book told how the builders built and the town inched inexorably northward; how it turned into a small city, then a big city and then a great city. It told about the Revolutionary War fighting and how George Washington took the presidential oath of office in New York, our country's first capital. It told how the grid was laid down for the future streets even when Broadway was still the road to Albany and most of Manhattan was forest and field. It told how the city filled with immigrants and tenements to house them. It told of the fine mansions, department stores and the Statue of Liberty sent by France to grace our harbor. Of course, it told about the creation of Central Park, the subways, the great skyscrapers, the Empire State Building, Times Square, and the hopes for peace embodied in the United Nations.

The book told most of all how the people arrived first as a trickle, then a stream, then a torrent, and eventually a flood: from every nation, every station and every race, religion and creed. Some stayed in New York and many went on to populate the great country that lay beyond. Again and again, the pages rang with Crazy Annie's prediction that the city would be great, until at the end it presented New York's crowning achievement. The last picture of the book was a two page spread of the World Trade Center, with the ghost of Crazy Annie, a tiny figure standing on the plaza, pointing skyward at the Twin Towers.

"People and stone! People and stone!" the ghost of Crazy Annie cried out.

Invariably, from the first time I read this book in the early 1980s, tears would well up, my chest would tighten and I would have to pause. Sometimes it took longer than others, but I could never continue until I recovered my composure. Then I would read this last page of the book to my son. If I paused too long, he gave me a frustrated "Mmmom!" making the three letter word into two syllables. I never knew why I choked up until the morning of September 11, 2001. But when I saw the towers collapse so perfectly on themselves like an amazing magic trick, I knew. Somewhere in the gift of my great-grandmother's second sight, I had known for years. Of course, by then it was too late.

That morning, I thought about the prescience of my great-grandmother who had died thirty years before I was born, mired in the troubles of the Old World and unable to escape, but saving her children and their children from the horrors of persecution and war. I thought about a wooden shack with an outhouse behind and how hard it must have been for her, first to lose her sight and then to send her children away, knowing she would never hold them close or hear their voices again. Yet she did what she had to do.

I thought about her courage as I saw the disgraceful display of people in other parts of the world dancing in the street as they watched the World Trade Center's demise. I realized with a shock how much this country is despised by some of its inferiors while they covet the riches that it produces and the lifestyle it enables. I thought about my old neighborhood in the Bronx, where the battle cry among children who bristled at being bullied was, "It's still a free country!" as they hit back or stomped away. I wondered if American children still say that.

I heard public officials speak words of comfort, encouragement and determination against terrorism. After a time, when the proposals for the New WTC were released, I wondered if the deed of rebuilding the fallen WTC would match the stirring rhetoric uttered within the first few days of its destruction. I'm still wondering. The chosen plan is long on high-blown phrases. Can it live up to its mission: to be bigger and better if its pinnacle is built only for show and not for people, not for ascent, not for business, not for world trade? With no possibility of meeting or exceeding the original reach of the WTC, this plan implies that we acknowledged defeat even before the first load of concrete was poured or the first beam set. Is this a vision to make us proud?

The bottom line is this: the World Trade Center was intended to last many lifetimes. In addition to the simple heinousness of the murders, the most shocking and distressing fact about the destruction was that many of us who saw the WTC go down also saw it go up. This was not a sight anyone in my generation or in several generations to come should have witnessed.

Some say we do not need the office space. Others do not want it. They want all of the trappings and effects of a 24-hour community without the engine of commerce to make it hum. If we plan to keep New York growing, firmly focused on the future, we will need all the office space we can build. Although the New WTC will be a tourist Mecca, the foundation of the plan must recapture the vibrant commercial community, the life of the World Trade Center that was destroyed. New York has never been a city of tombs and mausoleums, stuck in the past. New York is today. New York is tomorrow.

The New World Trade Center should be rebuilt bigger, taller and better than before: 10,000 years of civilization say we cannot surrender to the terror. Maybe someday, our politicians will realize this. *Our enemy is hiding in a cave and would like to reduce us all to his condition.* We must deny him any satisfaction beyond the momentary event which was 9/11.

When my great-grandmother sent her children to America, she was afraid for them. But she did what she had to do to insure that her children would survive.

We must match the politicians' rhetoric with actions that show the world our courage and determination in deeds. We do this not only for the people who died there, but in honor and respect for the dreams and hopes of all of those who came before us, for the people who are still here and for those yet to be. We do this out of respect and honor for our military personnel who fight for us, who are combing the caves and canyons of Afghanistan and risking their lives in many parts of the world where liberty is still a stranger. The New World Trade Center should be an icon of pride and honor to all of those who love freedom. The New World Trade Center should be rebuilt for all freedom-loving people of the world, wherever they may be. It is our symbolic invitation to them to participate in the incredible benefits of peace and freedom, including the freedom to trade.

If someday I could write an epilogue to my son's picture book, I would hope to be able to say:

"As the years went on, people from many countries visited and worked at the World Trade Center. It became the crowning symbol of freedom throughout the world as nation after nation abandoned isolation and embraced trade in the community of humankind.

"In 2001, terrorists destroyed the buildings and murdered

nearly 3,000 people. It was a trying time, and those few who knew the legend of Crazy Annie wondered if the sight of the falling Twin Towers had been her vision all along.

"But the courageous people of New York, encouraged by the entire world, were not to be denied. Although it took years, eventually, they redesigned the plaza and rebuilt the skyscrapers, bigger, taller and even better than before. Crazy Annie would have been proud. The New World Trade Center is a vibrant 24-hour community, always rushing and flowing with life. The New World Trade Center is open to the world, an exciting mix of people and stone."

Center of the World

By Alexander Butziger

John Dos Passos' *Manhattan Transfer* introduced the concept of New York's "center of things." To me, the World Trade Center was this center of things — and as New York is the capital of the world, also the center of the world. The World Trade Center Towers were my favorite place anywhere. I loved their boxy — that is simple, elegant, and efficient — shape and their incredible bulk in the sky: Unlike many other skyscrapers, they refused to apologize for their greatness by shrinking back in setbacks. The vast, beautifully textured rectangles of their facades afforded an impressive backdrop for Manhattan's skyscrapers and New York Harbor. Their tops towering high above most other buildings in the city provided a beacon when navigating the maze of Downtown streets. Every time I was in the city, I used to ride to the top of the Towers. The sense of being on top of the world, looking straight down at the World Trade Center Plaza and the small world below, is unforgettable — as is the view of the harbor and the Statue of Liberty at sunset from up there.

The Moral Meaning of Skyscrapers

To me, the most fascinating sight possible is the steel frame of a skyscraper going up — the ultimate puzzle where man joins countless steel beams and other parts into one of his largest and greatest works. Skyscrapers are man's thought given concrete shape. They are the most visible monument to his greatness and glory. Other wonders of man are less accessible due to their nature. Dams and bridges are often far away from city centers, and are not inhabited by human beings. Ships, aircraft, and trains are not as visible, as they spend most of the time under way, far from observers. Besides, they are rather a means for traveling to some place, while a building, or a city, is an end, the destination of a voyage.

That's not all. What makes a tall building great is that it is a *tall building*. Tall: Any band of semi-savages who have learned how to split rock or how to make bricks can build a large building. However, as wind loads increase exponentially with building height, it takes the full power of the human mind to defy gravity and make a building tall. Building: Among tall structures, there are guyed broadcasting masts and concrete broadcasting towers — both much less fascinating than actual skyscrapers. Constructing the Eiffel Tower or CN Tower was a much smaller achievement than building a skyscraper of equal height. Everybody will sense that if he compares the massive bulk of a tall building with the see-through skeletons and thin concrete shafts of other tall structures.

What's more, a tall building consists of hundreds of floors of offices and apartments occupied by human beings — instead of just an observation deck, a restaurant, or a broadcasting platform, if any. Thus the noblest building of them all is the office skyscraper, the place where man's noblest activity, his productive work, takes place. [1]

Or as Ayn Rand said it in her novel *The Fountainhead*:

"You've never felt how small you were when looking at the ocean."

He laughed. "Never. Nor looking at the planets. Nor at mountain peaks. Nor at the Grand Canyon. Why should I? When I look at the ocean, I feel the greatness of man. I think of man's magnificent capacity that created this ship to conquer all that senseless space. When I look at mountain peaks, I think of tunnels and dynamite. When I look at the planets, I think of airplanes."

"Yes. And that particular sense of sacred rapture men say they experience in contemplating nature — I've never received it from nature, only from..." She stopped.

"From what?"

"Buildings," she whispered. "Skyscrapers."

"Why didn't you want to say that?"

"I... don't know."

"I would give the greatest sunset in the world for one sight of New York's skyline. Particularly when one can't see the details. Just the shapes. The shapes and the thought that made them. The sky over New York and the will of man made visible. What other religion do we need? And then people tell me about pilgrimages to some dank pesthole in a jungle where they go to do homage to a crumbling temple, to a leering stone monster with a pot belly, created by some leprous savage. Is it beauty and genius they want to see? Do they seek a sense of the sublime? Let them come to New York, stand on the shore of the Hudson, look and kneel. When I see the city from my window — no, I don't feel how small I am — but I feel that if a war came to threaten this, I would like to throw myself into space, over the city, and protect these buildings with my body." [2]

This book was published during World War II, but one cannot but think how eerily prescient the last sentence is of the atrocity perpetrated on September 11, 2001.

Building Up and Tearing New York Down

The quest for the highest, the greatest, and the best is at the very core of man's existence and purpose. It is crucial to any discovery, science, progress, and achievement. Whoever claims that the Twin Towers were too big, not "human scale," relegates himself from the realm of man to the realm of the worm. Whoever says that one should be concerned only about the people who were murdered, but not about the buildings that were destroyed, divorces man from purpose. He implies that man should be glad to survive with the barest necessities, without any achievement, inspiration, pride, or joy. Countless visitors to the World Trade Center were inspired by the grand scale of the Twin Towers, as were billions of people around the world, due to the knowledge that such achievement exists.

The World Trade Center is close to my idea of the highest, the greatest, and the best. It was the largest office complex in the world. When the Twin Towers were completed, they were the greatest engineering marvel in history. A couple of taller buildings have gone up in the meantime, but none of those developments managed to truly trump the Twin Towers. None of them reached 110 one-acre floors — let alone two times over. These facts alone would place the Twin Towers among the greatest, noblest buildings in the world, but they were even more ennobled by their dedication to world trade. Commerce, or free trade, means the voluntary exchange of good for good, value for value, to mutual benefit. The only alternative to commerce is slavery and looting. It is exclusively through commerce, or trade, that human beings can coexist in freedom, progress, and prosperity. It is strikingly appropriate that the tallest skyscrapers are usually office buildings, the venues and symbols of commerce, the noblest activity of man.

Utopian urban renewal activists that had always hated the World Trade Center descended on the smoking ruins like vultures and called for less commercial and more cultural space in the new World Trade Center. Some would even replace the World Trade Center, the largest and greatest commercial buildings in the world, with a "World Cultural Center." The underlying idea is the notion harbored by the utopian vultures that commerce is somehow evil, that commerce is somehow not good enough for Lower Manhattan in general and for the Twin Towers' "sacred" footprints in particular.

Yet every dollar the vultures want to spend on "cultural amenities" must first be created through commerce. Nothing is found in nature except the most basic raw materials. Every good and product man needs or wishes to use has to be produced by the mind and work of some individual human being. This process of production and trade is commerce.

Under their mistaken morality of "altruism," everything commercial, everything involving profit, everything an individual does for his own benefit, is selfish and thus evil. Only what is done for the benefit of others, what is unselfish, is good. Every outrage is considered good, if it is only done "for the benefit of others." The identity of those others is hardly ever specified except for generalizations, like "the children," "the poor," or "the people."

In the final consequence, the morality underlying this thinking is a morality of death. Under this morality, if there was a flood and you wanted to save your girlfriend from drowning, that would be selfish and evil. Letting your girlfriend drown to save a complete stranger you value less than you value your girlfriend would be unselfish and good.

The individual's enlightened self-interest — whose attributes are reason, which entails innovation and achievement, and liberty, which entails profit and commerce — has brought man from the trees of a fetid jungle to the greatest city in the greatest civilization the world has ever known. Forsaking commerce to create "cultural amenities" that are of no earthly use to those who pay for them, for the benefit of unspecified others, is the first step on the way back up the trees.

If authorities are going to spend tax money confiscated from individuals on rebuilding the World Trade Center, the least they should do is let the residents of New York and New Jersey vote on whether they wish to see their money spent on rebuilding the Twin Towers of achievement or on experimental "cultural amenities" used only by a pseudo-intellectual subculture.

Yet the Twin Towers were not only symbols of commerce, but also of America. Which, one might argue, is one and the same, as the land of the free is necessarily the land of commerce, of free, voluntary, uncoerced intercourse and trade to mutual advantage.

As Lafayette had it, before there was a United States of America, liberty was homeless on earth. The history of the world was written in blood. Throughout untold millennia, all the countries of the world were ruled by looters — kings, dictators, fascists, communists. They all had two things in common: rule by force and contempt for the trader — for the man of justice. A trader neither takes nor gives the unearned or the undeserved. In all places, at all times, it was taken for granted, accepted as a matter of fact, and never questioned that men must be ruled, enslaved, exploited, sacrificed, and slaughtered. That the alternative is either to rule or to be ruled, either to sacrifice others to self or to sacrifice self to others, either to be a sadist or to be a masochist. The only exception, the only country founded upon the voluntary cooperation of men, is America, the land of the trader, the freest and noblest country of them all.

America, the noblest country in the history of the world, the only country founded upon reason, liberty, and the rights of man, deserves the highest, the greatest, and the best of everything. The tallest building in the world belongs to the greatest city in America.

Asian countries continue to build super tall — but the tallest building does not belong to a collectivist Asia, proclaiming a "Pacific Century," permitting collectivists to boast how they "beat the Yankees." Least of all does the world's tallest tower belong to the Arab world. "Hey, we knocked down their two tallest towers and built one twice as tall. Goes to prove that a culture that stones women is superior to reason and liberty."

Some propose to fight terrorism by not building any "targets." That makes about as much sense as burning down your house to prevent brush fires. If you surrender your achievements and the symbols of your values, your values and your life are next to go. The war on terror will not be won by surrendering. Neither can it be won by teaching unenlightened Arabs to build skyscrapers to pretend their backward, brutal culture based on faith and force spawning terrorism is equivalent to a civilization built on reason and liberty.

Like any war, the war on terror can be won only by ideas, by recognizing that reason and the liberty to apply the knowledge thus won is the only way to get things done, by proclaiming, "With our know-how we drilled oil wells in your neck of the desert. You confiscated our oil, you are selling it back to us, and you use that money to pay us to build towers for you with our know-how, towers to glorify your anti-reason, anti-liberty culture. You need us. We do not need you. If you knock down our towers, we'll rebuild them. If you build the world's tallest tower, we'll build one twice as tall."

Besides, New York is the skyscraper capital of the world. Of all cities, New York has probably the largest number of skyscrapers. It would be a pity for New York not to have the tallest one, too.

A Consolation Prize for Victimhood

Without rebuilt Twin Towers at least as tall as before, the adjacent memorial would only be a benefit and monument to terrorism. Without restoration on as grand or grander a scale of what was destroyed, a memorial would only assure would-be terrorists that terrorism will literally put them on the map. If there is to be a memorial, new towers by any measurement as tall and big as the Twin Towers must be built alongside, to put it into proper context, to demonstrate the ultimate futility of aggression. A memorial surrounded by buildings smaller than the Twin Towers says, "That day, the terrorists destroyed this and got away with it." New Towers at least as tall and grand as the ones destroyed say, "That day, the terrorists believed they could stop *this*."

What's more, it's hard to understand why there should be such an enormous memorial in the first place and why it should be the focus of the new World Trade Center complex. Victims' families say they feel the need to have a place to remember the dead, although it is hard to understand why they cannot remember the dead but in one dedicated place.

Frankly, I do not see any pressing need for a memorial at all. Why is memorialization all the rage now? Why does each and every crime victim need a super-size memorial? Why this fetish with suffering, death, and victimization? Why does someone who had his life tragically cut short by crime deserve a memorial, while everyone who lives on to a death of old age has to make do with a regular tombstone for memorialization? Is a memorial to be a reward for being a crime victim? Is it meant as a consolation prize of life (or death)? What a pitiful affair is then a crusade for memorials? If you could choose between one extra year to live and a memorial, even a memorial the size of Manhattan, what would you take?

And does life work this way? Would George Washington be forgotten if there were no Washington Monument? Would Thomas Jefferson be forgotten if there were no Jefferson Memorial? Would Abraham Lincoln be forgotten if there were no Lincoln Memorial? If there were no memorials, no places named for them, wouldn't it still be impossible to forget these great men? What about Benjamin Franklin, Patrick Henry, or Thomas Paine? Shouldn't they have long been forgotten due to a lack of a 555-foot marble memorial? No, the world does not work this way.

We are met on a great battle-field of that war. We have come to dedicate a portion of that field, as a final resting-place for those who here gave their lives that that nation might live. It is altogether fitting and proper that we should do this.

But, in a larger sense, we cannot dedicate, we cannot consecrate, we cannot hallow this ground. The brave men, living and dead, who struggled here, have consecrated it, far above our poor power to add or detract. The world will little note, nor long remember what we say here, but it can never forget what they did here. It is for us the living, rather, to be dedicated here to the unfinished work which they who fought here have thus far so nobly advanced. It is rather for us to be here dedicated to the great task remaining before us — that from these honored dead we take increased devotion to that cause for which they gave the last full measure of devotion — that we here highly resolve that these dead shall not have died in vain... [3]

Dead men tell no tales and do no deeds. The only memorial that matters every human being can only create for himself. By living a productive life in thought, word, and deed, he shall never be forgotten, but live on in the memory of posterity. If a human being lives such a life, no memorial is necessary. If he does not, a memorial with ten thousand angels sitting on it swearing the opposite will make no difference.

In Riverside Park stands the General Grant National Memorial, or as it is popularly known, Grant's Tomb, the mausoleum and memorial of Ulysses S. Grant and his wife. One could not wish for a fancier memorial, modeled after the Mausoleum of Halicarnassus and all. Now I could ask like Groucho Marx: "Who is buried in Grant's Tomb?" Or I could ask: How do more people learn more about Grant these days, by visiting his memorial, or by reading books, watching movies, and surfing the internet?

Through the lives they have lived, those who were murdered that horrible day have acquired a greater memorial than could ever be built by other men. But most people who worked in the Twin Towers were proud of their workplace and want them rebuilt. The only thing we owe both victims and survivors is to rebuild the center of their productive lives — the Twin Towers.

Blank Out

Nothing of this occurred to the authorities in charge of rebuilding, the Port Authority of New York and New Jersey, the Lower Manhattan Development Corporation, City Hall, and Governor George Pataki. "I think there is a developing consensus

— among everybody I've talked to — that it is not either practical or appropriate to build another 100-story building," opined LMDC chairman John Whitehead in early 2002. Apparently, he had talked to very few. In hearing after hearing, more and more people demanded that 110-story World Trade Center Towers be restored.

Thus, the LMDC promised to create a new "skyline element." Think about this word for a moment: "skyline element." It is not an engineering term, but a weasel word coined by the LMDC to cover up the fact that the people want their Towers back. Rebuilding the World Trade Center is not about a "skyline element." It is not about a pole on an office building. It is about engineering achievement. The new World Trade Center has to recapture the spirit of the Twin Towers. For that, it has to be the greatest engineering marvel of the twenty-first century, just as the old World Trade Center was the greatest engineering marvel of the twentieth century. At the very least, the new World Trade Center must not replace something great with something less. At the very least, it needs to consist of two towers of 110 one-acre floors each. Who in the world has come up with the idea that a seventy-story building with a "skyline element" could ever replace two 110-story towers?

Authorities say they cannot find any developer willing to build that tall. But have they really been looking for one? Or do they just take it for granted, because World Trade Center leaseholder Larry Silverstein is unwilling to rebuild the Twins? Silverstein's arbitrarily imposed, irrational height limit of seventy office floors for the new World Trade Center renders rebuilding monumental World Trade Center Towers impossible. Anything above that line can be only tiny token floors or "skyline elements."

This seventy-story limit has nothing to do with good business sense. The *New York Post* reported that one executive alone indicated a willingness to lease the top five floors in one of rebuilt 110-story Twin Towers. An asset management firm set up a billboard calling for the Twin Towers to be rebuilt, promising to move in. Former World Trade Center tenant Jonathan Hakala wants to return to his office on the seventy-seventh floor of One World Trade Center. He proposes that the LMDC should hold a worldwide auction for space above the eighty-fifth floor. He is sure that such an auction will be heavily oversubscribed. Hakala also vowed to rent space in the new World Trade Center only if the new buildings have at least 110 habitable floors. World Trade Center Restoration Movement volunteers regularly run out of supplies of "YES I'd Work on the 110th Floor!" stickers. David Emil, owner of the 107th floor restaurant, Windows on the World, is eager to reopen on the 110th floor of a new World Trade Center Tower. What is Silverstein's response to all this demand for high floors? He is "not comfortable with having people up there."

Not only is Silverstein determined not to build any office or other occupied space above the seventieth floor, he also wants to divide the office space into smaller buildings in order to minimize his short term vacancy risk. It is such short term thinking that breaks up our Twin Towers into five or six tiny buildings. The fact that five or six fifty- to seventy-story buildings take more land to build on than two 110-story Towers is at the root of authorities' planning problems and of their desire to annex adjoining sites into their new World Trade Center project. In the long run, all the office space of the World Trade Center is to be rebuilt and reoccupied. As Silverstein is going to rebuild, he should do it the right way: by putting ten million square feet of office space on the sixteen acres without crowding them. If he wants his space back, he needs to build giant new Twin Towers.

I do not wish to defend public ownership of land. But fact is, in the mixed economy we live in, Silverstein does not own the World Trade Center. He merely leases it. What would you think if you rent out your house to someone, it gets destroyed, and your tenant presumes to tell you how you must rebuild your house? That's preposterous? Well — it is. The World Trade Center is owned by the people of New York and New Jersey — yet the leaseholder wants to dictate how to rebuild it. If Silverstein wishes to build fifty- to seventy-story buildings, he should buy his own land. He cannot rent other people's 110-story Towers and replace them with his stumpy structures.

Silverstein did not lease just any ten million square feet of office space. He leased 110-story Twin Towers beloved the world over. It is questionable if his lease gives him any legal right — and it certainly is not morally right — to replace the glory of mankind with a mid-rise office park. He has no right to turn down those who want to go "up there." He obviously acts according to the bromide that "one sometimes has to protect people from themselves." But every human being is responsible for himself and for himself only. Every individual has to judge for himself which risks to take and which not. The timid have no right to "protect" the brave "from themselves."

If Silverstein is loath to accept the responsibility for rebuilding 110-story Towers, he should give up his lease in favor of a less timid developer. What if he refuses to do so? Under the terms of his lease, he needs the Port Authority's consent to build anything other than new Twin Towers. And in any event, the Port Authority has the right to cancel the lease. Why did the Port Authority never consider these facts, cancel the lease, and issue a call for tenders among developers for rebuilding the Twin Towers?

The Port Authority of New York and New Jersey is controlled by the two state governors. In World Trade Center issues, the governor of New Jersey deferred to then Governor Pataki of New York. The Port Authority was thus effectively ruled by Governor Pataki. When Silverstein refused to rebuild the Twin Towers in spite of public opinion, Governor Pataki failed to order the Port Authority to cancel his lease. Even worse, the governor selected the abominable Libeskind needle and death pit plan. Silverstein is not directly responsible to the public. But Governor Pataki was. He is to blame for the World Trade Center rebuilding train wreck. Voters should remember that at the polls if he should seek public office again.

Let us assume the worst case scenario, that not enough private capital can be found to rebuild tall enough. Why should tax money be available for expanding the memorial to nine acres, for improving transit infrastructure, for "cultural amenities," for "affordable housing," but not for rebuilding the world's greatest landmark? There is 1.3 billion dollars in Federal rebuilding funds left in the coffers of the LMDC. This Federal emergency aid has been granted for rebuilding Lower Manhattan. "Rebuilding" as in "rebuilding what was there." "Rebuilding" as in "rebuilding the Twin Towers." Not for building Downtown into something completely different from what it used to be. It is for rebuilding the center of the world. This money would be enough to rebuild one Tower, while the other one could be paid for out of the insurance proceeds. Why are the powers that be considering any option but rebuilding the Twins? Why are they desperate to find some other use for this 1.3 billion dollars than the most obvious one? Why were they willing to spend a billion dollars on burying West Street — a street residents do not want buried — but not on rebuilding the most recognizable landmark in the world?

Some folks say the Twin Towers killed people. That is wrong. The Twins saved lives. Virtually every other building would have collapsed on impact on September 11, 2001, killing all occupants. The Twins stood up long enough for untold thousands to escape. Any taller building is always safer than any shorter building, as a taller building must be built much stronger to withstand wind- and earthquake loads that grow exponentially with building height. Improved, state-of-the-art fireproofing would have enabled the Towers to stand up indefinitely after they got hit. Skyscrapers don't kill people. Terrorists kill people.

Some folks say rebuilt tall buildings will be a target. That is misleading. Rebuilding only one inch or one floor shorter, allowing terrorists to cut America down to size, will encourage future terrorists to launch similar attacks, knowing full well they will be guaranteed a place on the map, a gap in the skyline. Allowing terrorists to permanently destroy the Twin Towers is like allowing them to remove a star or a stripe from the American Flag.

The only way to combat terrorism is to go out and bring evil people to justice. Rebuilding smaller will not appease the terrorists. They do not so much hate skyscrapers as what they stand for — liberty, reason, achievement, and greatness. A shining city upon a hill cannot be hidden. Even if we stop building skyscrapers, every corner of the free world will remain a target — as long as we hold on to our values. We shall never abandon our values. So should we be proud of our values of liberty, reason, and achievement — and continue to build skyscrapers to symbolize them — or should we apologize for our values to savages who have no values? If we do the latter, we will soon discover that we have no values left.

We should do the obvious thing, the right thing, the principled thing: Let New York and America stand tall again. New York is not New York without the Twins. Let us rebuild our beloved Twin Towers — taller, stronger, safer, and better than ever.

Engineering Marvel of the New Millennium?

To restore what was lost, the new World Trade Center Towers need to be by all measurements at least as big and grand and tall — to highest floor, to roofline, to structural top, and to tip of antenna — as the Twin Towers. Preferably, they ought to be bigger and grander and taller. When the Twin Towers were built, they were the greatest engineering marvel in history. The new World Trade Center has to recapture the spirit of the Twin Towers. For that, it has to be the greatest engineering marvel of the twenty-first century, which raises the bar quite a bit.

Yet the Freedom Tower falls short by almost any measurement. The Twin Towers had a 1,368-foot roofline, a 1,377-foot rooftop observation deck atop Two World Trade Center, and a 1,728-foot antenna atop One World Trade Center. Daniel Libeskind's vaunted 1,776-foot spire will not be materially taller than the old World Trade Center antenna, and all other heights will barely be matched. What's more, the Freedom Tower has fewer floors, far fewer useable office floors, and merely 2,599,980 square feet of floor area versus 4,300,000 square feet in just *one* Twin Tower.

The degree to which authorities have corrupted this allegedly open and democratic rebuilding process is astounding. Early on, they decided that the new World Trade Center would be a complex of fifty-story buildings clustered around a memorial. Greenwich and Fulton Streets would be cut through the World Trade Center, dividing the site into four quadrants. The largest quadrant, including the Twin Towers' footprints, was to be dominated by the memorial. The three smaller ones would have to accommodate the rebuilt ten million square feet of office space in an L-shaped wall of short buildings. Six variations of this scheme were drawn up by the firm of Beyer Blinder Belle. To placate the public, one of the buildings was to rise to seventy to eighty floors with a needlelike "skyline element" on it.

At the Listening to the City II convention in July 2002, the public resoundingly rejected these plans. The most frequently uttered comments were: "Schemes are not ambitious enough. The buildings are too short. Nothing here is truly monumental. Looks like Albany." The latter should not be misinterpreted as criticism of the simple and elegant International Style buildings of Albany's Empire State Plaza, but rather of building height. A complex of a half dozen buildings with a floor count only in the double digit range is appropriate for a city like Albany, but it is not good enough as the financial center of New York City, the greatest city in the world. Neither is it a tall enough replacement for two 110-story Towers.

As one of the many people who submitted that "Looks like Albany" comment, I was dismayed to see that the Libeskind scheme selected by Governor Pataki was just Beyer Blinder Belle recycled. Libeskind had merely extended the 1,400- to 1,500-foot "skyline element" to 1,776 feet, added a death pit footprint memorial, and adorned — or rather disfigured — the buildings with unbuildable postmodern facades. Silverstein and his political enablers keep morphing every new World Trade Center design into a clone of the six plans.

As I am writing this, the new One World Trade Center is rising to eighty floors in the sky over New York. It would be a fine building in any other place in Manhattan, but it's not quite good enough to replace the Twin Towers. However, there is still time to redesign the other new World Trade Center buildings to be taller and larger.

New York desperately needs modern office space and in fact, if you look at the size of the average Manhattan apartment or hotel room, any kind of space. The construction of new super-tall buildings in New York should be welcomed and encouraged, not victimized by NIMBYism and politics.

Above all, New York deserves a new world's tallest building by every conceivable measurement. According to the American tradition, New York's new Towers should progress to an even grander state in size and appearance. After all, the New York state motto is Excelsior — Ever upward!

© 2007-2011 by Alexander Butziger

A Table of Two World Trade Centers

By Alexander Butziger

The point that George Elmer Fudd Pataki and the other Libeskind / Fraud'em Tower shills don't seem to get or don't want to get is that neither Fraud'em Tower nor the Libeskind scheme as a whole is a soaring memorial, as they would have us believe. Every building in the Libescheme is less than what one of the destroyed Twin Towers was.

Complex	Old WTC		New WTC			
Building	1 WTC	2 WTC	1 WTC	2 WTC	3 WTC	4 WTC
Tip height (ft)[1]	1,728	1,377	1,776	1,350	1,257	975
Roof height (ft)[2]	1,368	1,362	1,368	1,270	1,155	975
Top floor (ft)[3]	1,355	1,348	1,314	?	?	?
Official floors [4]	110	110	104	88	80	72
Floor range [5]	102-110	102-110	82-108	76-88	71-80	64-72
Office floors [6]	91	92	69	60	?	?
Floor area (million sq ft)	4.3	4.3	2.6	2.53	2	1.8

(1) Height of building to tip of antenna or spire.

(2) Height of building to rooftop, excluding antennas and decorative spires.

(3) Height of building's top floor.

(4) Official floor count.

(5) Possible range of floor counts, depending on what you count as a floor. E.g., a ten-story-high lobby as one floor or as ten floors; double-high mechanical floors as one floor or as two floors, etc.

(6) Number of office floors in the building. The old 1 WTC had one fewer than the old 2 WTC, for an extra restaurant level.

None of the Libescheme buildings exceeds either of the Twin Towers in any way, shape, or form, except for the spire atop Fraud'em Tower, which beats the communications tower of the old 1 WTC by all of 48 feet.

Replacing an engineering triumph with a bunch of random office buildings is not a soaring memorial, is not reclaiming the skyline, and is not a good idea. You don't replace something great with something less.

What part of "Excelsior!" don't you get, Elmer?

(Shhh. Be vewy, vewy quiet, he's hunting wabbits.)

A Tale of Two Cities

By Alexander Butziger

For what would happen to New York if the NIMBYs had their way, look at Paris. It died from what the French call museification. Sure, it's full of American tourists who want to see what they have been told to find romantic. So they do this original Disneyland with its Cinderella architecture. Sure, there are plenty of people and nightlife and whatever. But Paris is dead. It can't grow, it can't improve, it can't change. It's forever stuck in a period from the Middle Ages to the nineteenth century.

When Montparnasse Tower, the first and only skyscraper in Paris proper, was built, Parisians, or at least the majority of them, decided that they hated such buildings and banned them. Ever since, businesses have been leaving for the suburbs, like La Defense, where skyscrapers are allowed. What's left to the city is the tourist trade.

Now look at London. Just like Paris, the City of London outlawed modern skyscrapers with large floor plates to protect the views of its Baroque cathedral. The result was that the world's biggest banks moved their European headquarters from the City to Canary Wharf, where they can build beautiful, boxy, modern skyscrapers with trading floors as big as they want to. Suddenly, it became possible to build modern skyscrapers in the City. As I am writing this, the tallest buildings in London are going up in or just across the Thames from the City.

Now, Britain is no purely capitalist country. It's in fact a strange blend of capitalism, democracy, and monarchy. But it sure is way more capitalist than France, and observe the results. Capitalism = The market wants skyscrapers, so the City gets skyscrapers. Democracy = The majority doesn't want skyscrapers, so the frog town gets stuck in the past, a quaint little Disneyland for the majority that is afraid of change and likes to stagnate and the deluded tourists who believe vacation means watching stagnation happen. (That doesn't mean that slumming in Paris isn't fun. It just isn't exactly noble.)

Quo vadis, New York?

Only in New York — Not?

By Alexander Butziger

Looks like the sky is the limit everywhere — except in New York City, where zoning regulations, FAA height limits, and NIMBYs make it almost impossible to build the next world's tallest building. In the past, New York was the only city that could build the world's tallest building. Now it appears to be the only city that can't. The Skyscraper National Park is falling farther and farther back, while its inventory of up to century-old skyscrapers is becoming increasingly worthless for anything but residential conversion. New super skyscrapers with huge amounts of Class A office space are desperately needed to keep the city competitive.

The following table of the world's tallest buildings, existing and under construction, shows how tiny this allegedly tallest building in the world, the World Trade Center Fraud'em Tower, actually is in today's ranking of super skyscrapers.

Building	Location	Tip height	Roof height	Floors
Burj Khalifa	Dubai, UAE	2,717 ft	2,087 ft	163
Shanghai Tower	Shanghai, China	2,073 ft	1,856 ft	128
Abraj Al Bait Towers	Mecca, Saudi Arabia	1,972 ft	1,740 ft	95
Lotte World Premium Tower	Seoul, South Korea	1,821 ft	1,821 ft	123
1 WTC	New York	1,776 ft	1,368 ft	104

The world's tallest building belongs to New York City. Move over, zoning zombies, FAA, and NIMBYs!

© 2011 by Alexander Butziger

Are New Twin Towers Still Possible?

By Jonathan Hakala

New Twin Towers are still possible, but achieving them will require much better business and political leadership than we've had in recent years.

Boy Meets Twin Towers

I first became interested in the original Twin Towers at the age of thirteen when my parents gave me a brand new set of 1973 World Book encyclopedias that included photographs of the newly completed Twin Towers. At the time, the Twin Towers were the tallest buildings in the world, which made a powerful impression on me and on many other people.

The unapologetic, audacious design of the Twin Towers reached straight up, dwarfing all other buildings around them, and they appeared to act as sentinels protecting New York City. This appealed to my developing sense that my future career lay somewhere in one of the business districts of Manhattan. The fact that New York now had the tallest buildings in the world only enhanced my belief that this was the commercial capital of the world and the logical place to move to after finishing school, even though I had never actually visited New York City before. The geometric precision and power of the Twin Towers' vertical lines seemed an appropriate backdrop for the financial calculations and risks that took place in the neighboring Wall Street area daily.

After working as a bond trader for more than a dozen years, usually in Downtown Manhattan less than a mile from the Twin Towers but never actually on their premises, I struck out on my own. One of the first things to do was to find my own office space. Although I kept an open mind and looked at a number of locations, the office space I looked at on the 77th floor of One World Trade Center, in addition to boasting of amazing views, had an additional advantage: I would never have to give anyone detailed directions about finding my office again. Plus, my best friend Michael Taylor worked for Cantor Fitzgerald on the 104th floor of the same building, which made it easier for me to see him more often.

At the time, I wasn't married yet and had a furnished bachelor apartment across the Hudson River in Hoboken, New Jersey, with a window in the kitchen that looked out onto a fire escape and a closely adjacent building. Even with that limited view, the tops of the Twin Towers were visible and made my office seem somehow closer.

On September 11, 2001, twenty-five months after signing the lease for my Twin Towers office, I got onto the PATH subway train from Hoboken, New Jersey, to the World Trade Center in Downtown Manhattan. As usual, it was around 8:00 a.m. Right before the doors closed, I found myself walking off this train, across the platform and getting onto the PATH subway train from Hoboken, New Jersey, to 33rd Street in Midtown Manhattan.

Although I had planned to be in my World Trade Center office early that morning, and had emailed colleagues that I would be available in my office, for what seemed like no good reason I suddenly decided to go and revisit a company in the Chelsea neighborhood of Manhattan that I had spent the whole previous day with. This sort of spur-of-the-moment change in plans was unusual for me and indeed, I really had no further business there that day.

I only wish that Fate had somehow been able to spare all the good people who lost their lives that day, including my friend Michael Taylor.

From the roof of 231 West 29th Street in Manhattan, roughly three miles from the Twin Towers, some business acquaintances and I watched with a blend of horror and utter disbelief as the Twin Towers burned and then collapsed one at a time. After the first Tower collapsed, "my" Tower survived for another half hour as the only Twin Tower on the skyline before it also collapsed. It seemed so much shorter than half an hour. The human toll was what affected us all most, but the sight of the pillaged skyline after the debris cloud began to dissipate was even then jarring and obscene, as though a pair of legs had been forcibly removed.

The rest of that day and following days were difficult ones. There was the unwilling realization, after calling Michael's number again and again in the hope that he had somehow been able to get out, that my best friend was gone forever. There was the difficulty of learning more of the painful details of the terror plot, the dawning reality that there were few survivors in the rubble, and the painful accounts of many survivors and of the devastated families and close friends of those who hadn't made it.

In those early days I instinctively realized that there were a few things I needed to do to keep going. I needed to help the small and medium-sized businesses I worked with stay viable after the atrocities of September 11, 2001, because even more people would be hurt if I was overwhelmed with grief and one or more of these businesses failed. Two days later, on September 13, 2001, I found that I was the very first tenant to arrive at Larry Silverstein's offices in Midtown Manhattan with a copy of my World Trade Center lease in hand to try to start the process of getting a refund of my World Trade Center security deposit and advance rent. Earlier in 2001, Larry Silverstein and his partners had bought the leasehold interests in the World Trade Center from the Port Authority of New York and New Jersey. Mr. Silverstein's office staff greeted my lease with great relief, and asked if they could make a copy of it. Apparently their most conveniently accessible copies had been destroyed in the Twin Towers' offices of the Port Authority of New York and New Jersey.

I was soon offered temporary office space elsewhere in Manhattan, and looked out of my kitchen window in New Jersey less frequently for a while. The recovery efforts at the World Trade Center site continued.

Rebuilding

In the months immediately after the atrocities of September 11, 2001, I did not expect to become part of the conversations regarding rebuilding the World Trade Center, or that there would be any need for that. When the Twin Towers collapsed, in addition to a sense of shock, outrage and violation, there was also the widespread sense that an important symbol of our civilization had been savaged and that our Twin Towers needed to be restored, in order to start to set things right — or as right as they could be under the circumstances. In talking with a lot of people I consistently found, whether these people were from New York, from elsewhere in the United States, or from halfway around the world, that most people had this same instinctive sense that the logical, expected course of action, and the way to promote the most healing for the largest number of people, would be to rebuild new Twin Towers.

A narrow group of New York's business and political elite dominated by then New York Governor George Pataki had other ideas. Unlike most people, Pataki declared he had "...never liked the World Trade Center." [4]

Ordinary people had begun to mobilize to try to influence the outcome of the World Trade Center rebuilding process, and many people supported new Twin Towers.

Pro-Rebuilders Helped Make a Meaningful Difference

Many people volunteered considerable time and money in their efforts to help achieve new Twin Towers. These people were often referred to generically as "pro-rebuilders," and they helped make a meaningful difference. Their substantial efforts included letters to the editor, media appearances, rallies (including some organized by this book's editor, Joe Wright), and personal interactions with business and political leaders and other stakeholders in the World Trade Center redevelopment process. Without the many efforts of the pro-rebuilders, the World Trade Center site might have been saddled with the Libeskind designs that Pataki tried to cram down all of our throats in late February 2003. In my opinion, the original Libeskind designs would have been an architectural nightmare because they featured relatively short buildings sheared off at sharp angles that looked to me like pieces of broken glass after an explosion, with the so-called "Freedom" Tower (an Orwellian label bestowed by Pataki) topped off by what resembled a large switchblade. Libeskind's awful structures would have been located near what he insisted should be a deep pit, and his entire mess would have imposed significant pain and suffering on millions of people for generations to come. Thankfully, the many efforts of the pro-rebuilders helped consign Libeskind's architectural nightmare to the dustbin of history, and New York avoided becoming a laughingstock around the world.

Not Quite a Twin Tower

On June 29, 2005, *The New York Times* reported that:

New York officials unveiled a redesigned Freedom Tower today whose height and proportion, centered antenna and cut-away corners, tall lobbies and pinstripe facade evoke — both deliberately and coincidentally — the sky-piercing twins it is meant to replace... adjustments and refinements have been made to underscore the similarities. For example, the altitude of the floor of the rooftop observation deck would be set at 1,362 feet, the height of 2 World Trade Center. The rooftop parapet would reach 1,368 feet, the height of No. 1.

The so-called "Freedom" Tower was redesigned to look much more like one of the Twin Towers we lost, probably in response to the many efforts of the pro-rebuilders, which received strong public support from real estate mogul Donald Trump in May 2005. Construction of the so-called "Freedom" Tower is finally well underway, and the new building has since been renamed One World Trade Center. Unlike the Twin Towers, the higher floors of the new One World Trade Center are smaller than the lower floors, and the total amount of office space is considerably smaller than one Twin Tower had. There will also be only one tower that achieves the height of the Twin Towers we lost instead of two. After seeing one not-quite Twin Tower in the skyline again, it will be interesting to see how strong the public demand for a second similar tower will be.

A July 24, 2001 press release from the Port Authority of New York and New Jersey mentioned that, "The World Trade Center and its Twin Towers are among the handful of instantly recognizable structures on the entire planet, like the Pyramids at Giza or the Great Wall of China." The atrocities of September 11, 2001 made the Twin Towers a near-universally recognized symbol. Unlike the beloved Twin Towers we lost, I don't know anyone who has ever seen the new One World Trade Center building on a t-shirt, a coffee mug, or a postcard. It hasn't captured the public's imagination.

In a poll done by CBS News and *The New York Times* less than a year after the atrocities of September 11, 2001, a majority of New Yorkers said they would be "comfortable going high up in new buildings at the World Trade Center site" to do such things as "eat at a rooftop restaurant or visit an observation deck." [5] Roughly two of every five New Yorkers said they would even be "willing to work in one of the higher floors of a new building at the World Trade Center site" and similar results ranging from 40% to 43% were obtained in all three polls that CBS News and *The New York Times* conducted in 2005 and 2006. Given the large size of the New York area labor force, this would have been enough to fill the top half of more than 200 new Twin Towers. The argument that no one would work in new Twin Towers was always false, even in 2002.

Before the atrocities of September 11, 2001, the Twin Towers were 97% leased. Despite this, there is a myth that new and safer Twin Towers would have a hard time finding tenants. But having worked in our original Twin Towers, this strikes me as exceedingly unlikely, for the six different reasons I originally spelled out in my June 9, 2005, memo to Donald Trump.

First, consider what it's like to run a small or even medium-sized business. There are almost never enough resources for an adequate marketing budget. But when a small or medium-sized business leased space in new and safer Twin Towers, it would gain more free publicity than it could handle. This valuable publicity would act as a powerful incentive for small and medium-sized businesses to lease space in new Twin Towers. Every business card handed out to potential clients with a Twin Towers address would leave a powerful and lasting impression that would help a Twin Towers business stand out in a crowded competitive environment.

Second, some people would strongly prefer to buy some of the goods and services they desire from businesses located in new and safer Twin Towers. And to help such customers, there should be a single website for all participating Twin Towers businesses, organized by product or service categories. This would make it especially easy for people and organizations all over the world to favor Twin Towers businesses.

Third, even some large consumer products companies would want to lease space in new and safer Twin Towers as part of their marketing strategy. For example, there might be an international clothing company managed from an office in new Twin Towers. This company might deliberately choose to advertise in glossy high fashion magazines with the caption "Milan / Paris / World Trade Center Twin Towers."

Fourth, retailers in and around new and safer Twin Towers would be helped by commuter traffic and would benefit enormously from considerable tourist traffic. There would be substantially more tourism than there was prior to the atrocities of September 11, 2001. And the retail space near the Twin Towers we lost was already some of the most lucrative in the entire United States. It also seems quite obvious that new Twin Towers would attract far more tourism than a single not-quite Twin Tower would. When comparing dollars per square foot, retail space in and around new Twin Towers will rent for several times as much as office space would. And this would help make the entire World Trade Center self-supporting far faster than the pessimists realize.

Fifth, roughly 93% of the people who worked in the Twin Towers survived. Even though it had only been roughly a year after the atrocities, the World Trade Center Tenants Association did a survey of its members in 2002. Most said they were eager to return. Some Twin Towers lessees are now locked into long-term leases elsewhere, and they would not be able to return right away. As these leases expire, this would be a continuing source of strong demand for new Twin Towers for years to come.

Sixth, there are many people who would want to lease space in new and safer Twin Towers for something more than purely economic reasons, a desire to be personally part of something truly historic and meaningful. New Twin Towers would continue to stand for civilized values. As the lead architect of the Twin Towers we lost, Minoru Yamasaki, once said, the "World Trade Center is… a monument to world peace… a representation of man's belief in humanity, his need for individual dignity, his beliefs in the cooperation of men, and through cooperation, his ability to find greatness."

New and safer Twin Towers would likely be an economic success. Even right after the worst recession since the Great

Depression, demand for space on the highest floors of the best Class A Manhattan office buildings was surprisingly strong. For example, the December 4, 2009, issue of *Crain's New York Business* reported that Brazil's Banco Itau is paying more than $130 a square foot for 25,000 square feet of space on the top floor of the General Motors Building.

Although not an exact comparison, this is more than triple the rent per square foot that I was paying for office space on the 77th floor of One World Trade Center before it was destroyed in the atrocities of September 11, 2001. The Cassidy Turley Commercial Real Estate Services Market Research Newsletter for March 2011 reported that average asking rent for Manhattan Class A office space had "its sixth straight monthly increase," and that the Manhattan Class A office space vacancy rate was down to 11.3% from 12.8% a year ago. The large commercial real estate firm Cushman & Wakefield projects strong rent increases for Manhattan office space through at least 2013.

New Twin Towers Are Still Possible

New Twin Towers are still possible, but as construction proceeds at the World Trade Center site, the range of options for new and safer Twin Towers keeps shrinking. Business and political leaders might continue to ignore both public opinion and economic opportunity and remain unwilling to support new and safer Twin Towers at the World Trade Center site. I hope not, because new and safer Twin Towers at the World Trade Center site would also be a profound living memorial to the magnificent people we lost and an important symbol of our civilization. If any such opposition proves insurmountable, then new and safer Twin Towers might make sense on the underdeveloped Far West Side of Manhattan or even in Jersey City, New Jersey.

Myths of Rebuilding the World Trade Center

By Jonathan Hakala

You may remember the powerful beams of light that temporarily tried to fill the awful hole in our skyline. One of the two artists who designed this "tribute in light," Paul Myoda, said in *The New York Times*, "I fully want office buildings to be there again. Not a graveyard or a rose garden or a piece of art. There should be big buildings." Our goal: new World Trade Center towers that are even safer and taller. Our struggle will be long. Our struggle will be challenging. But when all is said and done, we will prevail.

To prevail, we need to overcome four myths. The first myth is that no one would work on the higher floors. The second myth is we don't need to rebuild eleven million square feet of office space. The third myth is that so-called "skyline elements" would somehow be an acceptable substitute for safer, taller towers. And the fourth myth is that all sixteen acres at Ground Zero should be left empty, either out of respect for the victims and their families or because new towers might be a terrorist target.

We will decisively defeat every single one of these four myths, starting with the myth that no one would work on the higher floors of new tall towers. I am reminded of a true story about John Whitehead that beautifully illustrates why we will be successful.

Mr. Whitehead is Chairman of the Lower Manhattan Development Corporation — the LMDC. Eighteen years ago, in late 1984, he was cochairman of Goldman Sachs and he hosted a large luncheon for new Goldman employees, at which the guest speaker was Dr. Henry Kissinger. I was one of the new Goldman employees in the audience. Mr. Whitehead and his staff had literally hundreds of outstanding Manhattan restaurants to choose from. So where did Mr. Whitehead choose to hold the Kissinger luncheon? At Windows on the World on the 107th floor of One World Trade Center. Mr. Whitehead knew, as did we all, that there was no location more impressive. Simply put, many people will always prefer the honor of occupying some of the highest floors in the world.

CBS News and *The New York Times* conducted a poll of more

than 1,000 people and asked them, "Would you be willing to work on one of the higher floors of a new building at the World Trade Center site?" Almost two out of every five people said yes, we are indeed willing to work on the higher floors. This magnificent result is far better than anything we could reasonably have hoped for.

The census bureau says New York City has a labor force of more than 4.2 million people, not including New Jersey or Long Island. Extrapolate the CBS News/*New York Times* poll and more than 1.6 million people are willing to work on the higher floors. But it gets even better.

There were thousands of us who worked in the World Trade Center who lived in New Jersey or out on Long Island. If you take the entire New York metropolitan area, more than three million people would be willing to work on the higher floors. And that's enough people to fill the top half of more than 200 new towers.

With such overwhelming potential demand, there needs to be a transparent process to determine who will have the honor of occupying the higher floors. The LMDC should hold a worldwide auction for space above the 85th floor. Such an auction will almost certainly be heavily oversubscribed. There will be overwhelming demand from people and businesses, and this will send a powerful message supporting safer, taller towers. There have even been media reports that one executive alone has indicated a willingness to take the top five floors of one of our new towers. We will prevail.

There is a second myth we will decisively defeat; the myth that we don't need to rebuild eleven million square feet of office space. Rebuilding is critically important for our economic future, as noted by Larry Silverstein in *The Wall Street Journal*: "About 50,000 people worked in the World Trade Center. Those jobs are lost, along with those of another 50,000 people who worked in the vicinity. Together, those jobs in lower Manhattan…produced annual gross wages of about $47 billion, or 15% of the annual gross wages earned in the entire state [of New York]." We need to bring the 100,000 jobs we lost back to Lower Manhattan. Tens of thousands of high-end jobs paying billions of dollars in taxes that pay for social services. And tens of thousands of entry-level jobs, which are also critically important, especially for

Chinatown and the Lower East Side. Not rebuilding would condemn us to a continuing vicious spiral of job destruction.

One of the largest Manhattan commercial real estate brokers is Cushman & Wakefield. If all eleven million square feet are rebuilt, Cushman & Wakefield projects that average Downtown rent at the end of 2008 will be $33 per square foot. If no office space were rebuilt, rent would instead be much higher at $42.55 per square foot. Many businesses will survive and expand paying $33 per square foot but would die trying to pay a much higher $42.55 per square foot.

We cannot allow a few wealthy real estate developers and landlords to take priority over the well-being of the entire New York City area. There are some good real estate developers and good landlords who understand this. Unfortunately, others are trying to delay rebuilding our new towers for as long as possible, to keep the rents they collect artificially high. We the people are determined to prevail over those who've made hundreds of thousands of dollars in campaign contributions in an attempt to corrupt this process and who would eventually desecrate Ground Zero with mediocre fifty- and sixty-story buildings from one end of Ground Zero to the other.

We will be constructive. We will always be law-abiding. We will behave responsibly. But do not underestimate our resolve. We will prevail.

Now we're going to decisively defeat a third myth; the myth that so-called "skyline elements" would somehow be an acceptable substitute for safer, taller towers. I have a cheap yellow plastic ruler in my hand. When I put this ruler directly on top of my head, no one thinks I'm suddenly seven feet tall.

Similarly, the six timid plans we rejected had so-called "skyline elements" resembling large drinking straws on top of short buildings. We weren't fooled. We know that people from all over the world for decades to come will judge New York by how well or how poorly we rebuild Ground Zero. These "skyline elements" — these large drinking straws — would have made New York the laughingstock of the world. The Jay Lenos and the David Lettermans would have had a field day at New York's expense, and we would have been judged a city in decline. "Skyline elements" are feeble and embarrassing substitutes for dynamic towers. "Skyline elements" would make a short World

Trade Center building even worse, not better.

Large drinking straws on top of short buildings at Ground Zero might have meant a few hundred million dollars in extra profits over time for a few already wealthy real estate developers and landlords. But that pales in comparison to building safer, taller towers, which will likely result in many billions of extra dollars for New York's tourist industries and economy over the years. We will prevail.

The fourth and final myth we need to overcome is the myth that all sixteen acres at Ground Zero should be reserved for our memorial. We passionately desire a world-class memorial that will show respect for the victims and their families. But we do not believe that all sixteen acres are required to build such a memorial. It is a political fantasy for anyone to believe that all sixteen acres will be preserved forever. That just isn't going to happen. But there is another option — rebuilding two tall towers allows us to preserve the maximum amount of open space for our memorial. The LMDC didn't seem to understand this; the six awful plans we so decisively rejected made it clear that their only real alternative to tall towers would have been the construction of lots of short buildings at Ground Zero, insulting the memory of all the good people we lost, and leaving much less land for our memorial.

The human beings we lost were bold. These people deserve majestic new towers as bold as they were. One of the best ways we can honor them is to carry on their work. Safer, taller towers will be a living testament that complements our memorial and helps make it one of the seven modern wonders of the world. We need a skyline that does justice to the wonderful people we lost. We will not sell these people short. Our new World Trade Center towers will be at least 111 stories tall. And we are profoundly grateful that many family members are already part of our movement or agree with us.

A few people say we should leave all sixteen acres empty because new towers might be a terrorist target. These people miss the point. Any building anywhere near Ground Zero might be a target even if just two stories tall. There are tens of thousands of possible targets all over the world, and we certainly haven't abandoned them. We will take full advantage of better safety features, better security measures, better structural integrity, better environmental standards, and other modern technologies that have become available over the last thirty years. It will take several years to finish building safer, taller towers, and many potential sources of terrorism will have been eliminated by then. We will prevail.

On May 23, 2002, the LMDC held its first public hearing. The result: *The New York Times* headline, "From Public, a Strong Voice for Rebuilding Twin Towers." On July 20, the LMDC held its second public hearing at the Jacob Javits center; 5,000 people gave up an entire Saturday and expressed strong support for tall towers. On September 5, the LMDC held its third public hearing, and the result? Overwhelming public support for tall towers. ABC News reported the September 5 hearing may have been a successful turning point in our struggle for tall towers. As you can see, our voices matter. We can influence the process. And we will prevail.

People from the New York City area are well known for being tough and resilient, and it would be a crying shame if our leaders didn't allow us to demonstrate that. We can help give our leaders more backbone. I didn't go from high school in a small town in the Midwest all the way to Manhattan to work in a short World Trade Center. I will do my small part by pledging to all of you that I will never sign any lease for any space in any new World Trade Center tower that is less than 110 stories tall.

In conclusion, then, these are the four myths we must all work hard to dispel. That no one would work on the higher floors. That we don't need to rebuild 11 million square feet of office space. That so-called "skyline elements" would somehow be an acceptable substitute for safer, taller towers. And that all sixteen acres at Ground Zero should be left empty. I know we can decisively defeat all of these myths. We will prevail.

Finally, I say that we have every right to expect more from our political leaders. A century ago, Theodore Roosevelt was President of the United States, having previously served as Governor of New York State and as the first Police Commissioner of New York City. If President Roosevelt had been alive today, his outstanding leadership would have kept the real decision-making process from being dominated by wealthy real estate developers and landlords. President Roosevelt would have insisted that we rebuild safer, taller towers.

Former New York Governor Pataki had ample time to act in the spirit of Teddy Roosevelt. Pataki's legacy and place in history will be largely defined by how poorly he managed the World Trade Center rebuilding process. Pataki's appalling judgment and his vague general statements designed to please all of the people all of the time were never a substitute for the specific leadership that New York so desperately needed.

The Twin Towers we lost on 9/11 were an almost universally recognized symbol. It has already taken far too long, but a great civilization will eventually replace the buildings we lost with something even more amazing like safer and taller Twin Towers. If the unnecessary mistakes already made at the World Trade Center site prove to make that too difficult there, then safer or taller Twin Towers could be built on the Far West Side of Manhattan or even in Jersey City, New Jersey.

To paraphrase former Canadian Prime Minister Trudeau: While it has already been ten years since 9/11, our hopes for safer and taller Twin Towers remain high. Our faith in our people is great. Our courage is strong. And our dreams for beautiful new Twin Towers will never die.

The Libeskind Plan Will Never Be Built

By Jonathan Hakala

Our goal from the beginning was new World Trade Center towers that are even safer and taller. Our goal has not changed. Our struggle has been long and challenging, but we will ultimately prevail. We have made enormous progress. Because of this magnificent progress, we can all be increasingly confident that we will indeed prevail, that this is not just some fantasy we all have but is instead an achievable reality.

All of us won a tremendous victory when it was reported that Danny Libeskind will never become the design architect or the project manager for any office building at our beloved World Trade Center site. As a result, we now stand a better chance of restoring our World Trade Center towers to at least 110 stories of occupied height.

An architect named Eli Attia designed the Millennium Hilton Hotel right across the street from our World Trade Center site. Eli, his wife Noa who is also an architect, and a brilliant writer and editor named John Lumea helped turn the tide with their study titled *The Nine Lies of Daniel Libeskind*, the most infamous of which was the so-called "wedge of light" being revealed as a lot of nonsense. For having helped to save us all from Libeskind's architectural atrocity, I would ask you to give Eli, Noa, and John vigorous support.

Our focus will soon shift away from Danny Libeskind, who is quickly becoming yesterday's news, and toward developer Larry Silverstein's favorite architect, a man named David Childs. The great city of London's *Guardian* newspaper seemed to be making a prediction this past Monday regarding our World Trade Center, "The developer will decide everything about the design."

I outlined the four battles we need to win to get the kind of new World Trade Center towers we all deserve. I am happy to report that we have already decisively won two of these four battles. There was still a big debate about whether or not we needed to rebuild ten million square feet of office space. That debate is essentially over, and we won. We will rebuild at least ten million square feet of office space.

There was still a big debate about whether or not to leave all sixteen acres at our World Trade Center site empty. That debate is essentially over, and again, we won. We will not leave all sixteen acres empty.

There are two battles still raging. The first battle is about the economics of tall towers. Winning this battle is crucial for us to get World Trade Center towers that have occupied height at least as tall as before. What is driving the entire World Trade Center rebuilding process far more than anything else is money. So last November, it was important to attack head-on the myth that no one would work on the higher floors. Last summer's CBS News/*New York Times* poll of more than 1,000 people asked each of them, "Would you be willing to work on one of the higher floors of a new building at the World Trade Center site?" Almost two of every five people said yes, we are indeed willing to work on the higher floors. Extrapolating the CBS News/*New York Times* poll to the New York City metropolitan area's large labor force, more than three million people would be willing to work on the higher floors. And that's enough people to fill the top half of more than 200 new towers. Many people will always prefer the honor of occupying some of the highest floors in the world.

Understandably, Silverstein wants to make as much money as he possibly can. Our opponents sometimes claim that Silverstein might make more money constructing mediocre fifty- and sixty-story buildings. Now it is true that a 120-story building would usually be more expensive to construct than two mediocre sixty-story buildings. But it is also true that high floors usually generate larger rents than low floors.

Since Silverstein cares about maximizing his profits, he needs to get the best information he can to discover whether or not the extra revenue would outweigh the extra cost. By far the best way to do this will be to hold a worldwide auction for the space on the high floors, before building them. Such an auction will almost certainly be heavily oversubscribed. There will be overwhelming demand from people and businesses, and this will send a powerful message supporting safer, taller towers. You may remember reading the *New York Post* reporting that one executive alone indicated a willingness to take the top five floors of one of the new towers. And it wouldn't just be Silverstein who would maximize his profits. Building safer, taller towers will likely result in many billions of extra dollars for New York City's tourist industries and economy over the years.

On the other hand, mediocre fifty- and sixty-story buildings would likely turn into a financial disaster for Silverstein and our tourist industries and economy. Market input from all of us who are potential tenants in our new World Trade Center towers can help Silverstein avoid making the wrong decision. I will do my small part by again pledging that I will never sign any lease for any space in any new World Trade Center tower that has less than 110 stories of occupied height. The second battle still raging regards the myth that so-called "skyline elements" would somehow be an acceptable substitute for safer, taller towers. These so-called "skyline elements" are the anorexic spires that resemble large drinking straws on top of short buildings. People from all over the world for decades to come will judge New York by how well or how poorly we rebuild our beloved World Trade Center. These anorexic spires — these large drinking straws — would make New York the laughingstock of the world. The Jay Lenos and the David Lettermans would have a field day at New York's expense, and we would be judged a city in decline. "Skyline elements" would be feeble and embarrassing substitutes for dynamic towers. "Skyline elements" would make a short World Trade Center building even worse, not better. The almost 2,900 human beings we lost at our World Trade Center were bold. These people deserve majestic new towers as bold as they were, not ridiculous, pathetic "skyline elements." We will not sell these people short. Our new World Trade Center towers will have at least 110 stories of occupied height.

In poll after poll, majorities of people support rebuilding our beloved twin towers. And yet you may have noticed what at first seems like an interesting contradiction, because similar polls say that majorities do not want to build the "world's tallest building." Libeskind's architectural nightmare featured the mother of all skyline elements, an anorexic switchblade spire that supposedly made the so-called "Freedom Tower" 1776 feet tall. And Libeskind kept claiming, over and over again, that this would make it the world's tallest building. Libeskind's architectural nightmare has always been deeply unpopular with the broader public. So it's not surprising that many people vote against the "world's tallest building" because they believe they're opposing Libeskind's architectural nightmare by doing so.

I mentioned earlier that Danny Libeskind will never become the design architect or the project manager for any office building at our beloved World Trade Center site. But we still need to get rid of the awful site plan Libeskind left behind. And probably the most effective way we can get rid of it is through the environmental impact statement legal process.

Libeskind's site plan would be an environmental nightmare. It fails to provide the open space we require, is much too dense, and would turn our World Trade Center site into a parking lot.

Libeskind's site plan nightmare is grossly deficient in community open space. Libeskind's so-called park of heroes is fractured into four tiny pieces, each of which is literally smaller than many suburban front lawns. It would be environmentally irresponsible to settle for anything less than the amount of community open space we enjoyed before our beloved World Trade Center was destroyed in the atrocities of 9/11. Taller towers equals fewer towers equals more open space.

New York City's zoning resolutions exist to protect our urban environment, to guarantee light, air, and open space for all. The six dreadful Beyer Blinder Belle schemes were decisively rejected by 5,000 people at Listening to the City over a year ago, and one of the biggest reasons why was they were much too dense.

Danny Libeskind obviously didn't bother to listen to the city. His site plan nightmare features a super-dense wall of mediocre fifty- and sixty-story buildings along Church Street, even though he won't be the design architect or project manager for any of them. Libeskind's site plan nightmare flagrantly violates the density standards set forth in New York City's zoning resolutions. His site plan nightmare would cause irreparable damage to our urban environment by subjecting us and our children to some of the worst light and air conditions in all of New York City for hundreds of years to come. We cannot and will not allow that to happen. Taller towers equals fewer towers equals less density.

Should we encourage pedestrian traffic at our new World Trade Center? Yes. Encourage bicycle traffic? Yes. Access for emergency vehicles? Of course. But Libeskind's site plan nightmare would desecrate our World Trade Center site by encouraging sport utility vehicles, trucks, buses, and cars to suffocate us and our children with traffic jams and air and noise pollution. It would be environmental insanity to allow this when our previous World Trade Center did not. Let us all agree — rebuilders of every stripe, victims' families, neighborhood residents, survivors, environmentalists, Democrats and Republicans and all those of other political persuasions — let us all agree that on these sixteen acres we will not replace blood with oil.

And now a brief message for Governor George E. Pataki. We applaud your decision not to allow Danny Libeskind to become the design architect or the project manager for any office building at our beloved World Trade Center site. But now it's time to get rid of the awful site plan Libeskind left behind, and remove him from the entire World Trade Center rebuilding project once and for all. Pay Libeskind his severance, and move forward.

Governor, we want you to be successful. We want you to earn a wonderful legacy and an excellent place in history. We want to have a productive dialogue with you. We will be constructive. We will always be law-abiding. We will behave responsibly. But do not underestimate our resolve to get rid of Libeskind's site plan nightmare.

We the people will prevail. We will stop Libeskind's site plan nightmare from depriving us of the environment we deserve, through the political process if possible, in a court of law if necessary. And we will enjoy new World Trade Center towers that are both safer and taller.

Our hopes are high. Our faith in our people is great. Our courage is strong. And our dreams for a beautiful new World Trade Center will never die.

* * *

Note from the editor: This essay was written several years ago and, because of that, may appear somewhat dated. But it also contains important information and commentary that is vital to understanding the history of rebuilders' efforts to see that the twin towers of the World Trade Center are rebuilt.

Better than Libeskind, but Not Yet Good Enough

By Jonathan Hakala

Ever since the atrocities of September 11, 2001, millions of people have been looking forward to seeing new Twin Towers on the Manhattan skyline, skyscrapers that would be safer and taller than the ones we loved and lost.

In a November 2002 speech, I warned the audience that the struggle to achieve new Twin Towers would be long and challenging. Two months earlier, in September 2002, architect Daniel Libeskind had unveiled a hideous plan for rebuilding the World Trade Center site. To quote the architect and author Philip Nobel, Libeskind's plan had "proposed to turn the site into a kind of shattered crystal city." [6] If Libeskind's "shattered crystal city" had actually been built, its constant reminder of destruction would have inflicted considerable and unnecessary additional pain and suffering on many people. A huge seventy-foot hole in the ground that Libeskind so desperately wanted to preserve would have severely damaged the neighborhood surrounding the World Trade Center site and would have made any economic recovery in the area far more difficult if not impossible.

The then New York Governor George Pataki was a strong supporter of Libeskind's awful plans. Pataki dominated a new government body formed in November 2001 that was later renamed the Lower Manhattan Development Corporation (LMDC). When the LMDC's own site selection committee voted against Libeskind's plan in favor of another one, Pataki quickly overrode their decision. Pataki even went so far as to give the tallest building in Libeskind's dreadful plans the Orwellian name "Freedom Tower." Almost three years of considerable effort by many different people forced Pataki to change course time and again. People in favor of building new Twin Towers, often referred to as "pro-rebuilders," were crucial in defeating Libeskind. As a result, Libeskind failed to become the design architect or project manager for any office building at the World Trade Center site.

Libeskind's plan featured a plaza that he named the "Wedge of Light." Libeskind claimed that each September 11, between the time the first airplane hit one of the Twin Towers on

September 11, 2001, (8:46 a.m.) and the time that Twin Tower finally collapsed (10:28 a.m.), the sun would shine on this "Wedge of Light" without shadow. An architect named Eli Attia designed the Millennium Hilton Hotel right across the street from the World Trade Center site. Eli, his wife Noa who is also an architect, and a brilliant writer and editor named John Lumea helped turn the tide with their study titled *The Nine Lies of Daniel Libeskind*, the most infamous of which was the so-called "Wedge of Light" being revealed as a lot of nonsense. In fact, Eli Attia demonstrated that at 10:28 a.m. on any given sunny September 11, the "Wedge of Light" would actually be 99% covered in shadow and only 1% sunshine. For having helped to save us all from Libeskind's architectural atrocity, Eli Attia, Noa Attia, and John Lumea all deserve our gratitude.

The focus began to shift away from Libeskind, who became "yesterday's news," and toward developer Larry Silverstein's favorite architect, David Childs. At first, Childs kept many of the undesirable elements of the various Libeskind plans, which the pro-rebuilders continued to oppose.

In November 2002, I outlined four battles that needed to be won to advance the cause of new Twin Towers. In 2002, there was still a big debate about whether or not New York needed to rebuild at least ten million square feet of office space. There will always be a few people who oppose even sensible commercial development and the jobs and economic opportunity that such development brings. That said, the debate regarding this issue is essentially over, and advocates of new Twin Towers were on the winning side of the argument. New York can eventually look forward to at least ten million square feet of new office space at the World Trade Center site.

In 2002, there was still a big debate about whether or not to leave all sixteen acres at the World Trade Center site empty. That debate is over, and again, advocates of new Twin Towers were on the winning side of the argument.

There was also a battle in 2002 about the economics of tall towers. Winning this argument was always crucial before any towers would be built that have occupied height at least as tall as the beloved Twin Towers we lost on September 11, 2001. It was important to attack head-on the myth that no one would work on higher floors. CBS News and *The New York Times* conducted several polls of more than 1,000 people and asked each of them whether or not they would be willing to work on one of the higher floors of a new building at the World Trade Center site. Almost two of every five people said yes, we are indeed willing to work on the higher floors. Extrapolating the CBS News and *New York Times* poll results to the New York City metropolitan area's large labor force meant that more than three million people would be willing to work on the higher floors. That was enough people to fill the top half of more than 200 new towers. Many people will always prefer the honor of occupying some of the highest floors in the world. For the last several years, the upper floors of prestigious Manhattan office buildings have commanded much higher rents than the lower floors. Data from Manhattan's commercial real estate marketplace make it abundantly clear that advocates of new Twin Towers were on the winning side of this argument.

Developer Larry Silverstein and the Port Authority of New York and New Jersey still hope to eventually finish building several office buildings on the World Trade Center site that would be shorter than the old Twin Towers. In the current difficult economic environment, there is insufficient demand for such space, which threatens to leave the World Trade Center area a construction site for many years to come.

The Twin Towers were an almost universally recognized symbol. In addition to being a wonderful way to honor the many good people we lost on September 11, 2001, new Twin Towers would be a worldwide "brand" with unique economic value to their tenants. One way to demonstrate that this is indeed the case would be to hold a worldwide auction for the space on the high floors of new Twin Towers before building them. Such an auction would almost certainly be heavily oversubscribed with overwhelming demand from businesses and from some very wealthy individuals. Building new Twin Towers would also likely result in a total of billions of extra dollars for New York City's tourist industries and economy over the years.

The fourth battle I described in November 2002 pertained to the myth that so-called "skyline elements" would somehow be an acceptable substitute for safer, taller towers. These so-called "skyline elements" were the anorexic spires that resembled large drinking straws on top of short buildings. People from all over the world for decades to come will judge New York by how well or how poorly we rebuild our beloved World Trade Center. These anorexic spires — these large drinking straws — would have made New York the laughingstock of the world, and New York would have been judged a city in decline. "Skyline elements" would have been feeble and embarrassing substitutes for dynamic towers. "Skyline elements" would have made a short World Trade Center building even worse, not better. The almost 2,900 human beings we lost at our World Trade Center were bold. These people always deserved majestic new towers as bold as they were, not ridiculous, pathetic "skyline elements."

In poll after poll, people consistently supported building new Twin Towers compared to Libeskind's architectural nightmare, which was deeply unpopular with the broader public. Libeskind's architectural nightmare featured the mother of all skyline elements, an anorexic switchblade spire that supposedly made the so-called "Freedom Tower" 1776 feet tall. After Libeskind was defeated, the anorexic switchblade spire was replaced by a proposal for a more conventional television antenna. The "Freedom Tower" became the new One World Trade Center, with the height of the building itself comparable to one of the Twin Towers we lost. That said, the new One World Trade Center will not have as many square feet as the old one. It's a lot better than Libeskind, but not as good as it could or should have been.

Unfortunately, there are still some elements of Libeskind's site plan for the World Trade Center that survive as part of the official World Trade Center rebuilding site plan to this day, and which if fully implemented threaten to be an environmental nightmare. The site plan fails to replace all of the open space from the original World Trade Center, is too dense, and threatens to turn our World Trade Center site into a parking lot.

Libeskind's site plan nightmare was grossly deficient in community open space. Libeskind's so-called "Park of Heroes" was fractured into four tiny pieces, each of which was literally smaller than many suburban front lawns. It would be environmentally irresponsible to settle for significantly less than the amount of community open space that existed before our beloved World Trade Center was destroyed in the atrocities of September 11, 2001. Taller towers can mean fewer towers which can result in more open space.

New York City's zoning resolutions exist to protect its urban environment, and to guarantee sufficient light, air, and open space for all of its citizens and visitors. The Port Authority of New York and New Jersey claims that it is not legally bound by New York City's zoning resolutions at the World Trade Center site. The six boring schemes for rebuilding the World Trade Center site from the architecture firm Beyer Blinder Belle were decisively rejected by 5,000 people at a major event called Listening to the City in the summer of 2002. One of the biggest reasons why they were rejected is that Beyer Blinder Belle's proposals were much too dense. Architects I have spoken to say that the site plan nightmare could cause irreparable damage to New York's urban environment by subjecting New Yorkers near the World Trade Center site and their children to some of the worst light and air conditions in all of New York City for hundreds of years to come. Taller towers could mean fewer towers which would result in less density.

Should we encourage pedestrian traffic at the new World Trade Center? Yes. Encourage bicycle traffic? Yes. Access for emergency vehicles? Of course. But the site plan would desecrate our World Trade Center site by encouraging sport utility vehicles, trucks, buses, and cars to suffocate us and our children with traffic jams and air and noise pollution. It would be environmental insanity to allow this when our previous World Trade Center did not. Those who favor left-of-center politics often oppose war with the slogan "no blood for oil." At the World Trade Center site, pro-rebuilders of every stripe, victims' families, neighborhood residents, survivors, environmentalists, Democrats and Republicans and all those of other political persuasions should all be able to agree that on the World Trade Center's sixteen acres we should not replace blood with diesel fumes or gasoline exhaust, especially if that would give potential terrorists unnecessary access to perpetrate another atrocity.

Ten years after the atrocities of September 11, 2001, the most recent plans for the future of the World Trade Center site are a lot better than those proposed by Daniel Libeskind, but are still nowhere near as good as they should be.

Anatomy of a Disgrace

By Louis Epstein

On September 11, 2001, ten murderous men in two airplanes gave their lives for their dream that gigantic landmark twin towers no longer dominate the skyline of lower Manhattan, that the city and America stand humbled and "cut down to size."

In so doing they extinguished the lives of thousands of good people, people who had and were entitled to every hope that those towers would continue to stand, that they would go on working there or protecting those who worked there, that the legendary Financial District of New York would survive. From that day forward there has been a struggle over whose dream would prevail, with insensitivity and incompetence combining to seek preservation of the terrorist vision of eternal enshrined devastation crying to the world that America dares not rise again, that the destruction of its icons is a fruitful endeavor.

In a war of symbols it is surrender to allow the destruction of one's symbols to stand, and closing one's eyes to this does not blunt the message to those who leave their eyes open. Redevelopment in a way that repudiates the act of destruction sends a message of defiance; redevelopment in a way that repudiates what was destroyed sends a message of submission that will linger on the ground long after any military response.

But these truths were lost on those officials who took it upon themselves to manage the vital matter of what would rise from the ashes of this catastrophic scene of mass murder and urban desolation. Quickly a "Lower Manhattan Redevelopment Corporation" was authorized, and then quietly that syllable "Re" disappeared without even an announcement. The implication that what was there before would return, be rebuilt, restored, was something they dared not preserve. To dare was not in them; they saw shrinking in the face of the short-term fears that had been the key goal of the terrorists as the guide for the long-term future, accommodation of those the terrorists had succeeded in terrorizing as appropriate response to the public. The hard fact of engineering that super-tall buildings are the safest of structures did not affect them; perceived risk was all and actual risk nothing.

In January 2002, John Whitehead, chairman of the renamed "Lower Manhattan Development Corporation," publicly announced that it was an emerging consensus among everyone he spoke to that rebuilding on the former scale was neither feasible nor appropriate. This jarring demonstration of how far removed those he spoke to were from a huge portion of popular opinion was the first public evidence of how wrong-headed the official planning process would be, a deficiency that has been regularly demonstrated ever since.

The opinions sought and listened to in the formative stages of the official process were far from representative. They involved preexisting lobby groups that had an intrinsic bias toward making the city different than it had been. After all, no one feels a need to form a group to save a status quo that seems under no threat, and until that horrible September day no one thought anything would remove the vastly profitable World Trade Center from the scene.

Groups that favored drastically different philosophies of urban design, groups that saw professional opportunities for themselves, and groups that saw any pool of funds dedicated to relief of the needy as best devoted to their own priorities swooped in to claim they spoke for all.

Allied to this was the most vocal proportion of those who had lost loved ones in the attacks, casting about in their grief for solace. Whether seeking to blame someone for their loss or seeking maximum public recognition of their loss, they made pleas of a kind rare in previous historical disasters that often amounted to leaving the site as the killers of their loved ones had desired rather than permitting it to be reclaimed for the purposes to which and for which their loved ones had given their lives.

To the vulture-like opportunists seeing an opportunity to remake the city, and to the emotionally devastated seeking to see its unmaking left as a tribute to the victims, the officials listened. To the wider nation anxious to see the restoration of what could be restored, they paid no heed.

A "Draft Principles and Preliminary Blueprint" document was released, based on workshops with handpicked advisory groups, and only then was public comment invited.

In May 2002, a public hearing was at last held — and strong demands for rebuilding of tall towers were heard. Some came from those who had worked in the towers or lost close friends there, some from people who had made long journeys to be heard. Only then was the "Blueprint" revised to include an appeasing "skyline element." Otherwise it was largely unrevised.

In June 2002, the Governor loudly and publicly shoved his oar into the process, pledging "we will never build where the towers stood" in front of a small audience dedicated to that goal, heedless of the significant portion of public opinion seeing this as a shameful act of surrender.

In July 2002, the "Phase I" designs were released — bland "massing diagrams" that inspired nobody, all named "Memorial" something-or-other in the hope that focus on the memorial would divert attention from their mediocrity. Every one of them was a flop with public opinion, including the one almost indistinguishable from the eventually anointed site plan of Daniel Libeskind.

Officials pledged at the giant "Listening to the City II" meeting to listen to those who had criticized every plan, who had singled out the buildings being too short and not monumental enough as the worst thing about the plans, who had called the site plans too crowded. They promised to be bold and come up with better ideas.

The September 2002 public hearing had a more resoundingly pro-tall-towers audience than ever, the officials repeating that they already understood that something better than the rejected concepts of crowded, stunted symbols of surrender was needed and would be offered.

They then turned around and made the three key reasons the plans had been condemned into binding program requirements for the next phase.

That Greenwich Street be extended completely through the site, slashing through what had been one of lower Manhattan's largest open spaces and dividing the site into a narrow eastern wedge, in which any buildings would necessarily be crowded and forced close to the streets, and a wider western wedge, was considered a must for any plan.

That both "footprints" of the former Twin Towers be left completely empty, making it impossible to site buildings on much of the western wedge, heedless of the implicit invitation to future terrorists to ensure a place in history by creating more such empty footprints, was considered a must for any plan.

And that construction proceed in small phases, only in response to market demand, rather than with the speculative boldness that alone had made the former Towers more than just ordinary buildings and proved spectacularly financially rewarding in the long term, was considered a must for any plan.

The word was sent out loud and clear that no plan that departed from official thinking on any of these three issues would be considered, and that only those willing to sign a comprehensive waiver of their intellectual property rights would be allowed to submit plans.

Further, it was demanded that the uses of the site be substantially different from before, the destruction of the distinctive character of the Financial District being seen as a public benefit. Highly profitable underground retail space was required to be sacrificed for weather-dependent street-level space.

What was left, they called the "innovative design competition," a rather wishful name considering their determination to stifle both creativity and any consideration of plans that did not depart drastically from the former design in certain specified ways.

The resulting designs were as a rule needlessly bizarre and yet straitjacketed by the unreasonable program requirements, putting too many twenty-first century buildings on a partial resurrection of the cramped nineteenth-century blocks that inspired past generations to move away from the area.

None of this range of choices was an overwhelming favorite, the most popular being the twin towers proposed by Lord Foster, a less marketable configuration than the old because of the obstruction of each other's views forced by the demand for total restoration of Greenwich Street.

(It may be noted that when the Project for Public Spaces opened a public comment board on the idea of restoring Greenwich Street through the site, every single person who bothered posting said not to do so.)

Public hearings on these plans brought forward criticism of their impracticalities, though Daniel Libeskind, smiling at front row center, made sure some shills praised his plans as part of his widely publicized self-promotion.

When the officials chose two of the nine design team plans as "finalists," they selected plans that were not particularly popular, but served the preconceived unreasonable goals.

The Libeskind plan, shattered shard-like buildings centered on a gaping pit that celebrated the mass murderers' destruction, differed only in that pit, the odd shapes of the buildings, and the intrusion of even more vehicle traffic, from the "Memorial Plaza" plan denounced in July.

The THINK team's "World Cultural Center" had coil-spring-like skeletal towers suspending bizarrely shaped inhabited sections — and the officials required that its height be reduced as consideration proceeded.

Public polls were offered to gauge popular reaction to these plans, and where "Neither" was offered as an option it was very successful. A poll offered by New York One had tens of thousands of respondents and a strong "Neither" majority and was slated to run until after the announcement of the official winner in February 2003 — so the official planners prevailed on New York One to close it down ahead of schedule in favor of one they would jointly sponsor as the official public poll of the official planning process.

"Neither" still won, and Libeskind finished last.

When the committee formally tasked with making the selection met to choose, its members leaned toward the modified THINK proposal — only to have Governor Pataki, amid rumors of bribery, compel them, mostly his appointees, to vote for Libeskind.

Thus, an architect who specialized in museums and had never built a high-rise building in his life was named master site planner of a project including some of the tallest buildings in New York, one of them marketed as the tallest building in the world though by some measures it fell clearly short.

Earlier, public hearings on the finally selected plan had been promised, but now it was announced that none would be held apart from environmental review hearings for the construction of the plan as it was. The environmental review process was intended to be compressed and streamlined to meet the Governor's politically motivated timetable, so the cornerstone for the main tower could be laid at the 2004 Republican convention and the topping-out ceremony be held the day before the 2006 party primaries.

Meanwhile, there was scurrying behind the scenes to find

actual building architects to produce practical detailed designs for what would fit with Libeskind's massing diagrams. Libeskind sought to require them to conform to detailed requirements and claimed public embrace of his largely disliked plan.

Governor Pataki sided with Libeskind's placement of the tall tower in the position least convenient for tenants. Mayor Bloomberg sought conformance to a "vision" that would further destroy the Financial District's distinct character. The Deputy Mayor Dan Doctoroff demanded the retail configuration be made even more street-oriented when it was already so much so that the master lessee, Westfield Properties, had demanded to be bought out rather than continue, that the lobbies of the office buildings be made harder for the office tenants to get to, that even more traffic jams on the site be made possible.

The first environmental review document, the "Draft Scope," at last included a "Restoration Alternative" that was to evaluate the impact of putting things back the way they were rather than proceeding with the proposed development according to the Libeskind plan. This seemed clearly intended as a straw man, with the intention of downplaying its advantages and overlooking the drawbacks of the Libeskind scheme in the final documents.

Public hearings were instrumental in ensuring that a fair comparison was stipulated in the "Final Scope," with new technologies being employed in construction of restored Twin Towers not necessarily placed on the old footprints. The "Final Scope" appeared on the planning website in September 2003, and then for some reason disappeared for a while. The old "Draft Scope" remained.

After infighting between site-planner Libeskind and building architect David Childs, a deal was announced that combined the worst features of each of their plans and negated concessions to public demand apparently made between the "Draft Scope" and "Final Scope" documents. The height of the tower's roof was announced to be hundreds of feet lower than the old Twin Towers, and the ornamental cage work above it was announced to be lower than the roofs of buildings already under construction in China.

In January 2004, the Draft Generic Environmental Impact Statement was announced, and the "Restoration Alternative" given the shortest shrift the planners could manage — three paragraphs of the 72-page Executive Summary and six pages out of the thousands in the full document.

Of the three Summary paragraphs, the first described the alternative, the second invoked terrorist-inspired fears as a justification for building smaller and made unsupported statements about open space, and the third asserted without foundation that separate development of the adjoining site whose condemnation the alternative would avoid would be done without "mitigation measures" to preserve historic resources.

In the full document's discussion of the Restoration Alternative, aspect after aspect was discussed in which there would be no adverse consequence of proceeding with new Twin Towers rather than the official plan, while the document was inconsistent with itself as to whether the streets would be reopened in the Restoration Alternative as they defined it. This definition was contrived to create some problems that a little imagination would have mitigated easily, but of course in a document designed to justify a different course of action they avoided doing so.

In its encouragement of rapid population growth and vehicular traffic, and advocacy of drastic alteration of the neighborhood's prior character, the Environmental Impact Statement departed enormously from any goals of environmental protection or preservation, but it was dumped in the laps of the public by an officialdom secure in their determination to whitewash the magnitude of their folly.

What responses were made in the final Environmental Impact Statement to the comments made highlighting the mistaken reasoning behind the plan presented the same blinkered mindset that the decisions that led to the situation had to be correct and only supportive sentiments were relevant. The basically flawed environmental review process by which the lead agency proposing plans was entitled to be the reviewing agency as well led to the inevitable certification by the foxes that the chicken coop could be in no better hands than theirs.

The same runaround was repeated in 2005 and 2006 as amendments to the plan addressed its worst impracticalities without admitting the flaws rendering the entire concept indefensible. The schedule dragged and dragged and the initial completion dates have receded into the past as excavation sites have awaited inappropriate structures and every throwing of good money after bad hailed as "progress."

Under Pataki's third successor as Governor, Andrew Cuomo, Mayor Bloomberg remains, determined to see through the wretched and counterproductive memorial (long renamed to remove mention of the World Trade Center even as images of the Twin Towers were offered to those unwise enough to donate toward its construction).

In popular culture, the Eagles came forth with a memorable lyric:

There's a hole in the world tonight,
There's a cloud of fear and sorrow,
There's a hole in the world tonight,
Don't let there be a hole in the world tomorrow.

In politics, officialdom is determined to guarantee that that hole left by Osama bin Laden, even after his death, remains as empty as he commanded and everything around it shows it off, screaming symbolic encouragement to future terrorists that all they destroy will stay gone.

Official determination to move full speed ahead in the wrong direction remains undimmed, placation of the short-sighted taking precedence over all common sense. Extravagant estimates for the peak traffic of a memorial are taken as guidelines for what is to be literally set in stone, the history of memorials losing public attention as the events they commemorate recede into history being firmly ignored.

Those behind the process see themselves as concerned for their place in history — but only abandonment of the fruits of their past incompetence can save that place from being in infamy.

Too Many Generals: The Man-with-a-Plan Syndrome

By Louis Epstein

In the wake of the catastrophic destruction of the World Trade Center, countless people were motivated to call for and work for its reconstruction... both on the scale befitting what was destroyed and, as told elsewhere, in more timid and disgraceful forms including the officially planned concept of Daniel Libeskind.

While some demanded replication, even demanding fanatically exact replication, of the original design, and others favored a more flexible approach, there were also those who saw the rebuilding movement as the chance to propose their own grand designs, even some apparently interested for no other reason.

Some designs were prepared quickly after September 2001, some not started for long afterward. Some spawned lavish web sites and some were publicized by hand distribution of simple drawings. But the number of self-nominated proposals for new World Trade Center towers was vast.

Some were careful to meet only the exact height of the old Towers, and some felt it proper to do so only symbolically; others exceeded the old Towers by margins ranging from "one brick taller" to double the old size. Some plans were orthodox architecture of contemporary or historical style while others were exercises in the extremes of futurism or abstraction.

For about a year the "Build the Towers" website invited submissions of designs and reviews of designs. Some offered their own inventions and others cast themselves as nominators of some form of rebuilding the old Towers. Its votes had little impact and were easily manipulated but offered a far more inspiring selection than the official process.

Certain themes were recycled repeatedly from various sources. The metaphor of the phoenix rising from the ashes was obvious and taken up by a number of visionaries, and when the six official "Phase I" plans with names all beginning "Memorial" were announced, various would-be designers declared their own plan the "seventh" and/or titled it something beginning "Memorial." More than one designer used "Memorial Tower," which was not used by any of the underwhelming official plans.

But these visionary designers, of whatever degree of style and skill, generally sought to present themselves and their plans as *the* alternative, to promote their plans without regard to any other means offered by anyone else of meeting their desired objectives. And it was this competing plethora of self-promoters that left the rebuilding movement with the problem of *Too Many Generals*. Many potential "generals" could see the problem themselves, but saw the solution (in each case) as getting everyone to unite behind *their* plan… often hostile to the idea of putting their plan to any test other than their self-nomination of it. But the search for the best design and engineering for a construction plan has never properly been a matter to be decided by self-promotion skills, like those that Daniel Libeskind managed to use on the incompetents tasked with making the decision by officialdom.

In the face of the official determination to consider only timid plans, the "generals" shared the frustration of all pro-rebuilders, but rather than seek fair consideration of plans with proper priorities, they saw the proper course for the rebuilding movement as uniting behind their respective efforts. Clearly the thing that should have been done was a contest open to all plans that built towers on the proper scale, and the circumstances demanded nothing less; nor can less ever be settled for.

In rejecting efforts to put their plans to an outside evaluation, the "generals" insisted that the pro-rebuilding movement would be better advised to present one particular plan as what should be built, when this would in fact fracture a broad coalition while placing at the head of what remained someone who had never earned leadership fairly and would largely on that account have no credibility against its opponents.

One "general," noted architect Eli Attia, actually departed from the rebuilding movement's best interests in the opposite direction… insisting on a design competition that was designed for the maximum freedom of architects, imposing none of the necessary preconditions to demand the full scale of the destroyed Towers being restored even though he favored such a design himself.

More typical, however, were the tactics of Illinois college student Justin Berzon and Bahamian market trader Derek Turner, who beat the drum for their designs and resented any implication that others should be measured against them. Turner repeatedly urged that the World Trade Center Restoration Movement abandon the effort to solicit qualified designs and place those chosen by a jury in a public poll in favor of letting Turner's nomination of his design make it a finalist. He finally dropped off the WTCRM mailing list in protest to its mentioning the efforts of Victor Marchese, another "general" who sought to establish a pro-rebuilding group that had no interest other than funding and promoting Marchese's design.

Berzon considered his photo-manipulation that portrayed new Twin Towers on exactly the old design relocated to the east of a restored Greenwich Street to be a major feat of urban planning. His arbitrary concession of the entire western site to the megamemorialists and the full restoration of the street to the urban-utopians he considered decisions that no one should question regardless of all their implications and impracticalities. After the rebuilding movement failed to reorganize itself as his fan club, he published a book, through an imprint created for that purpose, that declared this to be the reason for the movement's lack of success.

The designs of Berzon, Turner, Marchese, and many others would be far superior to the officially considered mediocrities. But the driven desires of each man-with-a-plan (very few women were in evidence as designers, Mary Ann Hart offering a building location plan and Marcia Esquenazi occupied towers with memorial atria and a skybridge being almost the only exceptions) to be considered to the exclusion of others without any impartial justification for that exclusion led to frustration for all, as the officials charged blindly ahead with their strict requirement of inadequate plans.

Certainly some of the visionaries have been appropriately willing to accept a verdict against their design if their designs were given the fair hearing denied by the officials. And some of the clamor to unite behind a single design has come not from designers but from pro-rebuilders insensitive to the damage this would do to their movement. But the general syndrome of discarding the goals that unite all pro-rebuilders in favor of one particular means of prioritizing and executing them has harmed the effort to make sure that those goals are finally realized.

The pro-rebuilding movement is united by basic principles of what should be built, and determination to overcome the refusal of the officials to commit to those principles or even permit plans fulfilling them to be considered. But to point to one specific approach as the incarnation of all we seek, to abandon hope of bargaining on any issue on which the designer has chosen tactical surrender either out of belief or priority, is to alienate one section or other of a necessary support base before the battles that need every effort of every member of that support base to be concluded successfully have even been joined.

Individual plans inspire particular zeal from different subsets of the movement, but to demand that others yield their preferences to support that one plan on a basis of holding their noses and taking a lesser evil is not the way to build morale. Also, a movement whose basis is the advocacy of one design, rather than the advocacy of goals which it will accept any appropriate incarnation of, will necessarily appear to others as being more self-centered and less dedicated to common benefit.

Enthusiasm for general principles is a different sort of enthusiasm than for that with a concrete image, but those favoring various ways to do the right thing must "hang together or hang separately." The continued commitment of all pro-rebuilders to what unites them is vital to securing success.

Who Opposes Rebuilding the World Trade Center?

By Louis Epstein

The opponents of the restoration of the World Trade Center are a disparate group, united only in their blindness to the symbolism of allowing the destruction of great icons of America and of world trade to stand as irreversible.

Most vocal and visible are the groups of activists founded by family members of those who were in the Towers and did not survive (the far larger number who were wounded or escaped have not busied themselves in such a fashion).

The groups themselves tend to be very small, a few people getting together at the instigation of one or two of them. Thus, the groups tend to form coalitions to appear more imposing. The implication that a gathering of groups constitutes the whole voice of everyone related to someone who died is, however, far from the truth.

Activists dedicated to ensuring the permanence of the success of the terrorists in emptying the "footprints" of the buildings that the activists' loved ones had every right, desire, and expectation to go on working in is never reversed are at most a few percent of those who were closely related to people who died on September 11, 2001. (And as noted, those who died and their families are a minority of those directly affected, albeit those most severely affected.)

The activists are unusual among family members in both the extent to which the attacks left them emotionally distressed for a long period, and their determination to ensure that their private grief guides public policy. Different people grieve their losses in different ways, see different actions as providing the most honor to those they lost. And there are in fact those who lost loved ones who would prefer that the Towers return, but their voices have been drowned out by those more insistent in grabbing the microphones.

As some of the groups are built around multiple survivors of one victim, the number of victims whose families are actively opposed to the restoration of the Towers is an even smaller fraction than the number of family members who are active rebuilders.

But those who have no objection to the Towers rising again are ignored, as those who do object raise their cries that to restore the Towers is violation of graves. Given that all human remains have been removed from the site with greater care than is customary in cemetery relocations, many of the activists demand the return of the remains to the site, both from the offices of the medical examiners seeking to identify the dead and from the landfill where many burnt remains are irretrievably mixed with toxic waste. This is actually a violation of city law but this has never occurred to them or to the politicians terrified of falling short in pandering to them.

Their emotional distress must be shared forever by the nation, these activists demand. No one should visit where their loved ones were that day and think that America ever recovered... The nation must be shown to have suffered an incurable nervous breakdown.

The invitation this makes to future terrorists to make attacks of similarly enduring effect does not occur to them; the distress to future families of future victims caused by sending such a message is something they cannot acknowledge. Doubtless they would offer such families assistance in procuring memorials as grandiose as possible, that the severity and incurability of the wounds be shown off to maximum effect.

This massive memorialization is a recent phenomenon alien to the history of great losses of life. The tradition has always been to rebuild what was destroyed and let the memorials, by being no obstacle to the restoration of what was, thereby be all the more effective. The site of the largest loss of life to the New York fire department prior to 2001, the Wonder Drugs fire of 1966, is marked by a plaque with the names of the dead firefighters by the entrance of the new, much larger building on the site of the one that was destroyed.

The shooting massacre in a San Ysidro, California, McDonald's in 1984 by madman James Huberty seems to have been the first place that the scene of mass killing was demanded to be forever deprived of its former use, when the restaurant the company wanted to reopen was turned into a memorial park. Other occasions of killers appallingly empowered by permanent places on the map include the Columbine High School library, where every book and every shelf was pulverized to ensure that nothing survived, and the Dunblane school gymnasium in Scotland, which was bulldozed within days by a local council pledging to ignore those opposed to their high-handed action.

Perhaps more effective than the family activists, however, have been those who have been described as urban-utopians. They have their own ideas of preferred forms of urban design that the World Trade Center did not match. They were sorry it was ever built and, given that their views have become fashionable, they want them implemented.

The vulture-like insensitivity of taking advantage of an act of mass murder to render the site of the victims' slaughter into something they would not have recognized is completely lost on them. They sing the praises of "24/7 communities," of "lively streets," of other buzzwords while regarding the priorities with which the World Trade Center was designed with clear distaste.

And given that these groups preexisted the attacks and were able to band together after it, they were able to ensure that any design that did not repudiate the basic elements of the old design was officially barred from consideration by the planners. These people did not represent majority public opinion, but the majority of organized activism seeking alteration in the city's existing planning. A status quo that seems under no threat — and the World Trade Center had been under a lease that pledged to keep it intact until 2100 — does not have organized backers because it does not need them. And when the existing reality was altered by the terrorists, those who were delighted at the opportunity to see that it never rose again swooped in.

Other opponents of restoring the World Trade Center cite their own fears of working on high floors as a reason, as if their personal misgivings should necessarily bind those who feel otherwise. And of course the desire of the killers to create such fears constitutes shorter buildings on the site into another monument to their success.

Still others may cite humility and piety... One correspondent who begged off further exchanges for Holy Week felt that it was wrong for us not to accept the destruction of symbols of our pride. Lost on him was his own church's erecting the largest cathedral in Christendom on the sites of the crucifixion and the burial of St. Peter.

And of course there are the bean counters, who see the budget of the present day as a valid reason to constrict the long-term future, again blind to the symbolic implications of being "cut down to size." Other buildings have been empty for years because they were too big for the short-term market, but in time they filled with more tenants paying more rent than the buildings that would have been dictated by prudence could possibly have produced... and solely because of their unusual size did they become the beloved icons that they were. The courage to build them is rewarded by not being forgotten as the constrained buildings would be.

Not one of these groups has produced an argument worth listening to, yet together they have monopolized the ears of the powerful listeners. For this state of affairs to continue would be the shame of our century.

Commentary on the Draft Generic Environmental Impact Statement for the World Trade Center Site

By Louis Epstein

This new document presented for comment in the process of rebuilding the destroyed World Trade Center is another illustration of the profound problems in the way the process has been conducted.

From Draft Scope to Final Scope to Draft GEIS, definitions have been altered back and forth as alterations are made to plans to appease various constituencies and confuse everyone. How are we to react to what is really planned while there is still time to stop it?

That is always a concern. Then Governor George E. Pataki remained determined to prevent anyone from having a chance to undo his mistakes. The acceleration of this review process drew protest from many quarters.

The Draft GEIS did not bear the imprimatur of the Port Authority, though it concerned the construction of Port Authority-owned buildings on Port Authority-owned land. The Port Authority did not bother sending the designated representative to the Draft GEIS hearings. Not long after, it was admitted that there is not yet any agreement with the development corporation to allow its plans to proceed. This is a good thing, as the development corporation is not likely to have to deal with the lasting consequences of its actions the way the property owners are. However, political pressure to pave the way for the horribly misconceived Proposed Action to proceed appears inevitable.

At long last a "Pre-September 11 Scenario" and the "Restoration Alternative" were explicitly recognized as benchmarks for the GEIS, after a prolonged process in which such strategies for redevelopment have been implacably opposed despite broad public support. However, given the history of official prejudice against redevelopment based on restoration of what was destroyed, it is no surprise that the Draft GEIS seeks to portray these scenarios unfairly, in a bid to justify the unreasonable programmatic requirements that have led to designs such as the Proposed Action.

In rebuilding where renowned icons of America have been destroyed, the presumption must be in favor of rebuilding in the same spirit and image, applying the latest technologies toward restoring what was there stronger than before, and the burden of proof that any new design is better must rest on the new design's proponents; in this regard, the DGEIS unconditionally fails to justify the Proposed Action.

The adverse environmental impacts of the official program requirements are evaded, and the environmental advantages of discarding the Proposed Action in favor of redevelopment based on updated reaffirmation of the design principles that produced the original World Trade Center are likewise obscured behind subjective sophistries.

An environmental impact statement needs to take into account responsible priorities toward superior environmental health, with particular suspicion toward anything that encourages population or traffic growth either at the location in question or as a result of the decisions made regarding what is to be built there. This DGEIS turns its back on these issues, and virtually glorifies the effects of this nature that would be caused by the Proposed Action.

The narrow-minded obsession with running streets completely through the site is a dramatic step backward, even apart from the disturbing insensitivity of using the occasion of the murder of thousands to repudiate the urban design principles that gave us the beloved Twin Towers.

To "integrate the site into the surrounding neighborhood" means to destroy the distinct nature of the site, and the official fixation with turning Lower Manhattan into a 24-hour community constitutes destroying the distinctive character of that part of the city in order to make it like countless others.

And contrary to the dubious representations of the City Planning Department, the way forward for Lower Manhattan surely lies in further de-vehicularization, not the creation of more space for future traffic jams and auto accidents. This is an area uniquely suited to being dominated by pedestrian traffic arriving by mass transit.

Chapter 10 begins by praising the neighborhood character created by the old World Trade Center, and then sets about implementing the above policies in order to ensure that that character is never restored, and the action of the terrorists in erasing it perpetuated.

Chapter after chapter tries to justify the Proposed Action, glossing over areas of concern. The last-place finish of the Libeskind plan in the official public poll prior to its selection is nonetheless vindicated.

While the exposure of the slurry wall has been reduced, it remains an objective of the design to perpetuate the terrorist-created exposure of this crumbling structure never intended to be exposed to the elements and designed to always have the weight of the Twin Towers holding it in place.

Pits remain as part of the design on the sites of the former Twin Towers, deep receptacles for the settling of heavier-than-air pollutants from the traffic invited through the site by the inappropriately restored streets and sources of chemically contaminated mist. Cold winters and deep snowfalls will present difficult challenges to these exposed below-grade structures.

The GEIS cannot be allowed to soft-pedal the hazards posed by leaving these open wounds as part of the plan. (What of suicide leaps into the sunken pools?)

Only in Chapter 23 is it at last admitted that "The Proposed Action is not, however, the only option considered by or open to LMDC." Yet, in the presence of other options, it does not then, as would be logical for many reasons, abandon the Proposed Action in favor of the greatly superior Restoration Alternative.

Rather it attempts to dismiss the Restoration Alternative in three ill-supported paragraphs of the Executive Summary. The first paragraph describes the alternative. The second shamefully invokes the fears that the terrorists sought to inflict as justification for submitting to their murderous will that we be denied the possibility of again working as high in the skies as before. The third for no reason assumes that environmental mitigating measures would not be a part of future independent development of the southern site.

Yet, if one looks at Chapter 23 for the detailed treatment of the Restoration Alternative, subheading after subheading admits that the Restoration Alternative would be no worse than the Proposed Action, even while avoiding the ways the Proposed Action would be worse than the Restoration Alternative.

In trying to come up with reasons to prefer the Proposed

Action, the Draft GEIS is driven to refuge in subjective design criticism. It is complained that the Restoration Alternative would need truck checkpoints to be on the site; but only in the Proposed Action can trucks, or truck bombs, rumble unchecked through the site, and on either side of every building.

Above-ground retail space, found all over the city, is extolled and the underground retail space as a distinguishing feature of the World Trade Center is denigrated. Yet the site has lost its retail operator because the plans called for too much of the retail space to be above ground when shoppers prefer it underground, the more so in bad weather. This was what made the World Trade Center mall among the most profitable in the world.

The Restoration Alternative's skyline impact is denigrated compared to the Freedom Tower, with its roof hundreds of feet lower and dozens fewer office floors. The space not accounted for in the envisioned towers is accused of making the project denser. Yet it would be wholly in the spirit of this Alternative to consolidate these functions into the new Towers to make them even taller, and the density less than the Proposed Action. Open spaces would be increased, where analysis shows that the Proposed Action reduces open space significantly.

The placement of new Twin Towers is said to be constrained by "the public's expressed desire for some meaningful recognition of" the footprints of the old Towers. Before Governor Pataki aggressively intervened to preempt public debate, polls showed New Yorkers evenly divided on building on the old footprints, and meaningful recognition does NOT have to be total emptiness.

Only with the placement contrived through this constraint is the shadow effect any worse off the site than that of the Proposed Action. Even placement of the new Twin Towers blocking Greenwich Street's course, since it would not be reopened in this scenario although the DGEIS seems inconsistent on this, would affect the open spaces and pull shadows away from surrounding areas as well as enhance the towers' security. But every effort is made to paint restoring the Twin Towers as more inconvenient than it is.

The safety technologies seen as advantages of the proposed buildings would of course be scaled up for new Twin Towers with more effectiveness than for smaller buildings. Engineering realities ensure that taller towers are necessarily built stronger and safer than smaller ones.

The new Twin Towers would be engineering marvels embodying the technologies of the new millennium to a degree only made possible by their breathtaking scale, which would also be the only way for them to generate revenue on a sufficient scale to pay for their construction. Neither the original Twin Towers nor the Empire State Building filled up in their first years, but had they been built more cautiously, they could never have been as profitable as they were in the long run.

The "Restoration Alternative" must be no empty "straw man" in the final GEIS. It must be fleshed out, regardless of official bias toward the Proposed Action, sufficiently to demonstrate its numerous advantages. The current effort reads like a rationalization for proceeding with the vastly inferior official design. There can be no assuming that, if the decision is made to proceed with the Restoration Alternative, no environmental mitigation or safety enhancement proposed in other contexts will be adapted.

Until September 11, 2001, the status quo had no established lobby because it did not need to be defended. Today a conspiracy of bureaucracy seems determined to leave the status quo of before September 11, 2001, defenseless. This environmental review process must not be perverted into another stage of that conspiracy, but must honestly weigh the drawbacks of failing to set ourselves back onto the course we were on before thousands of valiant lives were unconscionably snuffed out and iconic structures revered the world over collapsed into ruin.

Blinkered dedication to proceeding further down a wrong turn cannot allow the final GEIS to be a biased attempt to sell an eyesore imposed in the teeth of public disinterest and dislike, rather than the required fair evaluation of the consequences of the choices before us.

Commentary on the Amended General Project Plan for the World Trade Center Site

By Louis Epstein

The official planning process of rebuilding the destroyed World Trade Center has been a saga of uninterrupted incompetence and a constant succession of incorrect decisions.

We were asked to comment on the "Amended General Project Plan" in March 2004, with reference to a document prepared in September 2003 that looked forward to events that occurred months ago and does not reflect the constant "amendments" that happened since.

All through the process definitions have been altered back and forth as alterations are made to plans to appease various constituencies and confuse everyone. Whether one reacts to the plans as presented in the document or as they are believed to stand at this time of writing, it remains futile to "amend" a plan that was devised to meet indefensible programmatic requirements that arose out of inappropriate priorities.

The case for complete abandonment of the current plans in favor of ones much more evocative of what was destroyed in the attacks of September 11, 2001, was never clearer.

Public dissatisfaction with the proposals put forward by the official planners has been a constant throughout the process. Unfortunately, so has been official response aimed at deflecting the public concerns in favor of preconceived, misconceived official priorities.

In July 2002, the six Beyer Blinder Belle plans were uniformly denounced, the reasons people hated them were turned into official program requirements, and here we were nearly two years later presented with what is basically a warmed-over version of BBB's "Memorial Plaza." We did not get here by a process of taking public concerns into account, but by one of ignoring them.

That's why the Libeskind plan finished last in the official public poll, which was comfortably won by "neither" (of the last two plans considered), and was still selected by the Governor of New York against the advice of most of his own appointees.

This plan as it stands essentially completes the work of the killers in erasing the World Trade Center from the map, and thus honors the killers at the expense of the victims it pretends to honor.

Right now there is still an identifiable World Trade Center site. If the proposed plan is built, there will not even be that. Even the surrounding neighborhood's character is promised to be altered in a breathtaking triumph of opportunism over honor.

Renowned icons of America were destroyed, thousands of lives extinguished in an act of staggering brutality. What is suggested to rise where they — buildings and people — fell?

Where the Twin Towers themselves stood, officialdom has ignored the near even division of public opinion and decreed that both "footprints" must remain as completely empty as the terrorists left them, open wounds promising future murderers that when one destroys an American landmark, it will stay destroyed. The purposes to which and for which the victims gave their lives are decreed to be banished from those two acres forever, that land hence forward defined as nothing but what the killers sought to make of it.

Apart from that area, the site is ordered to be divided by streets, "integration" into the surrounding area translated into destroying the distinct identity that the site, even as an empty hole, has hitherto managed to retain. And the rebuilding is proposed to take in the Deutsche Bank block to the south, which was not part of the World Trade Center, further altering the definition of the site.

And what are these blocks, surrounding but not joined to the morbid murderers' trophy of a memorial, supposed to be filled with?

Most prominently, we are told, the "Freedom Tower" — a landmark in nothing but the history of pretentiousness. The "world's tallest building," we are told. Actually as a building, with walls rising to a roof, it approximates the height of the John Hancock Center, the third tallest building in Chicago. Above that was planned only an ornamental cage full of windmills topped by an observation deck lower than the solid roofs and walls of buildings now rising in Shanghai and Hong Kong, crowned by a spire lower than the structural top of the CN Tower. The actual height of the antenna we have yet to be told, and what we are told now may vanish as quickly as the 1776-foot observation deck promised in the Final Scope of the Generic Environmental

Impact Statement.

Compared to this structure each of the Twin Towers had a roof hundreds of feet higher and contained over 60% more office space, and this thin, twisted creation is set to be the largest structure anywhere on the site. In fact, it appears unclear that any others are securely funded.

Between Greenwich and Church Streets (which both ran between Liberty and Fulton Streets for less than a quarter of the city's history, the historical norm has been one of them or the other) we are told that buildings not much taller than others in the area will rise some day, but only in response to market demand.

In the meantime, urban designers encourage us to welcome street-level retail to this site that has lost its retail lease operator because of official insistence on moving retail to street level. We are told that it is a good thing that vehicular traffic will invade what was one of Lower Manhattan's largest open spaces, that becoming yet another of New York's countless "24-hour communities" is something other than destroying the distinctive character of the Financial District to a further extent than the terror attacks thus far managed.

And if we don't like this, we are ignored.

This is NOT the way to rebuild the World Trade Center.

This is NOT the way to honor those who died there.

This surrender is NOT the way to react to the murderers' desire to "cut America down to size."

Other cities devastated by war or disaster have not made sure their hearts cut out were never replaced. Not Halifax in 1917, not Hiroshima or countless European cities after 1945. At this time and in this place, it is absolutely vital that we rebuild in a fashion that sends the unambiguous message that the strength of our recovery outweighs the severity of our wounds, and the official plan does exactly the opposite.

We could not disgrace our fallen by continuing with the plans that, for all the empty rhetoric offered by then Governor Pataki, unambiguously signaled retreat, acquiescence, and timidity. No one will ever work closer than across the street from where they died, these plans said. No one will ever work as high in the sky. Where they died, and the terrorists did not wish them to be, we obey the terrorists and will never return.

If we truly wish to do the right thing for our dead, for our city, for our country, and for the free world, we must send the message that our courage and spirit were not among the casualties that horrible day.

We must build towers that rise every bit as tall as the old and beyond by every measurement, embodying a "can do" and not a "don't dare" spirit. We must cast aside the fears spinelessly invoked by the Draft GEIS as an excuse for not rebuilding, and build to the skies regardless of immediate market demand with the boldness exclusively responsible for the fame of the old Twin Towers, of the Empire State Building before them, and of the Woolworth Building even earlier. Only by being "too big" by market-driven standards did they become exceptional, and only because of that speculative boldness was it ever possible for them to produce as much rental revenue as they did when in time they did fill with tenants.

Let us not forget the Group of 35 report in 2001 that declared that the city needed sixty million square feet of new office space by 2020 even before 11 million square feet of Downtown's best space was destroyed and added to the shortage. Let us finance it however we must, but let us not stop short of full replacement of what was lost on the sixteen acres, and treat replacement of the Deutsche Bank separately.

It is towers built on a heroic scale, engineering marvels with standards of strength and safety that the laws of physics dictate no lesser structures can attain, that will inspire the world and show that it was indeed the terrorists and not their victims who died in vain. Nothing less can suffice.

If one needed even more reason to discard the Libeskind plan, surely the strong support for it voiced by Brookfield Properties at the February 18 Draft GEIS hearing should qualify. Why would a competitor owning buildings surrounding the site urge that this plan be proceeded with in haste, if it thought there would be stronger demand for space in the new buildings than in its own? Only if Brookfield was bitterly protesting the unfair competition from the new buildings would the plans be proposing buildings sufficiently inspiring of tenant demand.

In sum, the most important comment one can make about the Amended General Project Plan is that there is an urgent need to completely discard it.

We must instead have a plan with fewer, taller buildings, in terms of genuine height and not ornamentation on one of them. As with not tearing the site apart by running Greenwich Street all the way through it (unanimously opposed by everyone who bothered to post on a comment board on this subject opened by the Project for Public Spaces), this ensures more open space as well as greater structural efficiency.

We must have a plan that reaffirms and reincarnates, not repudiates, what was destroyed. In a war of symbols the destruction of symbols cannot be allowed to stand.

The World Trade Center must retain its identity and its Towers rise again undiminished, or history will record that America itself could not do so.

Commentary on the Final Generic Environmental Impact Statement for the World Trade Center Site

By Louis Epstein

This latest document presented for comment in the process of rebuilding the destroyed World Trade Center was yet another milestone in shameless official disregard for public opinion while brazenly pretending to be following it.

From Draft Scope to Final Scope to Draft GEIS to Final GEIS, plan definitions have squirmed back and forth while determination to push ahead with a plan tailored to preexisting misconception is rammed ahead full speed no matter what concerns are raised.

Then Governor Pataki remained determined to prevent anyone from having a chance to undo his mistakes, moving up groundbreaking despite the official review process still being underway. The accelerated timetable drew protest from many quarters.

The GEIS did not bear the imprimatur of the Port Authority, though it concerns the construction of Port Authority-owned buildings on Port Authority-owned land. That there was no agreement with the development corporation to allow its plans to proceed was a good thing, as the development corporation was not likely to have to deal with the lasting consequences of its actions the way the property owners will. However, political pressure to pave the way for the horribly misconceived Proposed Action to proceed appeared inevitable.

The "Pre-September 11 Scenario" and the "Restoration Alternative" were explicitly recognized as benchmarks for the GEIS, after a prolonged process in which such strategies for redevelopment had been implacably opposed despite broad public support. However, official prejudice against redevelopment based on restoration of what was destroyed ensures that the GEIS seeks to portray these scenarios unfairly, in a bid to justify the unreasonable programmatic requirements that have led to designs such as the Proposed Action.

Numerous public comments urging the abandonment of the Proposed Action in favor of the Restoration Alternative were received. Reasoned arguments were reduced to one-liners in the

Response section and flippantly dismissed with regurgitated falsehoods and invocations of unreasonable objectives.

It bears noting that no alternative drew close to the amount of public interest and comment as the Restoration Alternative. One entity each commented on the Memorial Only and Enhanced Green alternatives, eight on the Reduced Impact, and none at all on the others — but the Restoration Alternative was urged by nineteen. In the initial comments, more people urged the Twin Towers be rebuilt than expressed general approval of the Proposed Action.

What are claimed to be preferable attributes of the Proposed Action are NOT preferable to the Restoration Alternative in the eyes of the public regardless of the brazen claim that the Libeskind plan "achieved broad public support and fulfilled many of the goals articulated by the public."

The Libeskind plan finished LAST in the OFFICIAL public poll of the design process, which was won comfortably by "Neither" (of the last two plans considered). There is no question that the priorities decided upon by the planners led to plans that do NOT have public support, least of all this one.

To far more people than the development corporation will admit, that the new World Trade Center be centered on towers every bit as tall as the old by *every* measurement and representing an updated reaffirmation of the design principles that produced the original World Trade Center is:

More important than the extension of any streets into or through the site.

More important than "active enlivened street life."

More important than turning the distinctive quiet and low population density of the Financial District into yet another of the city's countless "24/7 communities."

More important than encouraging the disturbingly rapid growth of the population of Downtown.

And to many, *more* important than leaving the "footprints" of the former towers empty. (Before Governor Pataki aggressively intervened to preempt public debate, polls showed New Yorkers evenly divided on building on the old footprints.)

All these issues must be given lower priority, and their merit subjected to question rather than imposed as a design requirement. Honest evaluation of adverse environmental impacts of encouraging population or traffic growth either at the location in question or as a result of the decisions made regarding what is to be built there are a must for a responsible environmental impact statement. *This one fails!*

An environmentally conscious and appropriate redevelopment of the World Trade Center would see that the way forward for Lower Manhattan lies in further de-vehicularization, not the creation of more space for future traffic jams and auto accidents. This is an area uniquely suited to being dominated by pedestrian traffic arriving by mass transit.

An environmentally conscious and appropriate redevelopment of the World Trade Center would call for the concentration of the office space into a *smaller* number of *taller* buildings than in the Proposed Action. Such construction would use less materials, less land, require less construction equipment and activity with resultant disturbance and proceed faster. Once constructed, the scaled-up buildings would be more efficient in operation and safer for their occupants because they would be structurally stronger. Economies of scale would be possible in new Twin Towers that would not be possible in the much smaller Libeskind-plan buildings.

And such construction would leave more open space than before, rather than less, as is the functional consequence of the Proposed Action, which runs a street through what was one of the largest open spaces in the area.

The GEIS constantly soft-pedals the hazards posed by proceeding on the mistaken paths mandated by the development corporation.

Despite the substantial public pressure demanding a fair comparison, the Restoration Alternative remains a "straw man" in the Final GEIS, barely touched from the unfair rendering in the Draft GEIS. The same three slanted paragraphs of the Executive Summary attempt to dismiss the Restoration Alternative as before. The characterization of the Alternative, and the subjective design criticism, misplaced priorities, and conveniently incomplete comparisons it is judged negatively for not meeting, are barely touched in Chapter 23. The shameful use of short-term market conditions created by the murderers as a reason future development should implement their desires remains.

No flexibility is shown as to how the Restoration Alternative could best meet objections, such as combining other uses into the two main towers to increase open space. The placement of new Twin Towers is said to be constrained by "the public's expressed desire for some meaningful recognition of" the footprints of the old Towers, and "meaningful recognition" creatively construed to mean total emptiness. To many, reclamation of that space, even a symbolic portion of it, for the purposes to which and for which the victims gave their lives is the best recognition possible. And only with the placement contrived through this constraint is the shadow effect any worse off the site than that of the Proposed Action. Every effort is made to paint restoring the Twin Towers as more inconvenient than it is.

This document in countless ways failed to fairly address the issues, in the furtherance of its objective to ensure the implementation of a disastrously wrong planning decision rather than permit wiser action. Approval of the Proposed Action was a disgrace to the city, to the nation, and to the free world.

The bottom line for the Final GEIS remains what it was for the draft: *The GEIS unconditionally failed to justify the Proposed Action.*

Bring Back Our Loved Ones

By Deroy Murdock

On Tuesday morning, September 11, 2001, I awoke a bit earlier than usual. I had plenty to do before an evening flight to Pittsburgh to attend a convention of the National Conference of Editorial Writers. Beneath a cobalt-blue sky, a light breeze beckoned. So, I sat in a chair on my balcony to edit a newspaper column due that day.

A few minutes later, the silver belly of a commercial jet suddenly flew right over my Fourth Avenue apartment building. It was headed southwest over Greenwich Village rather than northeast toward La Guardia Airport. The low-flying airliner's enormous noise and vibrations triggered a car alarm on East 12th Street.

"My God," I thought. "He's heading for an emergency landing at Newark. I hope he makes it." The situation was serious enough that I checked the alarm clock inside my apartment. It was 8:46 A.M.

Little did I know that mere moments would bring the beginning of the end of the World Trade Center.

Since that horrid day, I have had many occasions to look back at that amazing landmark. I always do so fondly.

I remember my first time atop the Twin Towers.

Just days after I moved from Los Angeles to Manhattan to attend New York University's Graduate School of Business Administration in August 1987, I joined two other newcomers — from Baltimore and San Diego — on the observation deck high atop Tower Two.

Without saying a word, we realized we had come a long way from home to a city as grand as these skyscrapers were tall.

I am not one of those who fell in love with these 28-year-old identical twins *after* they left us. I believed the Twin Towers were amazing, majestic, and beautiful — from when I first laid eyes on them.

Lanky and unswerving, they stood at attention outside my window every morning as I awoke in my NYU apartment in the East Village.

From the Staten Island Ferry, my family and I marveled at the

Twin Towers from New York Harbor the day before I graduated from NYU in 1989.

High above those waters, I loved to peer at the Towers from jet windows. They greeted me like old friends as I approached La Guardia Airport. "Hey, you're back!" I almost heard them shout, with all the gentility a pair of Manhattanites could muster.

One summer afternoon in 1996, while attending the Further Fest concert at Liberty State Park in New Jersey, I watched the Twin Towers from across the Hudson River.

Gray throughout the day, they turned a blinding gold as the setting sun bounced off their steel beams. Then they became almost black at dusk. Finally, they filled with light as hundreds of desk lamps and thousands of fluorescent tubes brightened the offices of industrious individuals inside the World Trade Center.

The Twin Towers were gorgeous all along. I loved them very much, and miss them immensely. And I want them back!

The Twin Towers were things of beauty, not just for how they looked, but for what they meant. They were immediately identifiable as the premier symbols of America's free-enterprise system. The Twin Towers stood tall and every day declared America's independence as a free and prosperous nation.

Those bloodthirsty bastards — Mohammed Atta, Marwan al-Shehhi and their homicidal conspirators — did not slam jumbo jets into Tower One and Tower Two just because they were big buildings, although they were. These mass murderers did not destroy these skyscrapers just because they contained thousands of innocent civilians, which they did. These homicidal pricks demolished the Twin Towers because they represented American liberty and US economic prowess.

The best way we can "Just say no" to al-Qaeda is to put the Twin Towers back where they belong.

While the so-called Freedom Tower rises at Ground Zero, it is no more a replacement for what Muslim-extremists demolished than if they managed to destroy the White House, which then were replaced with a Spanish-style McMansion.

Whether they can be squeezed into Ground Zero or erected someplace nearby, the beautiful Twin Towers once again should climb towards the heavens above a nation filled with free people.

This has been the right thing to do since the last pebble was cleared from the debris pit at Ground Zero:

Rebuild the Twin Towers as they were before, only stronger!

New York State of Mind

By Jennifer Thorpe-Moscon

As the ten-year anniversary of one of the most profound and disastrous days in our nation's history approaches, we must again ask how we, as a city, should move forward. It is essential to remember the victims who lost their lives on that tragic day, but our tribute should be about far more than building a memorial or holding commemorative events. It must be about facing the future with a spirit of strength that would make the victims proud, that would prove to them that they did not die in vain. We must take September 11 as a lesson to stand guard against hatred at home and abroad, and never take for granted those whom we love. Importantly, we must never allow ourselves to appease the terrorists — we did not want to do so in 2001, and we should not do so now.

Yet appeasing the terrorists is what many politicians and urban planners would have us do. When Nazi Germany bombed London, the English rebuilt their torn and tattered city. When Japan attacked Pearl Harbor, we rebuilt what was there, a military base, alongside a memorial. But today there are those who would have us leave Ground Zero without our beloved Twins, and without them the site will be little more than a tribute to the terrorists. This may be a bold statement — after all, there will be a memorial — but as it is planned now, it will be one that does not do the victims justice. Rather than moving forward, there are those, such as former Mayor Rudolph Giuliani and Mayor Michael R. Bloomberg, who would have us remain in the past. Rather than build something to raise the spirits of New Yorkers and pay the best tribute to those who perished, they would create a memorial that would give no indication of the magnitude of what was lost that day, and would instead literally sink into the ground in submission to the terrorists' plan for our city. The Twin Towers are the only appropriate tribute to those we lost — anything less is a devastating failure.

Those who oppose rebuilding the Twin Towers fear that new towers would be attacked again, but that logic is severely flawed. By that logic, we should tear down our existing skyscrapers to avoid the possibility of attack. By that logic no moderately tall building should ever be built again. It would be far more sensible to try to thwart the forces that threaten us than live in cowardice. It is not the height of the Twin Towers that caused them to be attacked; it is what they represented. The Pentagon proved that short buildings could be struck. One plane into the Brooklyn Bridge would cause a catastrophe, but no one would suggest not building bridges. If terrorists destroyed the Brooklyn Bridge, would we not replace it? We must replace what was taken from us, rather than let terrorists dictate what our city should look like.

The current plans for Ground Zero involve building one tall structure, but this is not a true rebuilding. If you had two cars and they were both destroyed in an accident, would you consider the damage restored if I gave you one car? You would not — and I do not consider the damage downtown restored by giving us one building. The people of New York deserve better.

Residents of Lower Manhattan, more than anyone else, want a revitalized neighborhood. It is no wonder then that many of them want the Twins back as they were. Without the tourism and urbanity that the Twin Towers brought to the area, how could Lower Manhattan ever be the vibrant region it once was? Its residents do not want to live in a cemetery. There is no reason that a memorial could not be incorporated with the Twins. In fact, there would be no better tribute to the lives of those lost than to rebuild the pride and joy of our city, the symbol of the heights our nation is capable of reaching.

Contrary to what the small but vocal group of anti-rebuilders would have you believe, there are many family members of victims of September 11 who support the rebuilding of the Twin Towers. They know that their relatives loved those towers and knew better than anyone their value to this city. Why would anyone not want to bring back the buildings to which his/her relative had devoted so much of his/her time?

Just imagine it: One day we will bring our children and grandchildren to the site and tell them what occurred that morning. Without the majesty of a real tribute — new, strong Twins — how will they ever understand what happened? How will the site be different than any other place in the city? The important message taught to us by that day will be lost, and the experience of the soaring glory of the Twin Towers will be lost along with it. Tourists even today look at the site, trying to envision what was there, with no success.

The reasons to rebuild the Twin Towers are innumerable, but politicians and some media sources have let their biases and personal motivations stand in the way of the truth. One can only hope that the voice of the majority opinion in this city, that in favor of rebuilding the Twin Towers, will be heard through all of the media and city officials' filters. Even at this late time, ten years after the tragedy, it is not too late.

Rebuilding the WTC — the Greatest Tribute Possible

By Robert Murphy

> To the glory of mankind, there was, for the first and only time in history, a country of money — and I have no higher, more reverent tribute to pay to America, for this means: a country of reason, justice, freedom, production, achievement. For the first time, man's mind and money were set free, and there were no fortunes-by-conquest, but only fortunes-by-work.

> — Ayn Rand, *Atlas Shrugged.*

In July 2002, the Port Authority of New York and the Lower Manhattan Development Corporation announced six first phase designs to replace the World Trade Center towers. It is appropriate that this was announced in July, the anniversary of our nation's declaration of freedom. It was this very same freedom that was the cause of the attacks that brought down the towers on that black Tuesday in September 2001. The attacks were masterminded by those who hate America for what it represents: The freedom to make money. Therefore, there could be no more fitting tribute to those who died in that act of war than to rebuild the towers — and to rebuild them taller and more magnificent than they were.

America is often denigrated as a country of "materialistic capitalists" whose only concern is for their own happiness and how much they can produce. It is this invariable pursuit of happiness and production through hard work that has enabled America to surpass the rest of the world in both achievements and standard of living. The freedom to make money has allowed America to realize what most other nations can only dream about, because it is through money that men can trade honestly with each other. To quote Ayn Rand: "Money permits you to obtain for your goods and your labor that which they are worth to the men who buy them, but no more."

There is no free trade among those who wish to destroy America. For our enemies, strength is only achieved through the barrel of a gun. We love life, and they love death. To the terrorists, the towers were a blatant symbol of the freedom that they hate: The WTC mall was one of the most profitable in the country, and the WTC observation deck allowed views of freedom for 45 miles in every direction.

Among America's "materialistic capitalists" is Frank Lowy, whose family owns thirty-percent of Westfield Holdings. Westfield held a 99-year lease on all of the WTC site's retail space. Lowy's business partner, Larry Silverstein, holds the 99-year lease on the site's office space. Together, these two men could bring a symbol of America's freedom and capitalism's strength back to Lower Manhattan. Lowy knows the value of freedom. He fought to defend Israel in 1948, and he built his retail empire from a single delicatessen in Sydney, Australia.

Lowy and Silverstein faced an uphill battle against those who are opposed to using the site for commerce and against those who have called for the site to become a memorial park. While it is true that the WTC site calls forth an emotional reaction that needs some kind of memorial to those who died on September 11, turning the site into a mausoleum is the wrong action to take. It is an irrational emotional response. On the contrary, rebuilding the towers would be the most fitting memorial to America and what it represents. Finding supporters for reconstruction is as easy as looking to those who cleared the rubble from the collapsed towers. Many of those workers expressed a desire to work without pay to help rebuild the towers.

Would merchants and businesses be too afraid to occupy such a blatant target for another terrorist attack? Very few would harbor such a fear. Once people caught a glimpse of the towers rising out of the ashes, there would be an avalanche of businessmen rushing to sign leases or to pressure their employers to move there, if for no other reason than to boast on company brochures and annual reports about locating in the rebuilt towers. The men of commerce know what the towers represent, and they will not live their lives in fear.

Reason dictates that the most fitting tribute to those who died in the attacks is a soaring beacon to the rest of the civilized world — a beacon that represents freedom... and a country of money.

Rebuild the Twin Towers

By Robert Begley

Shortly after the World Trade Center was destroyed, there was a meeting open to the public, hosted by the Lower Manhattan Development Corporation. I was one of the audience members who had a chance to state my views, which were met with rousing applause. Here are some excerpts, with the opening inspired by an article written in *The Intellectual Activist*.

If we look back at history, there were many great buildings that were either damaged or destroyed in war. There is an important link between what society does to rebuild afterward and how they determine their own future.

When the Persians burned down the Parthenon 2,500 years ago, the Greeks did not leave a barren field memorializing those who died in battle. Instead, they constructed a new Parthenon with the best material available, white marble, and decorated it with sculptures of heroes. It was the greatest temple ever built and marked the beginning of the Golden Age of Greece.

Closer to home, America has examples to draw from. During the War of 1812, when the British burned the Presidential Mansion, we immediately rebuilt it, and a few years later President Monroe moved into the White House while expanded work was still in progress. Then, during the Civil War, while financing was scarce, the new, fireproof cast-iron dome for the Capitol Building was constructed. Forging ahead in this project gave Lincoln confidence that we would succeed in preserving the Union.

There is no doubt that 9/11 was an act of war.

Anything less than rebuilding the Towers will send a message to the public, our friends and enemies: New York is retreating. America is weak, living in the past.

Rebuild! Rebuild the Towers 119 stories high. Let's put a reverse spin on that barbaric act of cowards forever called 9/11. Give businesses tax-free incentives and believe me, the new Towers will fill up. In the process this will jumpstart the economy.

My advice to the LMDC about how not to be perceived as a bureaucracy is to read *The Fountainhead*, by Ayn Rand.

Does anyone know the state motto of New York? It is Excelsior!

Excelsior expresses the idea of reaching upward to higher goals. Let's live up to our motto.

I will finish by citing my recently published letter to the editor. I always wanted to quote myself in public.

The Pentagon has been restored. It was done with an appropriately sized memorial that did not overshadow the purpose of the building, which is the strategic military defense of this country. Let's do the same with the World Trade Center. Rebuild it again into the third largest business district in the US. And fill in the missing two front teeth of New York's glorious skyline.

Reflections on the World Trade Center

The buildings are lost in their limitless rise
My feet catch the pulse and the purposeful stride
I feel the sense of possibility
I feel the wrench of hard reality
The focus is sharp in the city

— "The Camera Eye" by Rush

Since the days of my youth these buildings had surrounded me. I miss them deeply. New York is not the same without them. And unless they are replaced in some similar, updated fashion, any alternative will be a letdown.

The first time I ever entered one of the buildings was in the early 1980s, to do a one day, manual labor job with my best friend Mike, who worked on the ninety-third floor. I took the lightning-quick elevator up, where we greeted each other and went in to get the work done. At one point we entered a room that had a clear view facing uptown. Staring out the window, tongue hanging, eyes riveted, I felt like I was in an architect's office looking down at a model of New York City, because that's how small the buildings below looked. No traffic could be heard through the thick window panes, but visually there was a buzz of activity. It reminded me of a plane circling in a descent, where you can see but can't hear the action beneath you.

In the mid-eighties, when I started working at Merrill Lynch, I told Mike that after my first landmark achievement with the firm we'd celebrate at Windows on the World. Less than six months later I was promoted to supervisor and we went to the restaurant. The food was good but the conversation and mood were better. The views weren't picture perfect, as it was an overcast winter evening. Many of the surrounding buildings could be vaguely seen below, and it felt to me like a bunch of little league kids gathering around one professional ballplayer. I vowed to come back in the daylight to get the 360 degree perspective and see the details which were missed at night. I wasn't disappointed. Then, for inspiration, I'd come back regularly to visit with friends, family and loved ones, whether it was at the restaurant or the observation deck.

Not much else was downtown at that time. Forty Wall Street and the Woolworth Building were two of the closest skyscrapers. Learning from my many trips to the Empire State Building, I would time my visits by arriving just before dusk and staying well into the night so I could observe the finer points of the city, which changed its wardrobe from a natural brightness to a sparkled darkness.

I spent my adolescent years living in Staten Island, but the focus on the city was sharp. I could see it every day on my commute to high school. Even while hanging out with friends at the beach, my gaze longingly turned towards those Towers, which dominated the skyline. As a paper delivery boy, one of the most thrilling days of work happened the morning after Philippe Petit's glorious wire walk, which connected the two Towers. It took me an extra twenty minutes to deliver the papers that morning because each time I threw a newspaper, before folding the next one, I'd read the entire front page story again.

Whenever traveling to Manhattan I'd run the two mile distance from home to the ferry terminal, often to save carfare. Once on the boat, drenched in sweat from the run, I'd sit down, leaning my back on the huge, circular, yellow metal column at the northernmost part of the boat. While the breeze cooled me off I'd enjoy an unobstructed view of those Towers growing larger and larger as the ferry carried me to my natural homeland. The tempo of my heartbeat increased in anticipation of the possibilities.

Upon turning eighteen and moving to Manhattan, I'd often go downtown, to SoHo, TriBeCa, or Little Italy. As these neighborhoods are not on the official grid of Manhattan, sometimes it's difficult to tell north from south when coming out of the subway. But the Towers always gave me my bearing as to what direction I needed to go. One of my favorite Midtown places to stand was on the corner of 59th & 5th, because I could look downtown and see both the Empire State Building and World Trade Center.

In 2001 I had a technical writing job, which brought me regularly to Pt. Pleasant, two hours south, on the Jersey shore. Whenever returning to New York, as the New Jersey Transit train was roughly one hour away, near South Amboy, I'd see just the tip of the Towers, way in the distance. This would inevitably cause my heart to beat just a little faster, telling me I would soon be *home*.

A few times I took helicopter rides around the city and when passing above the Towers the wind current seemed to pull us closer, as if those two gigantic lungs of the city inhaled deeply. Thrilling indeed!

I was in Rio de Janeiro for the Carnival festival in 1993 when the first attack on the Towers occurred, and I felt like I needed to rush back to make sure all was okay. A Brazilian friend who knew my love for New York told me my city was calling me home, to protect those buildings. Still working for Merrill Lynch at the time, I'd often go to their World Financial Center office so I could observe the progress of the reconstruction of the Towers.

Then came the hard reality of that fateful day on September 11. Watching the event on television was extremely difficult because I was outraged that we let our guard down, became too lax and didn't squash that Islamic Fundamentalist threat once and for all, when we should have, back in 1979.

My immediate thought was that I can't defend this city single-handedly, though I wish I could. My overwhelming feelings were best summarized by a character in the most influential book I've ever read, *The Fountainhead* by Ayn Rand:

I would give the greatest sunset in the world for one sight of New York's skyline. Particularly when one can't see the details. Just the shapes. The shapes and the thought that made them. The sky over New York and the will of man made visible. What other religion do we need? And then people tell me about pilgrimages to some dank pesthole in a jungle where they go to do homage to a crumbling temple, to a leering stone monster with a pot belly, created by some leprous savage. Is it beauty and genius they want to see? Do they seek a sense of the sublime? Let them come to New York, stand on the shore of the Hudson, look and kneel. When I see the city from my window — no, I don't feel how small I am — but I feel that if a war came to threaten this, I would like to throw myself into space, over the city, and protect these buildings with my body.

Guide the Future by the Past

There is no doubt that the terrorist attacks of 9/11 — where nearly 3,000 people died, along with those two massive, inspiring Towers — were an act of war. This was an attack not only to America's way of life, but was also a response to our contradictory foreign policy. Looking historically at our past, America's foreign policy started spiraling downward with SPAM, the Spanish-American War in 1898. This was the first time the United States ever went to war, not for self-defense, or self-interest, but instead to liberate another country (the Cubans from Spanish rule), in the name of humanity. This foreign policy of entanglement and internationalism has been dominant ever since Theodore Roosevelt urged us to walk softly and carry a big stick. However, for the past seventy years, America no longer declares war on an enemy (Korea, Viet Nam, Iraq, Afghanistan, etc.) and never calls for unconditional surrender. On top of the lunacy is the practice of providing material support to our future enemies (Germany, Japan after WWI, the USSR before, during and after WWII, and the Mujahedeen before 9/11), all of whom turned against us when they felt the time was right.

The only way to get out of this quagmire of entanglements, Islamic or otherwise, is to return to the brilliance of our Founding Fathers. The most rational foreign policy we've ever had can be found in the Monroe Doctrine, where America is once again for

Americans, standing as a beacon of liberty for the world to emulate.

This is not a war of arms. America's military can easily squash any adversary on the planet. But not if they are hamstrung by the moral uncertainty in which they are not told to achieve victory but instead to try not to hurt anyone's feelings. This is what we've experienced for much of the past century. The result is what we have today: young people valiantly fighting, not for America, but for some other country, financed by our tax dollars.

Domestically this same moral uncertainty has led to many disasters as well, including the prevention of the Towers being rebuilt. The World Trade Center should have been rebuilt immediately after the attacks but layers of bureaucracy, indecision and power grabs by various pressure groups prevented this. Perhaps it is a fear that the same thing would happen again if they were rebuilt, so why tempt fate? The answer to that is to squash the enemy so we don't live in fear.

America has lost its moral compass. The Tea Party movement is trying to return to the Founders' original principles, which upheld individual rights, including life, liberty and the pursuit of happiness. It is now time for a moral Declaration of Independence, so that the political one doesn't collapse. Fortunately there is a book which provides this: *Atlas Shrugged*.

Pax Americana

By Frederick Cookinham

When every person on the bus (except the driver and me) suddenly jumps up and lunges to the bus's port side, you fear the bus will topple over.

It never has, though, and as an experienced New York City double-decker bus tour guide, I know that even a top-heavy double-decker does not turn over when everyone moves to one side. It lists, but I have never seen one capsize.

This one — in May of 2003 — was a coach, not a double-decker, so I was sitting nice and stable on one deck and not standing on a pitching poop with the wind in my face, as I used to be on the Grayline buses in 1997. A "coach" means a single-decker bus that holds 52 passengers, as opposed to a double-decker, or a ten- or sixteen- or thirty-seater or a van.

Bus tour guides have their own lingo, like sailors do. "Pax" means passengers. The singular is "pas." A terminal is different from a station. A bus or a train stops at stations along the way from one terminal to another. If it is a terminal, your trip must either start or stop there. When a bus carries pax from Point A to Point B, that's a "maneuver," as from their hotel to the Empire State Building, for example. When a tour guide neither drives nor arranges a bus tour, but simply meets a bus full of pax, picks up the bus's microphone and guides the tour, that is called "step-on work," as opposed to having a "bid," which is a full-time, permanent job with Grayline, New York Apple Tours or New York Double-decker Tours, or "over-the-road work," which means staying overnight in a motel with the group and the driver and guiding them for days on end. Someone who does this is technically a "Tour Manager," not just a "Tour Guide."

This was a step-on job; a two-coach maneuver, following largely the route of Grayline's Downtown Loop. Mike had the tour, but he called me when he learned that there would be two buses. The group was a high school band and their teacher and chaperones and driver, all from Wisconsin. When they lunged to port, it was because we were heading up Church Street, past "Ground Zero." Nearly fifty pax on each bus — one hundred digital cameras whirring. (I remember when cameras contained "film" and clicked.) Every living soul on two buses, except the driver (who grumbled constantly that he had not been fed all day and had to stay with the bus), was pressed up against the port windows like leftover mashed potatoes in Tupperware — all to see down into, and photograph, the pit where over two thousand people had died violently twenty-one months before.

Except the driver and the jaded tour guide, that is.

I had seen "Ground Zero" before. After Grayline, I had returned to my former, and more lucrative, profession: proofreading at a Wall Street law firm. I now guide tours only on weekends. On September 11, 2001, I had been married for 2½ days and living in Queens for less than two months. I had moved in with my fiancée in July, from a cheap apartment in Jersey City, convenient to the PATH (Port Authority Trans-Hudson) train at Journal Square. If I had not moved, I figure I would have been emerging from the World Trade Center PATH terminal at Church and Liberty Streets just about the time the first plane hit. I would have heard the impact and explosion, I would have turned and seen the fireball, I might have been hit by a jet engine or wheel, and if not hit, I would have run, not walked, the half mile east to work. If I had gone to work from Queens that day, I would have been emerging from the Number 2 train at William Street, a safer distance away.

But I was, in any case, sick that day. My new wife woke me, saying a plane had hit the World Trade Center.

Now I was taking tourists to see "Ground Zero." It's totally different for them, I thought. They could not see the smoke plume from Wisconsin. I could from Queens.

They are curious. I am just heartsick. They had seen pictures and TV images of the World Trade Center, and then the rubble, and now the pit. But the World Trade Center had been, for twenty-nine years, one of my favorite haunts. It was almost the first thing I saw in New York when I was a tourist myself in 1972, and had been a hangout since I moved here in 1977. For two years it had been my port of call every morning on the PATH. I can still see, in my mind's eye, hundreds of details of the place: spots where I walked many times, faces I saw. I remember the sound the revolving door made as I entered the North Tower from the concourse, and the sound of rushing air in the elevator going up to the observation deck or Windows on the

World, and the feeling of my ears popping, and the smell of the carpets. I could walk blindfolded to the news stands and the pizza joint and the long PATH terminal escalators (replaced just days ago, as I write in December). I remember the fountain and the geode in the lobby of the Marriott hotel. I remember the crack in the concourse floor from the 1993 bombing. I still have a *Popular Science* magazine, dated July, 1993, that says that the towers were designed to withstand a once-in-a-century wind gust of 150 miles per hour, or a hit by a 707, the biggest plane in the skies when the Center was planned.

And I remember an acquaintance, John William Perry — you will find him under "P" on the list of the dead on the "Ground Zero" fence, and again on the Police memorial wall in Battery Park City. He had gone downtown that morning to file his retirement papers from the Force. He rushed to the scene to save people. The band members from Wisconsin probably didn't know John. Interesting fellow.

Someone called that fence on Church Street with its alphabetical KIA list "America's Wailing Wall." I have never seen anyone wail there, and I don't even think I've seen anyone pray, although red-tabarded volunteers are there to pray with you if you care to. I hate that term, "Wailing Wall," even worse than I hate hearing the term "World Trade Center" replaced with "Ground Zero." *My* America is not supposed to have Wailing Walls. America is not about wailing — it is about doing.

Americans are known for expressions like "Bigger and Better!", "Eureka!", "Excelsior!", "Sure thing!", "Gung ho!", and best of all, "Can do!" Chauncey Mitchell Depew, in his "Columbian Oration," said "The Cross on Calvary was hope; the cross raised on San Salvador was opportunity." Dan Rather wept when recalling the line, "Thine alabaster cities gleam, undimmed by human tears," after 9/11.

This nation and culture are about Progress and Success, and I would not live in any other. In a Brazilian movie I once heard a character say, after something had gone wrong due to incompetence, "What do you expect — this is Brazil!" Who would want to be identified with such a shameful national self-image — deserved or undeserved? Even the disaster itself suggests, to me, not fate and resignation, but the question: What could America have done to prevent it? And what can America do to prevent any repetition of it? Do a better job of hewing to, and exporting, our own revolutionary principles that defined us as a nation *and a culture* two hundred years ago, in the Enlightenment: the Age of Reason — that's what.

All this my pax were missing, as far as I could tell by watching them. They, on the bus, and thousands more I have seen at Grou... at the World Trade Center site, are engaged, not in wailing (I guess my last paragraph was my wail), but in looking, in trying to grasp, where everything *was* — in measuring distances with their eyes — in looking back and forth from the photos on the fence to the pit and the skyscrapers standing around the pit (as if mourning two of their own who had fallen; like an honor guard around a bier in the Capitol Rotunda), trying to get a mental picture of how *big* it all had once been.

The pax are looking at those surrounding buildings, too, to look for signs of damage. The coating of cement dust has been replaced with new black paint now on the Liberty Place Building. But they look also to appreciate the height of those buildings, the better to compare and grasp the still more amazing loftiness of the lost towers. The loved and lost. Several of these tourists have, in my hearing, looked at Liberty Place and said, in Southern and Midwestern and New England accents, that this building must be unsound and slated for demolition because look how it's bent! — obviously warped by the blast or something. I could not see this bending they described, and I decided that these visitors were simply astigmatic. The building is fine. Skidmore, Owings and Merrill's International Style buildings sometimes play tricks of perspective on the eye. They are meant to. With little or no surface detail to give the unaccustomed viewer clues as to scale and distance, a skyscraper can look narrower at the top and thus make you think that the walls are bending in as they ascend. Perhaps that is what these tourists were seeing.

Back and forth go the heads and index fingers, from the fence-mounted blown-up photos of the site to the surrounding, surviving buildings. "Here's this building, and here we are." Having established their own location in the football huddle of skyscrapers around the pit, and having satisfied themselves that one of those buildings is not about to fall, they say to each other, "Look how tall they are, but look how much taller the Twin Towers *were*!" Then they fall silent. They look and look at those photos, then at the pit. What is there to say?

Around them walk men with suits and briefcases, in twos and threes, who comment on what has reappeared lately, like the new PATH terminal now, or the Century 21 department store, which quickly reopened. These are men who work Downtown, with their out-of-town business guests. Being businessmen, they are supposed to speak to each other in businesslike appraisals. But all the tourists speak to each other in much the same tone, because of the nature of what they are mourning: This was the ultimate business building in the ultimate business city in the nation whose business has always been Business.

A laugh sometimes cuts the silence. Teenagers can't help having fun, even here.

The tourists rarely take pictures of each other here. They save that for a happier place: the Bull at Bowling Green. If they do, though, they do not smile for the camera very much. Their usual camera-smile is born, but then its growth gets stunted at adolescence, leaving a *Mona Lisa* or a dollar bill Washington-like strained grimace rather than a wide-open dazzler. The photographee with more presence of mind won't start to smile at all, but will relax his cheeks into a neutral poker face.

"This is History! Don't let it be a mystery!" chants the site map hawker, along with facts and statistics. "The World Trade Center had eight underground levels; five open to the public, and three utility levels…"

Twenty feet from him, an older, gray-bearded flutist plays "Amazing Grace" followed by "America the Beautiful."

The profusion of flags, teddy bears, and such has long since been cleaned from around St. Paul's Chapel, but on the World Trade Center fence I see a laminated 8½ x 11 page with the German headline *"AMERIKANER, WIR SIND BEI EUCH"* — Americans, we stand by you, the translation reads. The people of Hamburg sympathize. They are also grateful that America helped Germany out of her darkest hour, and that JFK, in Germany's hour of need, had said *"Ich bin ein Berliner!"* I write *"Danke, Hamburg!"* at the bottom of the page. Stapled to the page is an open book of matches. Two of the matches are left whole — the Twin Towers — and the others are skillfully cut into pointy-topped skyscrapers forming a skyline — but lower, always, in all pictures, whether in matches or watercolors or velvet — always the pre-World Trade Center skyline is lower than the Towers. People used to complain about that — before they lost those towers. The towers were of a scale to dwarf the skyscrapers that made skyscrapers famous.

Walking tourists are different from the bus pax. In a drive-by photo op, they instantly point their eyes and cameras at the pit. It's instinctive, and besides, they are four feet higher on a coach, and twelve feet higher on a double-decker, so they can see down into the pit better than the infantry ranked along the fence. Since the foot-tourists have more time, though, they take pictures in all directions, to get the context: this amphitheater of skyscrapers; this Greek chorus surrounding the missing star, the Oedipus Rex. The comparison is what gets them. They stand there concentrating so long on the fence-photos and the buildings because they want to grasp the size, the scale. It is the combination of the enormity of the crime and the enormousness of the lost achievement that keeps them rooted to the spot.

"Look, they're still tryin' to *fix* that one!" a traveler from the South says to his family. He is pointing to the Barclay-Vesey Building, designed by Ralph Walker in the 1920s in the Art Deco style. He is half right. The red plastic netting covers scars running down the side of the building showered and pierced by falling parts of the North Tower on 9/11, but the blue tarps at the top cover work that has been going on up there for years. That work was merely interrupted by 9/11, not unlike Man's rise from barbarism. Aren't we all just works in progress? Maybe Utopia should not be interpreted to mean perfection, but the hope for still greater perfection.

Funny, I never noticed that building much while the World Trade Center loomed over it. But now — and not just because I study Art Deco buildings for my tours — I do notice it. It is now the tallest thing in that vista, looking northwest from Church and Liberty. It no longer has something three times as tall next to it. The eye gravitates — or rather anti-gravitates — to the highest point. Like King Kong, we primates instinctively look for the highest tree we can climb to escape approaching predators. Cesar Pelli, who designed the Petronas Towers in Kuala Lumpur, Malaysia — now replaced by the Burj Dubai Building as the world's tallest — says that to him a tall building is not a "skyscraper" unless it comes to a pointy top, like the Empire

State Building, or the AIG Building, now once again respectively the city's and Downtown's tallest buildings. The point draws the eye to the top, irresistibly.

But a building with no point has a point, too. Unchanging vertical lines with no terminating point as you look up their length suggest infinite height. That is how I first saw the World Trade Center. In the fall of 1972, riding in my friend's car at night down the now dismantled elevated West Side Highway, I looked up to the tops of the Towers and could not see them. There was a low cloud ceiling. The Towers, with their lighted windows, lost themselves in the clouds. As we drove closer and closer to the World Trade Center, I tilted my head back farther and farther, just like the first-timers at the fence look up at the Millennium Hotel across Church Street, only more so. With no tops to the Towers apparent, it was easy to imagine them having no tops... just going up and up, forever, past the sun and the moon. Actually, what I thought at the time was: They are Atlas, holding up the sky.

The human eye always seeks the highest point. The skyscrapers are a command to rise that the eye instinctively follows. Life seeks other life. Mind seeks mind, just to have someone to talk to. We all need company; someone to reflect our view of ourselves, and share our values. Life is the process of filling holes, negating nothingnesses. The memorial to the loved and lost is not the hole — the hole is in our hearts and we need no other — the memorial is the *process* of filling and rising and building, itself, the healing of the wound — the resuscitation of the beating heart of the city, the nation, and the world.

Go and see for yourself. The pax are looking *up*.

What the Twin Towers Mean to Me

By Joy Goldberg

I am a private individual living in Brooklyn, N.Y.

I am one among many voices all over America and all over the world.

On Tuesday, September 11, 2001, I was off from work. I sat at the kitchen table thinking about what to eat for breakfast. It was going on nine o'clock in the morning.

We all were going about our affairs that morning, whether on our jobs, at home or homeless.

When I first came to live in New York City, I arrived with nothing but a bag filled with a few items and enough money to stay a couple of nights in a cheap residence hotel.

It was all I needed. I was in New York.

I spent two years in poverty, wound up in a few homeless shelters, spent times in furnished rooms all the while wondering where the next piece of bread was coming from.

When I got a very little bit more money, say a few dollars, I would buy a subway token and get on the train.

The A train is the longest run in the New York subway system, and is outstandingly scenic in places, extending all the way past JFK Airport, across Broad Channel where the Jamaica Wildlife Preserve is located, along the water and into Far Rockaway in the borough of Queens. To get a window seat on the right side of the train, to watch the sun set across the waters and to view, all the way in the distance, the Manhattan skyline, was heaven to me. This beauty knew no poverty, no want.

When I beheld the Twin Towers of the World Trade Center soaring tall from the furthest reaches of the five boroughs of New York City, I would have to pinch myself, not truly being able to fully believe I was here on earth, in the city I loved the most.

I was the wealthiest person on earth.

People from all over the world have desired to come to New York City to see the Twin Towers.

With the majestic grace of the Empire State and Chrysler Buildings to the north and the Twin Towers to the south, the skyline of Manhattan was perfect in its sweet, aesthetic balance of symmetry and asymmetry.

The names World Trade Center and Twin Towers have always, from the very beginning, been synonymous, without question.

There never was a question.

Until September 11, 2001.

Since the day the Twin Towers were blown away by cowardice and hatred, New York City and her people from all over the world have suffered and are still suffering immeasurably, to this very day.

Grief counselors told us we would feel better after a few months.

Today, they are at a loss to explain how it is that we do not feel any better and how it is that vast numbers of people who did *not* directly lose a loved one in the towers are as deeply affected as those who did.

Today, I have a good job and a beautiful railroad apartment on the first floor underneath the elevated J subway line.

One of my coworker friends lives in Far Rockaway. Before 9/11, she would tell me how, joyously, she would look at the Manhattan skyline on her way to Brooklyn every morning. For months after 9/11, she would drive home from work, park her van along Beach Channel Drive, which overlooks the water, across from which is the Manhattan skyline. She would weep profusely and ask, "*Why, why* did this happen?!"

My coworker did not directly lose a loved one in the towers.

Now, today, an even greater, compounding act of horrendous atrocity has loomed over New York City, an atrocity that would be the ruination of what was a beautiful, serene and uplifting place filled with *life*:

New York State Governor George Pataki and his appointed Lower Manhattan Development Corporation made the decision to erect *one* tower: a generic tower one would see in any other city, except taller.

And with this one tower, the "memorial" plan: the glorious Twin Towers, which before 9/11 stood tall, a true representation of freedom, now reduced to two sunken, abysmal pools with a mausoleum-like underground. The name of the planned "memorial" is "Reflecting Absence." A portion of Michael Arad and Peter Walker's (the designers) statement reads as follows:

Standing there at the water's edge, looking at a pool of water that is flowing away into an *abyss*, a visitor to the site can sense that what is beyond this curtain of water and ribbon of names is inaccessible.

Rebuilding the Twin Towers is what is normal.

Independent poll upon poll has shown that the majority of the people in New York City, and people all over the world want the Twin Towers to be rebuilt.

But we were *never, not once* given the chance to directly vote between rebuilding the Twin Towers and any of the LMDC proposals.

The LMDC prepared a Generic Environmental Impact Statement (GEIS), a huge 2,000 page report glorifying their "Freedom Tower" proposal and vilifying the Twin Towers, which they called "the Restoration *Alternative*."

The public, in general, does not have a clue about this. They have no idea that there were public hearings about the GEIS, this because the legal notice published in the newspaper was very small, and calculatedly worded so that the average Joe couldn't understand what it all meant.

The statement about their proposal not being the only open option is in Chapter 23.

The deadline for public comment passed on May 24, 2004, and a sad, depressed and grieving people who would have spoken were silenced.

Each successive governor, on both sides of the river, has furthered the weapon of choice: the huge battle wall of silence built by an unholy alliance of politicians, mass media, religious leaders, celebrities, corporate CEOs and special interest groups alike. "Hand has joined to hand" and purse to purse, to erect hideous edifices of arrogance and self-will, overlooking a twin pit.

Little wonder is this, among a mentality refusing to so much as release the landfill containing a near 100% potential for remains of victims of 9/11, to their devastated loved ones. Instead the landfill lies out in the open in Fresh Kills, Staten Island, garbage dump.

A better match than this to a lady of royalty such as New York, the feet of Cinderella's stepsisters forcing their way into her glass slipper, as they strained to declare it a perfect fit.

At this time, there exists a solid plan for new Twin Towers and for an honorable, peaceful and respectful memorial with flags from nations represented in the 9/11 tragedy. The plan has been designed by architectural engineer Kenneth Gardner and by architect Herbert Belton, Jr.

The new Twin Towers are at least one story taller and are of a "tube within a tube" construction, which is far stronger than the original Twin Towers.

I have had the privilege to meet Mr. Gardner and to view a model of the new World Trade Center. When I saw it, it gave me an exhilarating feeling of hope and closure. (The model can be viewed at MakeNyNyAgain.com.)

The World Trade Center, a.k.a. the Twin Towers, was a landmark, the signature of our nation's greatness set upon the very shore beside which the golden lamp of the greatest city of all time is lifted to welcome the peoples of every nation.

New York, America and all the nations of the earth deserve far better than a sentence worse than death itself, a huge gaping wound to our land, to our lives and to the American spirit itself, a wound fated never to heal unless the Twin Towers are rebuilt.

A Christmas Wish for My Country

By Cherie L. Fernandez

At thirty-four, I realize I may be a bit old for the whole Santa Claus rigmarole, but I'll make one last go of it: This year, all I want for Christmas is my Twin Towers back, bigger if possible.

This is not just a wish for myself, but for my world-weary parents and for my nephew and nieces, the eldest of which is seven. It is for my fellow Americans and thoughtful citizens of that part of the world which holds free inquiry, scientific endeavor, and honest human effort in places of esteem as the true deliverers of improvement in the lives of the lot of us.

In a nation obsessed with the humdrum details of daily life, a fixation exacerbated by the events of September 11, the answer cannot be more "human scale" building. Too many of us are trapped in mediocre environments and far too many, if we are not drawn to look up beyond our own navels, probably never will.

Human cultures have always built monuments. Before this atrocity, the Twin Towers and their kind were monuments. More than that, they were living monuments. Most others are not. They are tombs for royals, reminders to subject peoples, or the province of bored students and gawking tourists. Living monuments touch the realm of daily life. Everyday people work there, form friendships there, find life partners there. Over half a dozen babies were born in the original World Trade Center. Living monuments, rather than being dedicated to some distant, sainted historical figure, are beacons to which ordinary people can and do aspire.

From all over the world people came, drawn to take their place among the living monuments and those who built them. That some have met a tragic end should not be taken as a lesson. An immigrant worker who died while working for a building-services firm in the Twin Towers could've just as easily met his fate as a victim of an unscrupulous human smuggler, suffocated in a cargo container or left desiccated along a desert border. Accidents in motor vehicles happen every day. Nobody would have remembered his name then, so tragedy does not deserve the place at the head of our table.

Over thirty years after our first successful lunar landing we are still experiencing trickle-down benefits from the technology developed for that effort. The original Twin Towers were part of a dramatic break from the skyscraper building techniques that reached their zenith in the 1930s. Nobody planned for this heinous attack. We must pick ourselves up and go forward despite our wounds.

I spent the first few days of December 2001 in Toronto, Canada, at the Continental Automated Building Association's first Intelligent and Integrated Buildings Conference. I met many people there who are not willing to concede defeat and who are still reaching for the sky.

The work that we are doing to make tenants safer and building operations more efficient is complex and far-reaching. We are sure of that work. All we need is a public that is open, supportive, unafraid to look deeper instead of jumping to the wrong conclusions and, most importantly, possessed of the willpower to do great things no matter what others may think, to keep a chain of human achievement unbroken for the next generation.

"Can't" never brought us anything. "Modesty" never pushed us forward. Stagnant water turns foul. Dream no small dreams. After the conference, I went up the CN Tower, a beautiful, wonderful, though not "living" monument. It served to remind me of how important it is to have majesty in one's environment, a marker of achievement to show us what is possible. I loved the view, and as the sun set, I felt a hopeful serenity. During the construction of the CN Tower, all the way to completion, Canadians were there to cheer the crews and show their support for their people. Their hearts knew what they were doing it for, and it was not just a fancy antenna. Please, America, reclaim this triumphant spirit before it becomes a stranger to your soul.

Stand for a Future of Excellence

By Cherie L. Fernandez

I am writing to prevent a second atrocity from being inflicted on Lower Manhattan, and I am not alone. Between friends, family, email pen pals, coworkers, to people I talk to on the trains and buses I ride, hundreds in all, not one thinks the Libescheme is worth the paper it's written on.

It is essentially a rehash of the rejected Memorial Triangle design of July 2002. Back then people complained it looked like Albany. Nearly two years later, it still looks like Albany. Buildings of this stunted scale could be built anywhere. Perhaps this plan would work well in Cleveland. New York City is one of the few places that can easily support exciting, majestic, ultra-tall buildings, so the proposed plan is unworthy of consideration. It is a wasted opportunity, an encouragement of mediocrity where excellence belongs. Mediocrity diminishes this great city. No amount of capital-A Architecture can hide it. Also, name-brand designing is not what people care about. After all, how many people can name the Empire State Building's architect?

Our number one request in rebuilding was that our skyline be restored. "Restored" does not mean "replaced with an obvious joke," at least not in my Webster's. This seventy-story building with sixty stories of scaffolding is the equivalent of a very bad comb-over of weak hearts, small minds, and cowardice. Plus, as far as height titles are concerned, this is reopening a debate in the official arbiter of building height, the Council on Tall Buildings and Urban Habitat, of which I am a member. When the Petronas Towers were completed, the debate began over the relevance of structural top vs. highest occupied roofline. A significant group favored the latter over the former, with the argument that developers would erect buildings with progressively taller yet still insignificant crowns or spires. This displayed little engineering or design effort, would grow to ridiculous proportions, and, honestly considered, is a form of cheating just to get the title. I am of this camp favoring highest occupied roofline as the standard, and by proposing such a ridiculous structure, the LMDC has proven our point.

Plus, how can you possibly replace two super-tall towers with one? The LMDC is showing that we are less than half of what we were before 9/11.

There will be no shortage of occupants for the upper floors. Last time I checked my *Commercial Property News*, higher floors were still going for a premium compared to lower floors. As the founder of a start-up business, I hope to be able to afford an office on as high a floor as possible. Not only will I be inspired by the awesome views, but I will also have an easy time weeding through job candidates. Any who would be afraid of coming up to my office for an interview, yet think nothing of the safety of the cab ride they took to reach the building, would be unfit to work for me.

I am disappointed by the waste of resources for acquiring and ripping down the repairable Deutsche Bank Building. This structure was a survivor, and the LMDC is treating it like it is treating other survivors, deeming only the dead worthy of consideration.

We have the opportunity to build a multi-use complex like the Time Warner Center, or the John Hancock Center in Chicago, on an even grander scale, giving the concept the showcase it deserves, but instead the LMDC favors more of the same old, same old.

Their obsession with streets and street-level retail is unseemly. It fixes what isn't broken. I work outside. When it is not winter, I can enjoy being out in the elements, but it is nice to have a choice. I am relatively young and healthy. I have not tried to navigate the crowded sidewalks of Manhattan with a mobility device. Demographics show an increase in the elderly population. More will choose to gravitate to cities, where public transit, medical facilities, cultural and educational institutions, and amenities for visiting family members abound. The elderly will be even less nostalgic about street level retail when it's raining or the sidewalks are iced. What on Earth is wrong with such people taking a subway to an underground mall? And why is the LMDC determined to deprive harried commuters of the opportunity to grab a few items on the way down to their trains? The original WTC mall was one of the most profitable in the world. The success of the Time Warner Center enclosed mall also provides hints that people want choices in their shopping experiences.

These shortcomings are compounded by underestimates of the

impact of more automobile traffic on already choked nineteenth-century streets. Downtown does not and will not have the flow of Midtown. Midtown was designed to be more open, with its grid street pattern, yet it is painfully choked. Automobile dependence will be recognized as the "cigarette smoking" of the twenty-first century. We have the responsibility to discourage, not encourage, this nasty habit in the city.

The LMDC overestimates the long-term impact of the memorial. Historically, nobody has come to New York for memorials. They come to New York for modern marvels, for a taste of the world, and a glimpse of what is possible. There are dozens of memorials and memorial parks throughout the city. Almost unanimously, they have become at times vandalism targets and roosts for vagrants and dope fiends that deaden, rather than enliven, surrounding areas. Contrary to some of the bilge we have heard, this site where innocent people died cannot be compared to Gettysburg or Pearl Harbor. The latter are sites where soldiers died serving their country, a reminder of the sacrifices required for freedom. Far more people visit the Empire State Building observation deck than Grant's Tomb. This will not change to any meaningful degree.

Like hundreds of thousands of others, I do not want to "Reflect Absence." Terrorists celebrate absence, and it is incongruous to commemorate the lives of those who worked in the sky by descending down into a pit.

We need show some spine to the emotionally overwrought among the family members and to the anti-development utopians in our hair. I will give you the argument as to why the value dichotomy they've drawn is a false one. This is not a matter of commerce vs. reverence for life. These people utterly lack historical perspective, and are immersed in the very confusion they claim to rail against. Consider first the loose network of charities that provide proper funerals and burials for the bodies of abandoned children. This would not be a priority without the disposable income and free time made possible by our system of commerce. Then consider the Triangle Shirtwaist Factory Fire of 1911. Innocent working people died en masse there, but the building has been repaired. The incident is commemorated with a plaque within the structure. The lack of an elaborate memorial does not mean we have forgotten this incident. Instead, the legacy of the workers' lives is carried on in the unions, the regulations, and agencies like OSHA that protect our safety on the job to this very day.

I offer the following as a member of the civil engineering and building automation community. I operate my own startup company, Project AVATAR. I am a member of the Council on Tall Buildings and Urban Habitat, the Continental Automated Buildings Association, and the Skyscraper Museum. I do not stand to gain financially as a result of any of these comments. In fact, I stand to lose financially, for I have pledged to do any work on new Twin Towers at cost, and I intend to stand by that pledge.

While I applaud the interest in the newest generation of green building technology, please be aware that no amount of energy and resources saved by these technologies would be able to make up for the waste caused by the operation of those two huge waterfalls in the memorial.

Fewer, taller buildings are also far more efficient and safer, as well as potentially far more attractive, than the equivalent space in smaller buildings. The gains made through economy of scale are the most obvious. Fewer materials overall would be needed. Mechanical systems operate at a higher level of utilization. Energy efficiency improves, aided by the fact that larger structures lose less of their heating and cooling to the outside environment. As a contrast, the so-called "Freedom Tower," with its sixty stories of scaffolding on a plebian seventy-story building, is not only space inefficient, but a waste of steel.

Safety is greater in taller structures than smaller ones. We who are members of the engineering and construction community have a responsibility to educate the public about the truth, rather than passively catering to their ignorance. The structural redundancy inherent in taller structures is cost-prohibitive in smaller ones. Smaller structures simply cannot generate enough revenue to justify the higher level of design effort. Fireproofing methods are about to take a great leap forward, just like seismic engineering design did in the late 1980s. Give us the confidence and the support we need to advance the state of the art and we guarantee you great results.

Building automation is evolving at extreme speed and will handily remove the complications inherent in managing anything large. Here is a case where available technology has run so far ahead of applications, but now, a new generation of visionaries is showing us what can be possible in this field. Let us prove what we can do.

Silverstein's comfort and experience with buildings of a certain size does not matter since what he "lusted after" was not just another mediocre piece of Manhattan, but the only two 110 story buildings in New York. If he has suddenly found doubts about his ability to manage structures of this size, I stand ready to bring him the immense benefits springing from building automation. This technology would make managing new Twin Towers far easier than a single conventional mid-rise and I promise to install such a system in new Twin Towers at cost and at no profit to myself.

Finally, I also offer a bit of common sense regarding Silverstein's insurance situation. My plan has three steps.

Replace the sixty stories of scaffolding in the first tower with rentable office space, turning the building from a white elephant into a cash cow.

When sufficient money has accumulated from the first tower, recycle its plans and build it a twin.

Scrap plans for the other three stumpy, undistinguished buildings for something of higher value, like more retail space.

I'd like you to know that I have written this on an airplane. This is not the first post-September 11 flight I've taken. This airplane was so full I did not get my preferred window seat. Now you know how little regard I have for the LMDC's concern about ultra-tall buildings not being able to find tenants for upper floors. Their transparent short-term cowardice will deprive the current and future generations of go-getters of our inspiring workplaces in the sky. We built taller than seventy stories in the 1930s. Are we less than we were then? If they lack the stomach for greatness, they should at least have the generosity of spirit to step aside for those of us who do, and take Daniel Libeskind and the rest of his potty-minded de-constructivist cabal with them.

The Gardner Plan, which could be considered an improvement on the Restoration Alternative, is a hands-down winner compared to the Proposed Action. This was a completely private effort with a result far better than the horse-and-pony-show of a public process that made a studied effort of ignoring what the people really want. Twin Towers merchandise is still popular. The

World Trade Center was one of the few building complexes to have a nickname. The public still has affection for those magnificent buildings. I can only imagine derisive nicknames for the so-called Freedom Tower, which resembles nothing more than a junkie's needle from a distance.

I plead to you again to make New York whole, and not leave the LMDC's planned hole in our skyline and in our hearts.

Rebuild the Towers!

By Stuart Mark Feldman

If they are at all victorious, the Islamic, terrorist states' victory will not have been that they knocked down a couple of skyscrapers, but that they will make us afraid to build skyscrapers. It will not have been that they killed thousands of us, but that they will have made us afraid to be alive.

The towers were a symbol of the power we have in the world. Power that the elite of these terrorist states don't have, and don't think anyone should have: the power over material scarcity, and with it, the power to alleviate perpetual suffering. The power to eliminate this suffering is hubris and dangerous to their societies, and they hate us for having it.

They hate our easy confidence. They hate the casual way in which we move through the world. They hate that economic disaster, drought or starvation doesn't threaten us daily. They hate the symbols of our material success. They hate it when their own youth start wearing jeans and listening to Western music. They hate that every day we don't have to be afraid, waiting only on the afterlife for happiness. They hate that we can create our own happiness, here and now. They believe that man isn't supposed to have control over this world, and that without God and his mercy there is only misery. It threatens their worldview to see us have that control. It is *not* that they envy our lifestyle; it's that they don't want it to exist. Its presence defies their beliefs, and it enrages them that we are not ashamed of it.

A caller to a radio talk show thought we should not rebuild the WTC towers. The caller added that, in the future, maybe we should rethink building any more skyscrapers to become targets for terrorists. Other callers believed we should get used to scaling back our freedoms in order to protect ourselves. Still others simply believed that from now on, we will be afraid: afraid to travel, afraid of foreigners, afraid of packages, afraid of the unseen and the unknown.

If we don't rebuild the twin towers, that will be their victory. The victory of bringing to America the kind of world they live in every day. We will no longer build skyscrapers, because we will be afraid to build them. We will no longer walk so confidently through the world, fearless of death and disaster, because we will be afraid to walk. Our faces, hidden behind veils of apprehension, will no longer sport our easy smiles, because fear doesn't wear a smile. We will feel safe only within walls, not the walls of office buildings, but of churches, kneeling before *our* God, begging for *his* mercy, and expecting happiness only in *our* hereafter. We will have become like them. Their worldview will have prevailed. They will have won.

As a postscript, I wish to make this observation. This New Years Eve, in Times Square, in the face of threats of planned terrorist attacks in New York City on that day, a mere two and a half years after the original attack in that same city, and in the midst of a war on two Islamic states, hundreds of thousands of Americans showed up to celebrate the new year. The wild, fearless, and joyful expressions on the revelers' faces that night must have been seen as an incredible affront to the goals of the terrorists. Nowhere in the Arab world would you find such expressions of happiness even on a good day. This is what a new and taller pair of WTC buildings will speak to the world, "You will not be able to destroy our drive to build a world of happiness! Your threats will not keep us in our homes, and your bombs will not prevent us from rebuilding, higher still!"

Just Another City?

By Margaret Donovan

> City of the World!
> (For all races are here, all the lands of the earth make contributions here.)
> City of the Sea! City of wharves and stores — city of tall facades of marble and iron!
> Proud and passionate city — mettlesome, mad, extravagant city!
>
> — Walt Whitman

New Yorkers and tourists alike used the Twin Towers as literal landmarks — to help them get their bearings. And for people around the world they epitomized the brash, exuberant spirit of New York.

So, it is striking that the current design for the ho-hum "Freedom Tower" would effectively turn downtown New York into a Boston, or a Savannah, or a Providence — attractive boutique cities, sedate and oh-so seemly — leaving us to wonder where, in fact, we are.

The Twin Towers were immodest proof of New York's extravagant spirit and if our response to their destruction is to replace them with the current slick, derivative design, then our city will be trivialized in the process — it may seem like New York, but it won't really be New York.

If what we finally put up at Ground Zero is not at least as majestic as what the terrorists took down, then it will probably be just a matter of time before the blight of diminished expectations creeps northward and turns a once peerless city into a common place.

If we substitute the insipid, lowest-common-denominator building now on the drawing board for those legendary towers, then New York will take on a theme-park character. The Empire State Building, and the Chrysler Building, and the Statue of Liberty will still be here, but the spirit will have vanished.

It is time to stop playing politics with Ground Zero. It is time to determine what it is the people really want to see there, to stop trying to salvage the mess made by special interests in our name — and then to break records making it happen.

After all, this is the place where many of the construction workers who cleared away the vast mountain of debris expressed a desire to work without pay, if only they could help to rebuild the Towers!

No, this is not just another city.

A Nation That Never Dies

By Margaret Donovan

As early as I can remember, New York was the center of my universe — and from the time I first moved here from Boston in 1970, the Twin Towers' construction lights captured my attention. It seemed like I could see them wherever I went. What a thrill it was to finally stand on the observation deck for the first time.

Alistair Cooke, the Englishman who hosted the seventies' PBS series *America* once said: "People, when they first come to America, whether as travelers or settlers, become aware of a new and agreeable feeling: that the whole country is their oyster." Nowhere was that more true than when standing a quarter of a mile in the sky, on the Twins' outdoor observation deck, with the most fabulous city in the world at one's feet and the steady light of the nation's premier icon shining in the background, framed by the curve of the earth.

The Twin Towers had a spirit — a personality. They were the quintessential expression of the exuberant, immodest, excessive, confident, generous, invincible, "city so nice they named it twice." They were the establishing shot in dozens of movies, but it was the Mike Nichols classic *Working Girl* in 1988 that really captured their essence.

The film opens and closes with stunning shots of the Twin Towers and they were used throughout as a metaphor for the longing and aspirations of a young woman with gumption who set her sights high and conquered the city. One has only to imagine the same film being set against the Freedom Tower "icon" instead to recognize just how puny the current plan is.

But they had an other-worldly dimension as well. *The New York Times* bio of the Trade Center, *City in the Sky — The Rise and Fall of the World Trade Center*, related a trip that Guy Tozzoli, the newly appointed Director of the Port Authority's World Trade Department, made in 1962 to the Seattle World's Fair as a scout for the titan in charge of planning the 1964 World's Fair in New York, Robert Moses.

The book relates how the edgy engineer strolled into the Federal Science Pavilion and was suddenly transported into an oasis of tranquility. That pavilion had been designed by an architect he had never heard of — the Japanese-American Minoru Yamasaki — and the palpable sense of being in a cathedral or an Eastern palace was Yamasaki's trademark. He mastered the craft of making soaring spaces seem intimate and enshrined it in the Twin Towers.

Intellectual snobs never understood the Twin Towers' appeal and have been busy in the years since they were destroyed trying to diminish their appeal and downgrade their impact. Their disinformation is all over the Internet because they want people to think that most people shared their prejudice. But it is not so. For people throughout the city, the Towers were our friends. No one ever expressed that better than Nicole Gelinas in a May 5, 2005, *New York Post* column:

> It is shocking — almost inconceivable — that we haven't snatched back from our enemies what belongs to us. Americans always understood the Twin Towers. They were us: stark capitalism, power and beauty without explanation or apology.

In October of 2000, I had the good fortune to work in Tower Two and loved every minute I spent there. I can still remember how wistful I felt when my train pulled away at the end of every day. When I climbed the stairs to Columbus Circle on 9/11 and heard a radio blaring that the South Tower had just collapsed, I was sickened by the thought that it might mean 10,000 horrible deaths. But I also remember a sharp stab of pain for the North Tower standing there without its mate. After they were both gone I recall thinking the now ironic thought that it was better they were hit than the Empire State Building because they would be so much easier to rebuild.

Another urban fable is that the Twin Towers were white elephants, ignoring the fact that they were built in the middle of a financial meltdown and lifted the whole city up as they rose. It took years to get that much space tenanted, but by the nineties they were extremely profitable buildings. The know-it-alls sagely insist that hubris is what drove the builders of the Twin Towers, when it was actually the exact same wanting-to-be-great spirit that put a man on the moon. On September 12, 1962, President

Kennedy announced:

> We choose to go to the moon... in this decade and do the other things, not because they are easy, but because they are hard, because that goal will serve to organize and measure the best of our energies and skills, because that challenge is one that we are willing to accept, one we are unwilling to postpone, and one which we intend to win, and the others, too.

Hubris and achievement are not the same thing. Taking pride in mediocrity is an especially rancid form of hubris. The obstacles and challenges that were overcome to build the Twin Towers are legendary. In spite of all the back-slapping going on at the WTC site today, the current accomplishments pale in comparison.

Those who only saw "Ronzoni boxes" in the Towers' majestic profile or Gothic "kitsch" in their detail revealed more about themselves than about the Twin Towers. There was a reason that they were the favorite subject of many professional photographers and even Paul Goldberger, the *New Yorker*'s doctrinaire architecture critic and arch-enemy of the Twin Towers had to admit in his Pulitzer Prize-winning book *Up from Zero* that the Towers "did wonderful things in the light. They did not glare, like glass, but they did not absorb all the light either, the way stone or brick buildings often do. They reflected it back, softly, with a gentleness that belied their size." Well said. When I worked high in the Empire State Building, I thought the best part of every day was watching the sunset bouncing off the Towers and then the twinkle of the city's lights being lit. It was a daily magic show.

But the movement to rebuild the Twin Towers is not rooted nearly as much in affection for the buildings as in devotion to the country. Those who were murdered on 9/11 only died because they were Americans (or honorary Americans). And yet the rebuilding process is mired in an institutional arrogance that is the antithesis of what this country has always stood for. It is no stretch to say that on 9/11 Freedom was attacked and then Democracy got mugged — by our own people.

When Richard Hughes and I started Rebuild-the-Towers.org

we assumed that there was a short-circuit somewhere, and that doing what we could to help repair it was certainly worth a year of our lives. It seemed incredibly bizarre that so many people we knew, both in New York and across the country, on the right and on the left, old and young, rich and poor, just assumed that in due course the Towers would be rebuilt and yet none of the news reports or documentaries on the Towers made the least mention of the public support for the most obvious course.

Nicole Gelinas' smart and tough columns in the *New York Post* would periodically throw the public a lifeline just when we were going under, but the rest of the watchdogs were eerily silent. Either the people who claim to inform us live in a bubble — or else they are easily manipulated and/or intimidated — not impressive media credentials. There can be little doubt that the fix was in from the start, but the investigative journalists weren't going to look behind that curtain. *The New York Times* and the *Daily News* had major real estate interests that conflicted with quickly restoring the space downtown. And since *The New York Times* decides what is "fit" for the rest of us to know, that was a bad blow.

But we have come to believe that at the dead center of the keep-the-Towers-down narrative was New York's cranky billionaire mayor, Michael Bloomberg, who takes everything personally and thinks that his opinions and tastes are really all that matters. Those are dangerous qualities in a man whose media empire and targeted "philanthropy" function like the tentacles of a tarantula.

Through the years he has tried to keep a low profile at the site but his fingerprints have been all over it from the beginning. In September of 2007, I called Congressman Rangel's Counsel, George Dalley. Richard and I had met Mr. Dalley on a trip to Washington a few months earlier and I called after the summer recess to stress the urgency and propriety of getting Congressional oversight of what certainly appeared to be the massive misappropriation of taxpayer funds at the WTC site. I remember how startled I was when he said, "You don't really think the Congressman is going to cross the Mayor, do you?" I can still hear myself exclaim, "The Mayor! What does the Mayor have to do with it?" I don't remember the answer, but it was a real awakening.

The "year of our lives" was up by the time we launched The Twin Towers Alliance in March 2006, but the five years that have followed since then have been the privilege of a lifetime. With the blessing of Randy Warner and Robin Heid of Team Twin Towers and Louis Epstein of the World Trade Center Restoration Movement, who used their supporter lists to drive traffic to the new site, and WordPress maven Mark Jaquith, who designed the petition, we were off to a good start. But it was the devotion of Fard Muhammad, an early signer on the petition, that gave the TTA website its header, its logo, and its polish.

Both TTT and the WTCRM had garnered a lot of support for rebuilding in the years following the destruction and they were only too glad to endorse our efforts — I remember Robin Heid and I spent an hour kicking around ideas for the slogan. But both organizations were fundamentally opposed to endorsing a specific plan while, by the fall of 2007, Richard and I were convinced that the only likely pathway to new Twin Towers was with a real, not just a theoretical, plan.

We did not think that any politician would be willing to start the process all over again, no matter how compelling a case could be made, simply on principle. So we decided to reach out to Ken Gardner to find out how bona fide his plan really was and how much more work was yet to be done. We had the impression that it was little more than a plastic model and I will never forget the thrill of discovering how inspired and intelligent the "Twin Towers II" plan really is. It was like waking up on Christmas to find a pony and a sailboat and everything you ever wanted around the tree.

I know I can categorically state that if we had not discovered "Twin Towers II" when we did, the efforts of The Twin Towers Alliance in recent years would have been severely hampered. We have received a lot of high-level attention primarily because we could assert that there was a plan that could rescue Americans' hopes for the site and save money and time while doing it.

The more one learns about the plan, the more impressive it is, both structurally and aesthetically. So we could appreciate the dilemma it posed for the Port Authority's Executive Director Chris Ward when Ken, Richard, and I met with him in September, 2008. Although Ward undoubtedly told others that spending the better part of an hour with us was a mere courtesy, he learned more about "Twin Towers II" than he could casually dismiss and then made the calculated gamble of lying about the project instead of looking into it.

He answered public inquiries into rebuilding the Towers, on the PA website just a few weeks after meeting with us, and a couple of months later on MSNBC, by insisting that it would mean "turning back the clock," wasting all the work that had been done, and would add years to the project. Those were lies and officials were never authorized to lie their project into being.

The hard facts were that he was presented with a far more popular plan than the official one, at a time when most of what had been invested had to be done no matter what was built, and heard credible claims that a transition could save billions of public dollars and years off their most optimistic timeline. What's more, it could be built beside the currently planned 9/11 Memorial, so there was no conflict with what he cynically refers to as the sacred heart of the site. How many of those facts he conveyed to the PA Commissioners or to the Governors is anyone's guess, but it is hard to imagine what authority he or anyone thought they had to ignore such consequential information.

Mayor Bloomberg faced the same quandary the following May, after he announced the Gracie Mansion Summit to get the stranded project on track. We informed a top Bloomberg aide of the reasons why it made so much sense to look into what the "Twin Towers II" plan could offer. Ken offered to bring the model to the Summit, make a presentation, and answer questions. After a good many discussions, emails back and forth, and weeks of delay, we were turned down. By now it was becoming clear that officials didn't dare give the project the slightest glance, because there was no way to justify going forward with the less popular, less buildable, less affordable, and less inspiring plan instead.

If they had thought they could discredit "Twin Towers II," they surely would have done so, but a cost/benefit analysis would only confirm how much more practical and feasible it is. So all they could do was push ahead with construction and pour PR dollars into making their project seem inevitable. But the numbers don't work and the middle two towers may never appear, leaving a permanent hole in the skyline. Meanwhile, our public "servants" sit meekly by and let the public pay, while Larry Silverstein lives off the Towers' insurance money. After all the insurance money that has been siphoned off to pay Mr. Silverstein's architects, his attorneys, and his rent on the property, there is not much left to actually build anything with. He even got to pay off his mortgage and reimburse himself for his initial down-payment from the insurance proceeds. What would the court of public opinion think of that? He keeps turning to everyone's lender of last resort — but if the public is going to underwrite buildings that next to no one wants, the least they deserve is a chance to examine the unvarnished facts.

There are so many more angles and details that I would like to include in this tenth-anniversary synopsis, but it would be at the risk of overload. The simple equation is that if officials were proud of what they are doing, they would take the hard questions and defend their project, instead of ducking and weaving. But instead, the whole project depends on keeping the public in the dark. How can they really think that they can keep that cat in the bag?

We have been spending a lot of time in the past year filing and tracking a good many Freedom of Information requests and will soon connect those dots. One of the most notable discoveries was that the LMDC cannot provide the documentation to substantiate the cause-and-effect relationship between the public process and the current project. The foundation of all they have built is a fiction that cannot be substantiated. That is a prime example of the rule that has characterized the travesty all along and still does: Say whatever sounds good, whether or not it is true — and it usually isn't.

It has taken a long time to get to this point, but I honestly believe that officials are going to find that they cannot get away with lying their counterfeit World Trade Center into existence — no matter how much public money they misappropriate. They are betting that no one will break the true story and we are betting that someone will — and will win a well-deserved Pulitzer Prize for his or her efforts. It's bad enough to rob the people of their money — even though we are used to that. But to build a World Trade Center on misappropriated public hopes and public trust is a crime. No one will admit it, but that is what it is — a crime against government of, by, and for the People.

When we formed the Twin Towers Alliance, we were discouraged from including people's comments in our petition, but we didn't want it to just be another list of name after name, knowing the numbers would never tell the story, but that the comments and categories would. And the thousands of comments have formed an incredible treasury. They are like an x-ray of the heart of the world. Two comments from "Citizens of Other Nations" that were left on April 4, 2011 — the thirty-eighth anniversary of the Twin Towers' official opening — capture the camaraderie that people around the world still feel with us a decade after the attacks and how they see the World Trade Center.

Raffaele Guido wrote:

Hi, I'm Italian. I love your Country and New York too. You know that the Twin Towers were the symbol of your great City in all the world, people of other nations love them, and me too. I hope so much you will rebuild them in all its splendor and stronger than before soon, because Twin Towers were also the symbol of freedom, progress and human strength. At the bottom, all the world miss them! A special thought for all victims of 9/11! Great luck!

And then Abdussalam Aljoffe wrote:

New York would never be the same again without those titanic magnificent towers rebuilt again. This is the only restoration of New York image and reputation. This is the best revenge that Americans can do to humiliate terrorists and honor those who paid their lives in that site. New towers that are identical to the ones attacked would be the best memorial and best symbol of a nation that never dies...

© 2011 by Margaret Donovan

Twins for a Reason

By Richard Hughes

The Twin Towers were twins for a reason. They represented the spirit of peaceful cooperation without which world trade and world peace can't exist. If we are to cooperate with each other, we must treat each other as equals. You must see yourself reflected in me and I must see myself reflected in you. That was the idealism behind the World Trade Center. That is why Minoru Yamasaki designed his towers as Twins. Each saw itself in the other. Just as we must see ourselves in each other if we ever hope to live in peace.

In much the same way, if the Twin Towers Alliance were a political party, what would we be for? Well, we'd be for the best of both political parties, since both parties represent important aspects of America. We'd be for self-criticism, since that has always been an important part of being American and has helped us to right various injustices in our country. But we wouldn't be afraid to be self-confident either, since that is also an important part of being an American. Without self-confidence nothing great would ever have come out of America.

We wouldn't be afraid to be different from other countries, since difference adds to the richness of the world. But we wouldn't be afraid to cooperate either, since cooperation is the prelude to peace. We wouldn't be afraid to point out what's wrong with America. But we wouldn't be afraid to point out what's right with America either. In other words, we'd try to be balanced. To be balanced, you have to have two opposite poles.

The Twin Towers represented this perfectly. They were not one monolithic building that proclaimed to the world, "We are the one and only truth!" Instead, they were two identical buildings that proclaimed the duality, the polarity, the yin and the yang of life. Perfect symbols of a great democracy. It's not your way or my way, but *our* way. America isn't either/or. It's both. That's why the Twin Towers represented us so well. And that's why it's so urgent that they be rebuilt, instead of allowing something that in no way represents what is best in us to rise from what has become, for most Americans, sacred ground.

There Was a Better Way

By Richard Hughes

In the years following 9/11, Margaret Donovan and I always thought public officials would eventually come to their senses and the Twin Towers would be rebuilt. But one Sunday afternoon we were sitting around Margaret's kitchen table when it finally dawned on us, much to our shock and chagrin, that, no, they were not going to rebuild the Twin Towers, they were not going to do the right thing, they were not going to do what most Americans wanted them to do.

Shortly after this painful, if belated, revelation we set about creating Rebuild-the-Towers.org. Later, we started The Twin Towers Alliance.

As long-time New Yorkers, we were used to the corruption and malfeasance of Albany and City Hall. But we never dreamed that the pols and their bagmen would be so callous as to treat Ground Zero as nothing more than "business as usual." Surely they would exercise *some* restraint. Surely they would show *some* respect. Surely they would bring *some* dignity and consideration to the rebuilding of a site where nearly 3,000 Americans lost their lives. Every American felt 9/11 in his or her gut. Surely they would understand that all of us had a stake in what was built on that now-hallowed ground. But no, they didn't. Cronyism, corruption, arrogance, and stupidity have defined what has occurred at Ground Zero from September 12 on. A few despicable men were allowed to hijack what was sacred to us all and bend it to their own selfish ends. It is a disgrace without parallel in our history.

And yet there was a plan — a fully developed plan — that could have regenerated Ground Zero, made Americans proud, and pleased even the fussiest investors. But from the moment of its completion in 2004 (when sanity might finally have been expected to prevail), no one in power would even look at it and judge it on its merits or flaws.

I am speaking, of course, of Ken Gardner's "Twin Towers II" plan. In an act of real patriotism, Ken put his life on hold for years and committed his life savings and thousands of hours of his time to doing what he believed had to be done — fill not only the gaping hole at Ground Zero with something worthy, but fill the gaping hole in our psyches as well.

His plan was a noble reinterpretation of the original World Trade Center that was engineered in conjunction with Herbert Belton, an architect on the original WTC team. Together they re-imagined the Twin Towers for the twenty-first century, making them greener, safer, and mixed-use instead of pure office space. They saw these new Twin Towers as a way of connecting New York and America to the rest of the world on a 24/7 basis. The world had changed since the first towers had been built. New York's financial preeminence was being challenged. People in international trade and finance needed the convenience of being able to live where they worked. The global marketplace was open all night as well as all day. Ken's plan for new Twin Towers would have helped New York stay competitive with London, Tokyo, Hong Kong, and Dubai while keeping American jobs in America.

Ken Gardner and Herbert Belton not only created dozens of blueprints and design drawings; Ken, a structural engineer, also created a highly detailed ten-foot model so that the vision of the new Twin Towers could be easily grasped by the politicians and the public alike. (Such models cost hundreds of thousands of dollars.) The model was seen on Fox and MSNBC and displayed in both the lobby of Trump Tower and years later in the head office of the World Trade Centers Association. But not one official had the decency to come see it.

Christopher Ward, the executive director of the Port Authority and the man in charge of everything at Ground Zero, was invited to view the model. He did agree to come see it. But time and again Ward cancelled his visit at the last minute. Instead, to use Margaret Donovan's phrase, Ward put the building of the Freedom Tower "on steroids" after construction had languished for years. This after Ken, Margaret, and I had met with Ward in his office at the PA and explained how "Twin Towers II" could save billions of dollars over the current plan while giving the public what they had always wanted. (Some of the top people in skyscraper construction had vetted the plan and enthusiastically backed up Ken's assertions.)

Ward promised to evaluate the plan, promised to come see the model, promised to get back to us in a timely fashion. Instead, he did none of these. As we soon discovered, he went full-speed-ahead on the disastrously conceived, wildly unpopular, endlessly modified Libeskind plan with the easily predicted chaos and cost overruns and uncertainty that have since resulted.

It is now nearly ten years since 9/11. In place of the inspiring new Twin Towers most Americans would have expected to see rising above our country's greatest skyline a decade after the worst attack in our history, all we have is a grotesque muddle, billions of dollars wasted, and a plan that with each passing month gets smaller and smaller and is mired in more and more problems. It is the perfect metaphor for what has happened to America.

Ward and his minions still refuse to consider the simplest, the easiest, the most elegant, and the most popular solution: Rebuild the Twin Towers! As recently as 2009, an MSNBC poll found that *more than 90%* of Americans wanted to see Ken Gardner's plan built over the current plan. Over 90%!

Why? Because the Twin Towers meant so much to all of us. They were American icons. They were the goalposts at one end of the great American playing field. They were the entryway for millions of immigrants and visitors to our shores. They were the welcoming arms outstretched to countless Americans returning home. They were, quite simply, *us*. And we will not be the same until they are rebuilt.

Ten Years Gone

By Gary Taustine

On May 1, 2011, President Obama announced that Osama Bin Laden had been shot in the head by an elite team of Navy SEALs. Four days later, the president went to the World Trade Center site and stood in front of the unfinished 1 WTC building to eulogize 9/11's chapter in history. Up to this point, history would write that Bin Laden had destroyed the Twin Towers and gotten away with it — and while the latter is thankfully no longer true, the former is painfully evident every time you look downtown. Bin Laden will forever be the man who erased the Twin Towers from our skyline, certainly a point of pride amongst his followers, but it didn't have to be this way.

By the morning of September 12, 2001, New Yorkers were already discussing what would be built at the WTC site once the recovery was complete. People were understandably skittish at first, but before long, a majority of New Yorkers supported rebuilding the Twin Towers, and were it not for then Governor Pataki's own political ambitions, our skyline would be whole again today. Instead, New York ended up with an ill-conceived plan for an unwanted building designed by an egotistical snob, Daniel Libeskind. Fortunately, his original design has been reworked beyond recognition, and even the ridiculous "Freedom Tower" name has been abandoned for the more befitting, dignified, and appropriate "1 World Trade Center."

Perhaps it is the fate of anything meant to replace an iconic structure taken away so painfully to be doubted in proposal, delayed in construction and despised in completion — much like the original Twin Towers were. Familiarity with the Towers had bred contempt among many New Yorkers before 9/11, but their absence has made many more hearts grow fonder.

Every time I see the Twin Towers in an old movie, there is an overwhelming sense of loss when I realize they are gone forever. I can't help being angry at the people who destroyed them or the politicians who refused to rebuild them, but NYC has always been about accepting change.

Whether we are replacing an icon with an eyesore remains to be seen; I do however take some comfort in the knowledge that at least one building is heading skyward. Something tells me that most New Yorkers will eventually grow to love the new building, but to me, there will always be that nagging feeling that it was built as a result of the attacks and not in spite of them.

Can't Rebuild or Won't Rebuild?

By Tal Barzilai

It was just another Tuesday morning as I was heading to my classes over at Adelphi University, located in Garden City, New York. I had to make it to my morning classes there as I was encountering the traffic. While I was driving, I heard on the radio that a plane hit the North Tower of the World Trade Center. At first, I thought it was some kind of a joke, but then as I crossed the Throgs Neck Bridge, I noticed the smoke there realizing that it wasn't just some joke. Many of the classes I had that day were cancelled due to the attacks. The only thing showing on screens throughout my college was about the attacks. Later on, I heard that the South Tower was attacked as well. However, I didn't know that they collapsed until only after I came back that day seeing that they were no longer there.

At the same time, I heard that the Pentagon got attacked as well when part of it was taken out. There were rumors that the plane that crashed near Shanksville, Pennsylvania, was to hit the United States Capitol or the White House, but thankfully the passengers there were able to thwart that one. I then saw that this was no coincidence, but an attack on this country. Terrorists had hijacked planes and used them to make attacks on places that were symbolic to the country both politically and financially. It was later on found out that the group that carried out the attacks was Al Qaeda. Many of its members hailed from the Middle East, mainly Saudi Arabia, and its mastermind was Osama Bin Laden, who is now dead.

Ever since the Twin Towers had fallen, I felt that the only way to show that we can't be kept down is to have them back. Why should we let a group of people from lesser developed countries destroy something so important to us, and let their group live to talk about it? When I looked at *New York Times Magazine*, I couldn't believe that they tried to act as if you couldn't have both the Twin Towers rebuilt with a memorial, and showed two other possibilities. The second one said that we should just make it a memorial, while the third one was to build something completely different with a memorial. However, why wasn't a memorial shown with rebuilt Twin Towers as the other two were? It made me feel as if some were trying to act as if they were always a mistake, and used their destruction as an excuse not to have them back. Some of the claims for saying that they were gone were almost similar to those that didn't want them around in the first place. When my essay got selected on the one year anniversary of the attacks over on PBS's *America Rebuilds*, I stated why the site does not need to be mutually exclusive to just having to decide on whether to have rebuilt Twin Towers or a memorial when you can easily fit in both.

When the Pentagon was hit, nobody made it a debate that the destroyed side should be done differently or even shifted off to respect the dead yet here there were endless debates on what should go when it should have been obvious. Hearing after hearing, the same thing came from the crowd, and that was to have the Twin Towers rebuilt, but it was ignored constantly. Governor George E. Pataki never liked the Twin Towers, and would make sure that they would never be rebuilt, never allowing them to be an option despite all the support for it. He even appointed a committee, the Lower Manhattan Development Corporation, to help address the issue, but it was really to do his bidding. Their major event, Listening to the City, was nothing but a sham and also exclusive. I have tried to enter that group, but I have never gotten back anything in return from them. I have emailed them several times as to why I wasn't picked, and they have never even bothered to respond. Although I wasn't in the country when they had the six original plans and presented them at the Jacob K. Javits Convention Center, I did hear how many rejected them and saw them all as nothing more than an insult to what was there. Most of the buildings in them were only about half as big and made many of them feel as if they were trying to erase what was there. Meanwhile, some said things such as "Looks like Albany," as many of the designs resembled Empire State Plaza, which is located in that city. Others just said that they were too short and felt as if they could have been done anywhere in that the designs were barely that special compared to what had stood at the WTC. Then again, why should we replace something that was so grand with something that is less? Unfortunately, this is what Larry Silverstein, the majority leaseholder, wanted rather than to just have the Twin Towers rebuilt.

When the LMDC heard that the original plans were rejected,

they tried to use the claim people didn't want anything commercial when in reality, it was that they would rather have the skyline restored to what defined it so well rather than change it. Most of the nine new plans were hardly even realistic to build, while some of them were just similar to one of the six original plans that were already hated. Even with the new plans introduced, many still wanted to have the Twin Towers rebuilt rather than any of these. Pataki personally loved the Gardens of the World, designed by Daniel Libeskind, so much that he would make sure that it would win at any cost even if it meant rigging the process for it to happen. He thought he could pull a fast one by making it a finalist, despite the fact that it was ranked the worst according to Imagine New York, and using another plan, World Cultural Center by Rafael Viñoly, to make people think that the Libeskind scheme was the lesser of the two evils. When the votes were cast, his favorite plan lost, but it was still declared the winner even after the WCC had more votes with the majority of them going for neither. I went to the Winter Garden over at the World Financial Center with a printout of the LMDC's official poll to show that it wasn't the winner. Pataki saw that poll and just continued to walk by me, while Alexander Garvin, one of the LMDC members, told me that he wasn't even going to comment on that. Pataki didn't like the name and renamed it the Freedom Tower in that it reached 1,776 feet when including the spire, but the truth was that it was really a mockery in its name to give it that when freedom didn't describe the way it was picked. Many did not see it as a symbol of freedom, but more as a symbol of death, and its resemblance to the Statue of Liberty at a certain angle didn't make it feel less like death, while others thought that it looked like the North Tower just before it hit the ground.

In 2004, the LMDC made a Generic Environmental Impact Statement that discussed what was going on. Despite how much rebuilding the Twin Towers was despised, it was still kept as an active option when stated in Section 23.4 under Article 23 as it still is even today. Throughout the years, to so-called Freedom Tower was given numerous changes to help make it better when it really made it worse. At some of the hearings involving the GEIS, many had said that they would rather end it than amend it. One of the leading causes for a redesign was the concern that in the original design, it was almost impossible to have gardens at such an altitude, and when this was exposed, they were no longer planned. Although it was supposed to use green energy, the idea for a concrete bunker as the base for the first twenty floors became a contradiction to that in which the sunlight could not penetrate those floors. The reason for the base was the idea to restore the street grid, which though it was clearly opposed meant that a possible vehicle bomb could go there. Pataki was hoping to get the building started after laying what he called the Freedom Stone, but instead the building went through setbacks leading to what it looks like now. Chris Smith, who writes for *New York* magazine, called Pataki out for being nakedly selfish in believing that he could have this building done by the time he considered running for president in 2008, but he dropped out in the early part of that year after seeing that it was hardly there. Despite the costs increasing from time to time, he didn't want to stop having it.

The memorial was no better, either. Michael Arad's design, Reflecting Absence, was seen more as a vapid reminder of what had been there. As a matter of fact, it was found that the cost of running the fountains was so expensive that they would only be running on certain dates rather than daily like all the others. When MSNBC's David Shuster interviewed some of the families of the victims, they said that having an underground memorial was not only expensive, but insulting as well. Nobody wanted to be left in the dark as some had described it. The museum was actually going to charge people to see it rather than invite them for free. More recently, it was even said that the museum won't even have restrooms. The reason for such a memorial was that Libeskind wanted to have pits in his plan.

During the time of the redesign, I attended other events on this. It was definitely a big one when I went and spoke out over at the Aftershock Hearing at Pace University. When I was stating my question on the fact that they were aware that the Freedom Tower was picked behind closed doors and why rebuilding the Twin Towers wasn't an option, Stephen Pryor, another member, just cut the microphone off on me, and claimed that everything was all set and done. Just like any other time, another LMDC member refuses to give a straight answer. In 2005, Shuster conducted a poll and found out that at least three-quarters of the votes favored having the Twin Towers rebuilt over the Freedom Tower, showing that it is still supported despite what was going on, and again more recently when it was shown that nearly ninety percent wanted them back. Rather than accepting it as a fact, the LMDC refused to acknowledge it and continue with what they wanted, while others who supported the official plan tried to dismiss it as nothing but a popularity contest.

It was unfortunate that other politicians went along with the official plan even though they had some concerns about it. Although Elliot Spitzer, who became the new governor of New York, didn't like the idea of the plan, he still went with it when he could have stopped it right there. That brought the question on if he truly was the people's lawyer as he claimed to be. David Paterson, who succeeded Spitzer after he resigned, was no different and accepted the plan as well. Although State Assembly Speaker Sheldon Silver had concerns about possible false starts, he never showed any signs of actually stopping it and calling for the Twin Towers rebuilt despite being in his district. United States Senator Charles Schumer had some questions about what was going on, but didn't bother to be proactive on the issue, while Hillary Rodham Clinton, the other US Senator, took no stance and stayed neutral on the issue. New York City Mayor Michael R. Bloomberg didn't like the plan, but wasn't pro-Towers and offered the Port Authority of New York and New Jersey a swap to build something residential there. Then-Mayor Rudolph Giuliani was only interested in having a memorial and believed that it should be the focus of the site, and for the most part didn't want any buildings whatsoever in that he claimed it would be disrespecting. Amanda Burden, who is the head of city planning, not only supports the official plan, but she even denies the process that was being used for it. Despite the fact that Kent Barwick, the head of the Municipal Arts Society, didn't like the process that was being used, he still went with it anyway. How can one say they have major concerns and still be in favor of it? This is very similar to the Patriot Act or the Iraq War where despite a number of Congressmen having questions and concerns, they still voted for it no matter what.

In the end, nobody is saying that they can't rebuild the Twin Towers; it's more like they are saying that they won't rebuild them. Mayor Bloomberg goes on record for saying, "Mr. Trump, we are not going to rebuild the two WTC Towers." Those in charge never liked the Twin Towers, and would use whatever it took not to have them back despite how much the people were in favor of that. If the support for the official plan is true, then why do those who are in favor of it always tend to act defensively, repeat the same rhetoric already said by Pataki and his cronies, say how much the Twin Towers were a failure, or just say all of the above? Unfortunately, one can never get a real answer from any of them. Sometimes I wonder, what if the Empire State Building or Statue of Liberty had been destroyed by terrorists? Would there even be a debate on what should go there, or would they just be rebuilt to resemble what was there? Then again, what if those in charge said that they weren't going to rebuild them, would everyone fight tooth and nail to have either of them back or just go with whatever goes there instead, just like what is going on here, and accept it?

Excuses Rather than Reasons

By Tal Barzilai

Over the years after the attacks, I have heard statements from some people on saying why the Twin Towers can't be rebuilt. However, some of them didn't even sound like reasons, but rather like excuses. From time to time, I have compiled a whole list of such claims and even debunked them to show how false some of them were. Just read on — here are some of the most repeated myths that those who are against the rebuilding of the Twin Towers have used.

Some have claimed that since the official plan has already progressed this far, it is no longer an active option to have them rebuilt, especially because those in charge have said so. I tend to think of hearing this as if some don't know what is really going on. Just about every few months, I keep hearing that the costs have increased and caused some setbacks. Don't forget that back in 2004, Governor George E. Pataki thought he could start the Freedom Tower by placing the Freedom Stone, but it was found to be nothing but a false start. Other parts that have gone up in costs include Reflecting Absence, which is the memorial, and the station house for the PATH trains. Meanwhile, the remaining two office buildings have no set construction date; their sites are left empty indefinitely. However, rebuilding the Twin Towers is actually still considered an active option according to the Lower Manhattan Development Corporation according to Section 23.4 under the Restoration Alternative in Article 23 of their very own Generic Environmental Impact Statement that was done back in 2004, especially if they can't get it all done. Those who say it can't be rebuilt because a group of politicians say so tend to forget the fact that the decision was done in a backroom and behind closed doors, hence an act of elitism. Why should we accept something that was picked against the principles of democracy?

Another commonly repeated myth is that rebuilding the Twin Towers would be a step back rather than forward because their design is outdated, not to mention their engineering. There is no call to build it as *status quo ante bellum*. If the Twin Towers do get rebuilt, they will have to use updated engineering, just like the WTC buildings now planned. Keep in mind that older skyscrapers are being renovated all the time to meet updated building codes; otherwise they would have to be demolished. The only thing that would match the originals would probably be the design, but the rest would be different. Also, it will be possible to make it use green energy with some of the new technology as well as updated fireproofing rather than what was originally used.

There have been those that have used that its design was ugly, but this statement is really an opinion rather than a fact. In reality, beauty is really something that is in the eye of the beholder. To some, it may have been the best, while to others, it was the worst. In my opinion, I thought that they were great just looking simple and didn't have to show off to be the best. What they lacked in design, being of the International Style, they made up for in engineering, especially for being advanced at the time. Regardless, this is not a reason to not have them back.

It was very common to say that rebuilding the Twin Towers where thousands had died was disrespectful. If this was really the case, then why build the official plan, which consists of buildings as well? Isn't that just as disrespectful as having the Twin Towers rebuilt? It seems as if some are just trying to be selective here. As a native of Israel, where terrorist attacks are daily fare, I know what it's like to lose someone in a terrorist attack, but we shouldn't let terrorists change our way of life. Also, in Israel, many of the places that were attacked by terrorists, either by suicide bombers or by rockets, weren't preserved out of respect for those who died there. The sites were cleared and reused. By that logic, maybe the WTC should have been abandoned after it was attacked back in 1993, when terrorists perpetrated a failed attack that only affected the garage, but it wasn't. Let's not forget that New York City has a history of rebuilding places that were destroyed rather than just declaring them memorials. Keep in mind that the Pentagon got rebuilt and people died there as well on that same day.

Other excuses have included that rebuilding the Twin Towers would either forget or remember the attacks. I have never understood what this meant. My guess is that to some rebuilding them was just trying to act as if the attacks never happened, while others thought that they would always be reminded of the attacks and would never want to go back there. Either way, I never bought into any of these. Was rebuilding the destroyed part of the Pentagon done to either remember or forget the attacks? I would say no to that. If anyone would forget about the attacks, it will be because of time itself, not because we have the Twin Towers back.

More recent myths have said the official plan is popular. As a person who has attended many hearings on the very issue, I have never heard anyone outside the panel say this. If it was really so popular, then why when under its original name and design did it rank all the way at the bottom according to Imagine New York? Also, why didn't it win when polled as a finalist? David Shuster of MSNBC ran two polls, one in 2005 and another in 2009, and both showed that the majority preferred Twin Towers II over the Freedom Tower. Why support a plan that was hardly popular to begin with? If the Freedom Tower is really popular as some put it out to be, then why have they been acting so defensive on it rather than cite evidence that proves their point?

I can remember those trying to use the claim that the Twin Towers were poorly constructed and engineered, which is what led to their collapse. Actually, the reason why they collapsed wasn't their structure; it was what they had to take. Nobody assumed that someone was going to hijack planes and literally slam them into them. At the time, it was believed that if a plane would ever hit them, it would be only by accident, like the one that hit the Empire State Building in 1945. Seriously, if they really did have poor engineering, then they wouldn't have won the Outstanding Civil Engineering Award back in 1971, and an award such as this one isn't given to just any building, especially those that don't meet certain codes. Again, when they were being built, they were considered advanced for their time, using technology that had not been used before, such as the kangaroo crane, which can be extended up as the height increases, while even the Empire State Building used mere derrick cranes.

The claim that the Twin Towers were money losers and failed to help their neighborhood has been overstated numerous times. When they first opened they were 70% occupied, which was faster than any skyscraper before them. Even the Empire State Building took twenty years to fill up. Part of the reason they may have been seen as money losers was because just like Rockefeller Center, they were built when the economy was in bad shape, but they were built anyway, as it was believed that they could be beneficial in the long run, even though there was no apparent demand. As a matter of fact, they helped reduce unemployment not just in the Financial District, but also in nearby areas such as Downtown Brooklyn. The towers were fully occupied by the 1990s and tenants were paying triple digit rents. Despite being mostly a place of business, the complex also became an area for culture as well as retail and recreation in its way of being a mini city. The neighborhood known as Battery Park City would never have existed if not for the presence of the World Trade Center. The very landfill the former stands on came from the excavation of the latter's "bathtub" foundation.

Others have said that nobody would ever work there especially since many have died there. By such logic, the Pentagon should have been abandoned because it was hit as well. While I do give my condolences to those who lost loved ones, it's not a reason to not rebuild the towers. Was the Brown Building just left as it was after the Triangle Shirtwaist Factory fire back in 1911 or was it rebuilt? Wasn't the Equitable Building rebuilt bigger and better and reoccupied after it collapsed in the 1912 fire? As a native of Israel, I can tell you that there are many places in my native country where people have died due to terrorist attacks, but hardly any of them were just left abandoned out of fear that another attack will happen. According to the Twin Towers Alliance petition, there are a number of returning tenants, other businesses, and construction workers that will gladly work there. Even a number of families of victims, survivors, firefighters, policemen, and other responders said that they would support having the Twin Towers rebuilt despite losing someone there on that day.

There have been those who claim that even if the Twin Towers could be rebuilt, whatever is there right now would have to be demolished, that the whole thing would have to start over. This is not true at all. There is no reason to demolish anything, just to integrate it. The latest Twin Towers II Plan actually calls for the two buildings that are being done right now to be capped off where they are and incorporated into it. Since the other two buildings have been placed on hold indefinitely, their lots can make perfect spots to have the Twin Towers rebuilt. I have seen the idea for this on the Twin Towers Alliance website, and they show exactly that. Due to the foundation that is there, whatever goes there, be it rebuilt Twin Towers, the official plan, or just a memorial park, there will have to be extensive foundation work no matter what. Then again, if the Freedom Tower is so prestigious, then why haven't there been businesses lining up to work there at the office of the Port Authority? If some like Condé Nast locate there, it won't be because they see it as a good place to work; they will go there only for the subsidies they get, which will actually hurt the neighborhood, not help it.

Others have claimed that rebuilding the Twin Towers would cost just as much or more. Studies have actually found this to be the other way around. Rebuilding the Twin Towers actually costs a small fraction compared to what is being built. If majority lease holder Larry Silverstein had just gone for rebuilding them, rather than build something completely different, it would have been covered by insurance. He was underinsured when the attacks happened and tried to get the courts to rule that it was two attacks so that he could get double the money. However, even if that was so, he still wouldn't have enough money for it no matter what the outcome would be. Also, many of the buildings cost a lot to build because every couple floors, the floor plates change, which takes even more money and time to build. The memorial has also gone over budget so much that a $25 admission now needs to be charged to cover it, and most museums that charge admission for memorials hardly go that high if ever. The station house for PATH is not just expensive, but completely unnecessary to have since it won't generate any money. Due to the fact that there is the idea to run streets through the World Trade Center, a lot of money will have to be spent on security against a possible vehicle bombing, while keeping the superblock can easily prevent it. To make matters worse, the Port Authority now has to raise tolls on all of their crossings as well as fares on PATH just to pay for the WTC scheme. Many commuters opposed it, but the PA went ahead with it anyway. One other thing, rebuilt Twin Towers wouldn't just cost less to build, they can also be done even more efficiently for having the same floor plates.

More importantly, I have heard this myth, "If you support rebuilding the Twin Towers, you are against new designs." What is that supposed mean? This is just a way of taking a cheap shot at those who tend to disagree with the other side. It's sort of like

172

saying that if I am against other projects, I have to be anti-development or against others getting jobs or housing. Next, I can't seem to oppose congestion pricing or many bike lanes unless I am against air quality. Does opposing the wars in Iraq and Afghanistan mean that I have to be against the troops or be a traitor? Does voting for the Democrats mean that I have to support the terrorists? Can only heretics support same sex marriage and abortion? Do I have to support apartheid and oppression of the Palestinians just for believing that Israel can exist as a country? Do only communists believe in keeping social security and healthcare public, supporting affordable housing, or even wanting the rich to pay their fair share? The list can go on, but I will stop here, because it was to prove why some will stoop to such a level as saying that. If you ask me, statements like these are really the path of the weak and cowardly, especially if one has nothing to rebut with.

Overall, many who support the official plan will always have a tendency to ride the myths even if they have proven false. It is the typical attitude of a yes-man, who is always known to rush to the defense of someone or something whose claims are being disproved. After reading all the debunking of these claims, it is now seen how some like to downplay the other side rather than actually state facts. Of course there will always be myths that some will believe, especially if they are repeated enough times to a point where part of it would seem true even though the rest of it is still false. It's sort of like what P.T. Barnum used to say, "There's a sucker born every minute." However, there will always be those who tend to ride the myths no matter how many times they have been debunked.

Comments Made to the LMDC

By Joe Wright

I attended the May 23, 2002, hearing at Pace University and also the Listening II session at Javits Center in July. In advance of that, I made these comments about the status of rebuilding so far. This, I believe, would be considered a response to the so-called Phase I plans.

First, the most important thing to do is to rebuild the WTC Twin Towers as tall or taller with buildings incorporating all of the safety features that are feasible from an economic standpoint.

Like anything else, you can overdo things. If you build a solid concrete structure with one office per floor and ten elevators encased in concrete and steel in the center, you'd have a safe building. And an economic disaster. And a disaster from other aspects. No business would want to operate in such a bunker.

By the same token, you can under-build. To exactly duplicate the original Towers as they were without incorporating any new materials and ideas since they were originally designed would be severe under-building. Some support the idea of duplicating the original towers to the letter, down to the exact doorknobs. I don't for several reasons, not the least of which is that I thought they were ugly and undistinguished architecturally. (I have a different view of them now.)

I am unalterably opposed to replacing the WTC Twin Towers with a series of stunted buildings. If that happens, not only will it be a disgrace architecturally and culturally, it will be an insult to and a defamation of those who lost their lives in the WTC attack. It will also be a victory for the terrorists. They will have succeeded in cutting us down to their size. They will have won because they will have succeeded at destroying one of the most treasured symbols of NYC and of the USA. They will have stolen from us a symbol known worldwide.

We must not allow the terrorists to philosophically, morally, culturally or economically kneecap us. If stunted buildings are built instead of towers as tall as or taller than the original WTC Towers, that's exactly what will have happened. We will have admitted defeat at the hands of terrorists.

We will also be defeated if any substantial part of the site of the original WTC Towers is given over to anything but new towers. Anything less than a total rebuilding will be a defeat at the hands of terrorists.

I know there is a great desire to have a memorial to the victims of the attacks and their families. But I believe they would be better honored by rebuilding the towers as tall or taller. That would be a celebration of their life and their work which was so tragically destroyed on 9/11. A memorial is a celebration of death. A cemetery is a permanent place of death. The WTC site should be thought of as neither. While thousands were killed on the site, no one is buried there and consequently in no way can it be called a cemetery. You can think of it as hallowed ground, but that should not stop the resurrection of the business and commerce that was the life of the area.

There is no stopping those who believe a memorial should be built. I admit that. But I argue that the memorial should not be the focus of rebuilding. It should at most be an acknowledgment. A plaque with the names of the victims in a small park-like setting would be acceptable to me. But anything beyond that will be a misuse of the land and too focused on death instead of life. Sentiment and grief can't be allowed to overrule life, hope, optimism and heroism.

I don't happen to believe that a memorial will attract the millions of people some advocates think. I predict that within a few years after construction of any memorial, the visitor traffic will drop to near zero. I don't even think many family members will return except on anniversaries of that eventful day and even those numbers will decline very rapidly. Just as the number of visitors to the Oklahoma City memorial has declined.

Consequently, and I hasten to say that I don't mean to be crass, while the primary focus should be on restoring business to the area, the secondary focus should be on restoring tourism to the area. A memorial will not do that. A park will not do that. New cultural centers will not do that. But a rebuilt WTC with towers as tall or taller, an even better observation deck, a new Windows on the World restaurant and enhanced attractions will do that. And it's vital to our economy that that be done. If we don't do it, everyone's life will be diminished. Opportunities for those of us who have suffered from the terrorists attacks — and I mean all New Yorkers, not just the families and relatives of the victims — will never return if rebuilding is not done with the right criteria in mind.

Everyone agrees that Lower Manhattan has to be restored. But to restore it with anything less than the heroic vision that befits NYC will be a depressing and destructive mistake from which there can be no recovery. No one restores anything without some thought being given to improving what is being restored. Blind restoration is a rejection of the future and a trap from which you cannot escape.

Looking at things from a negative standpoint, what better way of poking a finger in the eye of terrorists than to rebuild what they have destroyed? What better way of saying we will not be defeated?

But more positively, what better way could there be to demonstrate what we as Americans, as pioneers, as New Yorkers are made of than putting those twin towers back on our skyline, a skyline known around the world as not just a symbol of New York, but a symbol of America and the spirit we acclaim and celebrate?

Stunted buildings and undue allocations of precious land to memorials, parks, museums, entertainment and other uses contrary to the nature of the area will destroy the possibility of ever recovering what was lost. You have to face the fact that Lower Manhattan is the financial capital of the world. While neighborhoods change over time, everyone thinks that Lower Manhattan is still the financial capital of the world. And it should remain so even though some major financial companies have for some bizarre reason decided to move to 42nd Street and other areas of town completely inappropriate for that kind of business.

It's been argued that there is no immediate need for the office space that was lost when the Trade Towers collapsed. How short sighted! How pessimistic! What nihilism!

Besides the fact that any replacement towers would not be on the market for years, when has NYC not built for the future? And from a planning standpoint, how can you not build on speculation? Was the WTC solidly rented before construction? Was there a demand for that much office space five years before they were opened? The same questions were asked about the Empire State Building.

The idea that we shouldn't build at all or that we should build stupid, stunted little buildings truly disgusts me. Are we mice or men? Are we Lilliputians in mind and spirit?

But strangely a more recent argument is that there will indeed be a need for new office space and that instead of building new towers as tall or taller, stunted buildings should be built to replace them and neighboring buildings should just be taken over as necessary to make up for the difference. I have long thought the vile power of eminent domain would come to play in rebuilding Lower Manhattan. It seems that my prediction may come true. I will fight that tooth and nail.

But aside from the immorality of eminent domain and the violation of individual rights that its exercise involves, there is no need for it whatsoever! We don't need backward thinking and small minds doing the thinking.

An even more idiotic idea is to build modular towers, i.e. small buildings with foundations strong enough and facilities good enough to permit expanding them in the future. This kind of building will be the end of skyscrapers. No expansion will ever take place. This is just a ploy to avoid rebuilding towers as tall or taller and a device to divert us from that focus. It is also a dishonest way of sneaking in those stunted buildings that should be opposed as the disgrace and insult to NYC that they would be.

An opportunity that will never again present itself exists to do the right thing, that is build new office towers as tall as or taller than the original WTC with all the confidence in the future with which they were built. Think of where NYC would be if every development was based on the pessimism exhibited by the advocates of these stunted buildings. There would be no NYC. We are a city of buildings and a city of builders. We should continue to be so.

So, I believe that new twin towers should be built. Second, I believe that they should be as tall as or taller than the original twin towers. Third, I believe that whatever is built must be economically viable. After that, it is a question of engineering and architectural design.

I'm not an engineer, but I like, at least from a conceptual standpoint, ideas I've read about how the buildings could be strengthened, for example the following:

- Fireproof polymer coatings applied to all columns and members that will not be removed easily. (It's ironic that the hated asbestos might have saved lives had it been left in place in the first WTC towers instead of being removed and replaced by the defective material that was used.)

- Sprinkler systems using foam with independent sources on each floor not dependent on sources or supply from other floors.
- I-beams instead of trusses for floor support.
- Stairwell walls made out of concrete, reinforced with rebar, rather than drywall.
- Bio-terrorism sensors in the HVAC system.

You cannot terror-proof any structure 100%. What you would end up with is a structure that is unlivable and totally uneconomical. Personally, I don't think there will be another attack such as occurred on 9/11. I think there's a possibility of another terrorist attack, but I think it will be different and perhaps far more destructive. But I'm not going to run scared from it. I will remain in NYC. I will not be driven out by terrorists.

By the way, I don't think any of the airport security measures being implemented would have prevented these attacks. But the heightened awareness of the possibility of a future airplane attack may be enough to ward them off. In other words, the billion dollar Nazi sounding Department of Homeland Security program is a waste of money and is the typical government reaction to a disaster. Throw money at it and you'll save face with the public. Whether it works or not is irrelevant. But that's another subject.

I was never a fan of the Trade Towers from an architectural standpoint. I always thought they were hideous, undistinguished boxes. After their destruction, and from being much more involved in thinking about them since 9/11, I have changed my view. Having seen so many photos of them in different seasons and at different times of the day, I have grown to appreciate their uniqueness and their importance.

I hope that that grandeur will obtain, not pygmyism. I hope we will rebuild on a heroic scale, not an inhuman scale. I have all the confidence in the world that the market will follow us to the top of the tallest buildings in the world. No one will be impressed or thrilled by anything less than that. I for one will be depressed and insulted as a New Yorker and as a human being.

On the subject of site planning and configuration, I think it should remain as is. I don't believe streets should be allowed to once again enter the site because that would make rebuilding even more difficult and would impede regaining the substantial pedestrian commerce that existed with the plaza concept. I do support putting West Street underground, but only because of the possibility of creating even more land on which to build, not to replace building on the WTC site. I mean NEW building.

I also support improving transportation in the area by which I mean that the subways should be better connected. But I would argue against creating a horror such as exists at 42nd Street where there are simply too many people trying to go somewhere in a maze that no one can figure out. So, I support connections, but not consolidations. I can't see the viability or the desirability of creating an environment that would be filled with herds of people. Good transportation management dictates that the herd be thinned out so that undue crowding doesn't take place. So, as I said, I support connections between subways, but not consolidation into a massive, inhumane terminal like Penn Station.

Regarding bringing the Long Island Railroad into Lower Manhattan, I'm against that. Especially if it means losing a tunnel between Brooklyn and Manhattan. This, like other transportation issues, must stand on its own and must be justified as a separate project. It has nothing to do with rebuilding Lower Manhattan. It would be tremendously expensive and a misuse of moneys allocated for rebuilding. And it would serve a very few people compared to what could be accomplished by better connections between the subway lines or alternative transportation modes like light rail or the extension of the half-assed AirTrain running from Jamaica, Queens, to JFK directly into Manhattan where it should originate.

But these items are trivial in the context of rebuilding though some of them have to be taken into account since no rebuilding can even begin without infrastructure being put back in place.

The bottom line question to me is then not whether the towers should be rebuilt but how do new towers get built in such a way that they are economically viable and safe?

The most important thing to me is to build a new WTC with office towers as tall as or taller than the original towers and with all of the underground retail space restored.

To do anything less than that will be to grant victory to the terrorists and to disgrace the spirit of New York City and everyone as Americans.

Facts You Cannot Ignore

By Joe Wright

Hallowed Ground versus property rights. Just because someone happens to die on another's property, that does not grant them any rights with respect to how the property is used. Of course you can exercise your freedom of speech and try to persuade the owner to do something you desire, but you must recognize that you have no rights in the matter whatsoever.

The only parties who have the right to build on the WTC site are the Port Authority, which owns the land, Larry Silverstein, who holds the lease for the WTC itself, and Westfield America, which held the lease for retail space.

Listening but not hearing. The Lower Manhattan Development Corporation (LMDC) sponsored several Listening to the City (LTTC) events. But if something was said that they didn't like, they chose not to hear it. For example:

- Well over half the people at the Javits Center meeting rejected the LMDC's six proposals for new buildings on the WTC site. "Looks too much like Albany," many derisively said of the plans.
- During the online LTTC program, 60% voted that the towers should be rebuilt as tall as or taller than the original towers.
- In spite of these votes, the LMDC refused to consider any proposal for the building of towers as tall or taller.
- They listened, but they did not hear. That is, unless you were a memorialist.

Memorials. Proposals ranged from dedicating the entire sixteen-acre site of the WTC to a memorial to not building a memorial at all. The LMDC, in this case, chose to listen to and hear only the memorial advocates. They turned a deaf ear to anyone who said there should be no memorial. And they listened with near deafness to anyone who said the memorial should be in proportion to the numbers killed and injured.

Alexander Garvin, LMDC Vice President for Planning, Design and Development, remarked at a NY1 Town Hall Meeting hosted by John Schiumo, "I'll guarantee you that the entire site will be a memorial." While this might not have been meant to be taken literally, it is an indication of the narrow-mindedness and shallow thinking of the LMDC. They lived up to the popular interpretation of their name, the Leave Manhattan Destroyed Corporation.

George E. Pataki, New York State Governor at the time, guaranteed that the footprints of the twin towers would not be built on. Ex-mayor Rudolph Giuliani caved to the victims' families and said he wanted the entire site to be a memorial.

All of this even though residents who live around the WTC pleaded that their neighborhood not be turned into a cemetery, that they not be reminded of the horror of 9/11 every day for the rest of their lives when passing by or through the site.

Memorials that have been built have been discrete and in proportion. None have consumed the entire "battlefield." Over 60,000 were killed in the Vietnam War. Compare that number to the space occupied by that war's memorial. Consider Hiroshima, where a modest memorial was built and the entire city rebuilt. Consider the Pentagon, which was made whole and not insanely memorialized.

To talk of anything other than a modest WTC memorial is to deal in the absurd. It is also absurd to allow the almost 3,000 victims' families to dictate the future of Lower Manhattan and thus the entire city.

No one will work in a WTC tower rebuilt as tall or taller. Some won't. So what? Jonathan Hakala, whose company was on the seventy-seventh floor, said he would return. And so would thousands of others. How many people have refused to work in existing tall buildings? Some did. So what?

There's no need for all the office space in this depressed economy. Such optimism! When the original towers were built, there was no demand. The Empire State Building was empty for years as was Rockefeller Center. Construction wasn't halted. In New York, we build on speculation and with confidence that we will succeed. Besides, new twin towers wouldn't be ready for occupancy for years to come. Should we just bury our heads in the sand?

Not so very long before the 9/11 terrorist attack, local politicians and representatives from New York City's biggest businesses met to determine how to secure the City's ability to grow in the face of the steadily diminishing supply of office space. Now that the WTC and its eleven million square feet of office space has disappeared from the market, doesn't that greatly exacerbate this problem?

Rebuilding the towers would create new targets for terrorists. This is said as if there are no other tall buildings that could be targeted. What about the Sears Tower in Chicago or the Empire State Building or the Transamerica Pyramid in San Francisco? Should we tear them down because they could be targets? Ron DeVito of Team Twin Towers said, "You can't walk two blocks in NYC without seeing a building that could be a target."

Affordable housing must be included in any rebuilding plan. Whenever you see the term "affordable housing," identify its real meaning: government housing or government subsidized housing. There ain't no such thing as a free lunch whether in housing or anything else. Subsidies will come out of everyone else's pockets whether *they* can afford it or not. Peter will be robbed to provide housing for Paul.

And, must it be said, that Lower Manhattan is and has been for years the *financial* center of the nation, if not the world? There are plenty of areas in the City for residential development. The WTC site clearly is not one of them.

Defending the towers. Many ignorantly characterized the Twin Towers as deathtraps. Many accused them of being responsible for the deaths of almost 3,000 people.

The World Trade Center Towers didn't kill anyone. The killers were the terrorists who flew planes into the buildings and those who supported and sponsored them. The terrorists were the killers. Let us never lose sight of that fact.

The towers saved lives. They stood long enough for tens of thousands of people to get out before their collapse. Certainly, more lives could have been saved if the buildings had been built differently, with modern techniques and materials. But that's classic Monday morning quarterbacking.

The towers stood and therefore tens of thousands of lives were saved. It is a defamation to call them deathtraps. Everyone who survived 9/11 should thank the designers, the engineers, the construction workers and the Port Authority personnel who operated the towers. You owe your lives to those many people. And to the towers themselves.

The Autocratic LMDC

By Joe Wright

What we don't need is the dictatorial LMDC armed with the power to destroy the Financial District and Lower Manhattan by general ineptitude but also by the use of eminent domain. They have a demonstrated ability to stand in the way of renewal and rebuilding, but no talent to create or even re-create the WTC that was destroyed by terrorists. For evidence, consider the pathetic plans they submitted. Their ambitions are low. Our ambitions are high.

If things go the way the LMDC dictates, you can honestly say that Mohamed Atta is the urban planner for Lower Manhattan because what will be built on the site — if anything — will be on his terms. [7] He and his terrorist comrades destroyed the World Trade Center towers. And the LMDC will have left them destroyed. Building stunted little buildings and a mega-memorial on the site is a capitulation to terrorism.

I object to the very existence of the LMDC. Why were they granted total authority over the lives, liberty, property and the economy of Lower Manhattan? As a speaker at a recent NY1 Town Hall meeting said, "I'm not afraid of another terrorist attack. What I am afraid of is the LMDC." She has a right to be. They have the power to Leave Manhattan Destroyed in a shameful surrender to the terrorists. And so far they have. They stand in the way of rebuilding and progress. The Pentagon has been rebuilt. What do we have? A hole in the ground courtesy of the Lower Manhattan (construction) Delay Corporation.

This is a classic case of authoritarian government at its worst. We have fought world wars to oppose regimes with powers like those granted to and arrogated unto itself by the LMDC.

Their actions are contrary to the sprit and the letter of American principles of individual rights and the free market.

Something must be said about the fixation on memorials by the LMDC, former Governor George E. Pataki and many others. They know nothing about the meaning of a memorial or the way they are used to honor the dead. But they are intent on wasting taxpayers' money by conducting junkets to not only national but international memorials. I heard recently that fifty people are about to take off on an international tour of memorials. I'm sure they're not eating at McDonald's and staying in one star hotels. This kind of memorial fetish must be stopped.

If a memorial is to be built on the site, it must be proportional. If you think of the some 60,000 who died in the Vietnam War and the size of the memorial to those veterans, you see that a memorial to some 3,000 does not justify a sixteen-acre or even a one-acre memorial. It is a shameful waste of property and in fact is a violation of the property rights of the Port Authority, Larry Silverstein and Westfield properties. I hasten to add that the Port Authority is also dominated by the LMDC and will not defend its property rights for fear of losing the entire site.

I for one do not believe there should be any memorial as such. I believe that the only way you can honestly honor the victims of the murderous terrorist attack of 9/11 is to restore what was taken away, restore what was destroyed. And that is the workplace and the environment to which those killed came on a daily basis to work and pursue their happiness.

We are also told that Ground Zero is hallowed ground. That is an evaluation of the person observing or relating to whatever is viewed as hallowed. It is not a fact of reality. One of the most prominent victim family advocates remarked at a recent meeting that she didn't know the meaning of hallowed or sacred, but she was certain that Ground Zero was both. Such ignorance, irrationality and emotionalism cannot be allowed to dictate the future of Lower Manhattan, the economy of New York City and indeed the entire Metropolitan area.

Dying on someone else's property does not gain you any rights to the property. You can use your power of persuasion and try to convince the owner of the property to see things your way, but you have to realize that you don't own the property and have no rights whatsoever to determine how it is used.

Yet that is precisely what is happening. And the vehicle for taking control of the property is the LMDC. They have no respect for anyone's property rights. Their so-called Listening to the City meetings were nothing more than exercises in pretense. They didn't listen to you. They're listened to themselves, politicians, urban planners and worst of all to the victims' families. They turned a deaf ear to advocates for rebuilding.

We do not need and do not want the LMDC. We must demand

that this rogue autocratic organization be dismantled. Power and control over the rebuilding of the WTC must be returned to the owners and the leaseholders where it rightfully belongs.

What we don't need and never needed is the LMDC. Yet it was in power long enough to stop the rebuilding of the WTC. To this day, ten years after 9/11, it is still a threat to rebuilding.

What we do need is a visionary architect like Howard Roark, the hero of Ayn Rand's novel, *The Fountainhead*. If you want to know philosophically what's wrong with the current process under the autocratic hand of the LMDC, I recommend that you read the book or watch the video of *The Fountainhead*.

The Cortlandt Street subway station, across the street from the WTC, has been reopened after six years of closure. I frequently used that station over the years. Since 9/11, every time I pass through it, I think of Cortlandt Homes in *The Fountainhead*, which Howard Roark dynamited because his design had been altered without his permission. I wonder if the right thing to do, the moral thing to do is to intellectually dynamite the currently under construction fake WTC because the Twin Towers and the rest of the WTC are not being rebuilt.

Let me say something in defense of the original World Trade Center Towers. Many ignorantly refer to them as deathtraps. Many accuse them of being responsible for the deaths of almost 3,000 people.

As I said elsewhere:

The World Center Towers didn't kill anyone. The killers were the terrorists who flew planes into the buildings and those who supported the terrorists. The terrorists are the killers. Let us never lose sight of that fact.

The fact is, the towers saved lives. They stood long enough that tens of thousands of people could get out before the collapse.

A Reply to a Victim Family Group Email

By Joe Wright

I've been reading all of the communication back and forth in response to your email. Since it was addressed to me, I want to reply in my own words. With respect to messages from those who don't want to continue these communications, that's fine with me. I have no intention to send email to recipients who don't want it. However, I will take this opportunity to reply to your email.

Dear Mr. Wright and Mr. Epstein:

As a widow of a firefighter killed on September 11th, I find it offensive that you are making an effort to rebuild the Twin Towers.

I find it equally, if not more, offensive not to rebuild the Twin Towers. Far more people worked there and lived than died or were injured. No matter what you say, it is a capitulation to terrorism not to rebuild or to rebuild stunted little buildings and/or mega-memorials.

I had customers and friends in 1 WTC who survived the first attack in 1993. In fact I was within 15 minutes of being in that attack because I was that few minutes late for a meeting with the Port Authority. (I provided the system that gave bridge and tunnel information.) I would have been as upset as you are if any of my business associates, who because of that 1993 incident became more than business associates, had been injured or killed. I worried about them for two weeks after 9/11 before I eventually found out that they were okay.

However, that would not have affected my view that the WTC should be rebuilt as tall or taller.

Clearly, you have learned nothing from September 11th if you think rebuilding the towers on top of our loved ones will change terrorism or strengthen our economy.

I beg to differ with you that anyone is building anything on top of your loved ones. The area has been thoroughly cleaned and any bodies or remains have been removed. No one is buried at Ground Zero. And consequently, it cannot be called a cemetery.

The best that you could say on this point is that the remains of your loved ones are in one or more of several places: (1) At the Fresh Kills Landfill in Staten Island, (2) in refrigerated trucks at the Medical Examiners facility, (3) scattered by the wind all over Manhattan, Brooklyn and out to sea, (4) washed down into the sewer system or swept up by street sweepers, or (5) inhaled into the lungs of anyone and everyone who visited or worked at the site.

Does this mean that every one of those sites, including my lungs, which were filled with the smoke and dust from Ground Zero, are hallowed? Or, since I have by now probably coughed out the particles, my lungs are no longer hallowed?

I could cite dozens of examples of rebuilding on sites of death. Andrew Oliff and Louis Epstein have mentioned some of them in response to your email. Of course the most recent is the Pentagon. Happily, it wasn't turned into a mega-memorial and taken off the list of inhabitable property as you apparently want Ground Zero to be.

As to learning anything from the 9/11 events, I didn't have to learn anything. I think the same way now as I did before about terrorism, domestic or foreign. You might say my desire to exterminate terrorists was heightened, but it didn't take the attacks on 9/11 or the death of your loved ones to make me think that all terrorism, especially religious-based terrorism, is evil. The current flavor of terrorism is as old as is religion. It is in fact a religious war. Although Osama bin Laden may think he's discovered something new, attacks on capitalism, individual rights and the free market are just as rampant in Christianity as in Islam. May I remind you that slavery in the US was completely endorsed by many who hewed to the Christian religion? And why not? God ordered his minions on many occasions to attack enemies, killing those of no value, taking prisoners and freely enslaving those who served his "benevolent" cause.

To the question of whether rebuilding will change terrorism, the answer has to be, I don't see how it could. Nothing will change terrorism. It is an irrational ideology that no amount of reason or rational argument will change. However, not to rebuild contributes directly to increased likelihood of terrorism.

If the WTC is not rebuilt as tall or taller, terrorists can easily say they succeeded in destroying a substantial component of NYC's economy and indeed the act has turned the national economy into a tremendous spiral downward. By not rebuilding, you will have accepted that as the normal state of affairs. You will have allowed us to be cut down to size and you will have decided out of fear or grief to let New York City, the nation and everyone who lives and works to stay in this depressed state. By opposing rebuilding, you are contributing directly to the malaise, depression and economic stagnation from which we all have suffered since 9/11. Believe me, you don't have to operate a business below Canal Street or 14th Street or wherever you want to draw the line to have your business affected adversely by the 9/11 terrorist attacks.

Rebuilding would cause an immediate upturn in NYC's economy. Not only would this help construction workers, but it would help us all. Mentally, physically and economically. Nothing could be more inspiring and hopeful for those who have suffered loss of business or who have had to shut down than to see a shovel going in the ground at Ground Zero as the first step toward rebuilding the WTC. There would be an immediate response.

And, yes, it would be a statement to any future terrorists that they cannot succeed, that no matter how many times we are attacked, we will put back what they destroy, we will refuse to cower in fear, we will persevere.

I'm sorry to see that you don't believe that it's important to restore the symbols and representations of our American heritage. I'm sorry to see that you have rejected the American way and, instead, have chosen to capitulate to what the terrorists have done to us. I'm sorry to see that you have lost pride in your country and the principles for which it stands. I can see that you would have been of no value during the Revolutionary War, you would have held up the white flag and surrendered the nation to the attacking British soldiers.

The reality is, that the Twin Towers were a death trap to the almost 3,000 people who were incinerated and crushed there.

On the contrary, the reality is that the Twin Towers saved tens of thousands of lives. They should be given credit for this. Sure, almost 3,000 people died, but consider how many had time to escape and live. The undeniable reality is that the buildings stood — despite a horrendous, hellish conflagration that no one could have ever imagined — and are responsible for saving tens of thousands of people.

To demonstrate how little you know about structural capabilities, ask yourself what would have happened if the planes had come down in Chelsea, a section of New York City characterized by low-rise buildings and nothing much that could remotely be considered a skyscraper. The number of deaths would have been uncountable. A fireball would have engulfed the neighborhood for blocks and blocks of homes and businesses. There would have been no possibility of escaping such an event. It would have been impossible for the fire department to either fight the fire or save anyone.

The fact is that a tall building is inherently safer than a short building, no matter what the threat, be it a storm or an aerial attack. Should a plane fly into one of the stunted little buildings you and others favor, there would be instant death for every occupant. Instead of standing for an hour, the buildings would collapse within minutes. Any architect can tell you this; any building contractor could tell you this.

One anti-WTC advocate is great at spewing out false information in addition to performing according to script at public hearings, including the faux tears almost immediately followed by joviality as soon as the play has ended and the camera shut off. Believe me, I've seen the performance. It is unfortunate that many are taken in by it.

Her particular falsehood ties in with your statement. She claims that the Port Authority built the WTC in violation of the building and fire codes. What she won't admit is the truth that, although the PA is indeed exempt from the codes, the Trade Center was not only built to code, but exceeded the code. If you and she don't believe that, you only have to check it out. And while you're at it, instead of lambasting the Port Authority, why don't you ask the fire department and the building department why they signed off on the plans? If they truly thought the buildings were unsafe, do you think they would have done that? Not unless you in fact hold the integrity of firefighters to a lower level than you indicate.

The undeniable fact is that the WTC was as safe as any building built at the time and was safer than many buildings built since. How many buildings in NYC or anywhere in the USA can you name that would have withstood the impact of a fully fueled jetliner flying at 500 to 600 mph? I would grant you that the Empire State Building might be one of them. And that's because it is built of heavy iron and massive amounts of concrete. But otherwise? Not a single building would have withstood the impact better or even as well. They would have collapsed, some immediately upon impact, killing far more people than were killed on 9/11.

> *My husband was at the 1993 bombing and knew then that a fire in a skyscraper as tall as the twin towers would be a major disaster and although he could have never anticipated the events of the 11th, the lesson is clear.*

Not to be churlish, but did your husband say or do anything to express his thoughts to the powers-that-be? And what proof did he have? Was this just speculation on his part? Is he a building engineer or is he knowledgeable about building engineering to the extent that his view would be accepted as an informed and an important view to take into account? If so, what did he do to alert people including those who worked in the Twin Towers about this condition?

The fact is that 1 WTC survived the 1993 bombing. Isn't that an indication of strength, not weakness or flawed design?

I think the only clear lesson from 1993 is that 1 WTC performed extremely well considering what it had suffered from an incredible truck bombing. Again, the building saved tens of thousands of lives. You seem incapable of giving the building credit for anything and are just fixated on the injured and the dead. You seem unable to focus and open your eyes to the facts of the case.

I will grant you one point, which in fact you didn't mention and one that is very important but has disappeared from the field of discussion: asbestos. I don't know if you know the story, but it was mentioned in an early *New York Times* report and on one other occasion somewhat more recently.

In short, the Twin Towers, like every building up until that time, was to be insulated with asbestos, a very effective, proven barrier to fire. Unfortunately, in one of those all too common events, it was declared a dangerous, cancer-causing substance and was banned. This ban took place as the Twin Towers were being erected. If I remember correctly, one of the towers had been treated with asbestos up to a pretty high level. However, because of the ban, it was ripped off and replaced with a decidedly inferior product. And even at that early date, the substitute product was known to be inferior because it simply wouldn't stick to the now rusted metal of the Twin Towers. Asbestos would have stuck to rusted metal.

The inspector for the manufacturer of this substitute material was interviewed on a television show (and I believe in addition to mentioned in that *NY Times* article) and commented that the material would fall off the steel just from a prick of a screwdriver. He had 230 photographs he had taken over the years that demonstrated how vulnerable this material was to flaking off from the metal it was intended to protect.

So, if you want to blame anything structurally about the building, (1) blame those responsible for banning a superior fire barrier, asbestos, and (2) blame those who decided to remove the asbestos and replace it with a known inferior fire barrier.

I'm not saying how many people would have been saved had the building utilized asbestos. I'm simply not competent to make such a determination. But from what I've read and seen on television and read in the *Times*, it would have contributed substantially to preventing the spread of the fire as well as have protected the fragile metal trusses that gave way and ultimately (and allegedly) resulted in the collapse of the buildings.

(As an aside, another banned product that would aid in human health is DDT, the most effective pesticide ever invented to kill the mosquitoes that cause malaria and would completely eliminate the threat of the West Nile Virus. It was a victim to unreasoned and unscientific attack in the same way that asbestos has been a victim. In case you don't know, asbestos is dangerous only in a certain, rare state in which it exists as a very fine particulate, a state referred to as "friable." Outside that state, asbestos is entirely benign. There are even questions from scientists as to whether or not normal exposure to asbestos in this friable state presents any danger.)

Turning to the subject of building new buildings, it is obvious that they would be stronger and safer just from the fact that better materials are available, better technology exists and experience over the last 30 years since the WTC was built has increased our level of knowledge. Certainly, for example, no one would attach the light metal trusses to the outer steel columns with bolts or rivets alone. They would be welded. Perhaps you could say that this is one lesson learned from the reaction of the trade towers to the fire that engulfed them on 9/11.

It was a mistake not to weld these trusses. But we know that only in hindsight. It's worth repeating that no one, no one would have ever thought that anyone would fly a fully-fueled massive jetliner into the WTC at 500 or 600 mph. The designers did investigate the consequences of a 707 flying into the building — but only under the assumption that it would be an accident, not an intentional act. So, the speed at which it would have hit the buildings would have been the speed it would have been flying upon a takeoff or a landing approach to one of the area's airports.

I'm sure that, if anyone would have thought about someone intentionally flying a fully-fueled 707 at 500 mph into the WTC, they would have done things differently. But no one even remotely conceived of such a possibility at the time. As feared as the enemy at that time, the Soviet Union, was, no one thought they would initiate an attack by flying a plane into a building. We were, during the Cold War, led more to expect a ballistic nuclear missile attack. (Are you of a certain age that would remember Nike Missile bases surrounding New York and other cities?)

Returning again to building new WTC towers, certainly there is a clear lesson or more accurately, two lessons. The first clear lesson is that the original WTC towers were built solid enough to stand for an hour and allow tens of thousands of people to escape safely and to survive.

The second lesson is that sure, things that would enhance safety could be incorporated into new buildings and will be. Stairwells will be better secured, built wider and there will be more of them. Lightweight materials will be replaced by sturdier materials. More fire-resistant materials will be used. New ways to escape from fires in tall buildings will be utilized. They already exist, but they are recent inventions. Alternate sources of water supply for sprinklers will be included as will methods for preventing a breakage in the supply from taking out the entire system.

As with the phony scare of a Y2K catastrophe, human ingenuity will resolve any problems and make new buildings better.

Skyscrapers are dangerous to firefighters and the people who work in them.

As mentioned above, low-rise buildings are far more dangerous in case of a massive fire such as resulted from the fully-fueled planes that flew into the WTC. They are inherently more dangerous because skyscrapers must be built far more strongly in order to support the entire structure than is required for shorter buildings.

But the fact is that no building is dangerous to firefighters or anyone else as such. That's like saying that streets are dangerous to pedestrians. Sure they are if you walk in front of a moving car. But you don't stop building streets.

We have to get away from the view that firefighters and policemen and policewomen are automatically heroes. I do my job and nobody calls me a hero. So why should a firefighter be a hero for doing what the job requires? I can't conceive of a single firefighter who wouldn't have known, before signing up, that the job is inherently dangerous. Likewise with a policeman or policewoman.

Rallying to rebuild them is a slap in the face to families, the murdered and my husband's surviving firefighter brothers who have to protect the people who work there.

And your efforts to block rebuilding are not a slap in the face to the tens of thousands of people who lost their jobs? And your efforts are not a slap in the face to tens of thousands of us who want the towers rebuilt?

Grief is a personal matter in my view. I've lived through death and suffered tremendously. But I never used that grief to tell other people how to live their lives or to deny them the things they want that would enrich their lives. You should be ashamed of yourself for inflicting your grief on the thousands of people who are still alive and suffering loss of jobs, income and happiness in their lives because you persist in blocking the rebuilding of what would in fact enrich their lives, a new WTC. You should be ashamed of inflicting your grief on hundreds of millions of people in the nation.

One might question how a relative handful, an infinitesimal number of people have come to be dictators of what happens not only in Lower Manhattan, but to New York City and the nation at large. This is a brazen takeover of the lives of thousands and millions of people by a handful of 9/11 victim families.

True, you have the ear of the autocratic LMDC, but you shouldn't have it. You are a decided minority exercising your bullying tactics to the severe detriment of the millions of people who live and work in Lower Manhattan and the rest of New York City.

Apparently you think that just because someone dies on a piece of property, you somehow gain total control over the property with the power to dictate for the rest of eternity what can and cannot be done with it. The notorious LMDC has caved to your demands in a show of unprecedented fascist power.

I remind you that you don't own a square inch of the sixteen acres of property that was the site of the WTC. As such, you have absolutely no right to control it. Yes, you can talk your heads off and say what you would like to see built there, just like we have the right to say what we would like to see built there. But neither you nor I have any rights in the matter whatsoever. Dying on another person's property grants you no ownership rights.

The families affected by this tragedy overwhelmingly support our efforts to not only build a profound and beautiful memorial, but to stimulate the economy downtown.

I'm sorry to inform you that a mega-memorial will in no way stimulate the Lower Manhattan economy to the extent that new Twin Towers would. What a memorial offers in economic value to a visitor and what visitors to the memorial would do for the economy fails to measure up to what new towers would contribute.

If you have any knowledge at all of how many people visit memorials, you'd understand that your ideas will destroy the economy of Lower Manhattan and indeed cause the New York City economy to stay in decline for years to come. What you're saying is that people will come to the memorial and then immediately go shopping or go for a drink in a neighborhood bar or go to dinner in a local restaurant. The problem with this equation is that there ain't going to be any neighborhood bars or restaurants and the shopping will be severely limited in the absence of a new WTC where some 40-50 thousand people worked and tens of thousands more visited for business as well as pleasure.

Your vaunted memorials will kill the economy just as effectively as the terrorists killed your husband. Consider the number of people who attend a relatively massive memorial in Oklahoma City. It attracts nowhere near the millions of people you think will visit a memorial at Ground Zero. Over time, the visitations by strangers and the curious drop off, eventually to nothing. This leaves family members who visit on a regular basis. But their visits drop to taking place only on anniversaries of the event.

Death is eventually overcome and life goes on, as it must.

And you may or may not know that many permanent residents in Lower Manhattan have expressed their opposition to the memorialization of their neighborhood. They have clearly stated that they don't want to live near or overlook a cemetery (which as I said earlier, of course that the WTC site is not). And they don't want to be reminded every day for the rest of their lives there about what happened on 9/11. I, if not they, see your efforts at turning Lower Manhattan into a permanent place of grief as macabre, as an unhealthy focus on death and destruction rather than life.

Utilizing the over one million people who visit there each week is a more productive and fitting way to stimulate the economy that was so adversely affected.

As I believe Louis Epstein noted, your numbers are way off.

Millions of people a week do not visit Ground Zero. Thousands perhaps, but certainly not millions. And there never will be millions. There certainly will not be millions a year for the time to come. The number of visitors will dwindle rapidly as time passes as in fact it already has. We have been petitioning near Ground Zero for a couple of months. After the anniversary of 9/11, the number of people has noticeably declined.

I'm sorry to inform you that your memorial will not be a winner. It will attract a steadily dwindling number of visitors and the result of your actions will have been to destroy the economy of Lower Manhattan, putting business people out of business and causing what few residents who live there to leave because the work that they moved there to engage in will have been destroyed by your memorial.

The reality is it took over 30 years to fill the towers the office space in the Towers and currently the office space presently available downtown is not even being utilized.

To which I say, so what! Every builder builds on speculation. Just a year or so ago, the city was facing such a crisis in available space that a committee was formed by the most prestigious businesses and local politicians of all stripes to solve this immense problem. If the lack of space a year or so ago was an emergency, how much of an emergency is it now that some ten million square feet of space has been destroyed?

I can see that you have no optimism whatsoever about the future of New York City. You're perfectly content to let the City wither away and, moreover, you're recommending actions that will contribute to this withering process.

The Empire State Building was unoccupied for many years after construction as was Rockefeller Center. Should they not have been built? Should we tear them down so that the available space more evenly matches your pessimistic and unreasoned forecast of the future business needs of the City?

Your irrational memorializing actions will create a shortage of office space for years to come. With the Holocaust Memorial, the Irish Hunger Memorial and the WTC memorial, what are you people trying to do? Turn New York City into a Disneyfied Memorial Amusement Park?

Will we soon have barkers on the street, yelling out to tourists, "Get your memorial ride tickets here, take a ride on the memorial roller coaster!"

Even if construction began now, it will be years before new Trade Towers would be available for occupancy. At that time — who knows? We might have overbuilt. But history tells us that we will have under-built.

You are also apparently unknowledgeable about economics. There is no such thing as too much office space. In a free market, there is only too much space at a certain price. If office space is not renting at $80 a square foot, that doesn't mean there is no demand for office space. What it means is there is no demand for $80 a square foot space. In the face of that, the market will force an adjustment in the cost per square foot.

So, I guarantee you that, if the higher floors of a new WTC are not renting at an initial offering price, they will rent and will be completely filled up at a lower price. The market will make it all work. As people can afford to move into better or more prestigious buildings, they will move out of lesser buildings. Those buildings will be reduced farther in value and will either attract new renters looking for even less expensive office space that they might not have been able to afford or they will change or go completely out of business, clearing the way for new uses for the building or the property on which it rests.

Your view of the economy is static and assumes that the only possible change is downward. History tells us that that's not the case, but you insist on New York City being entrapped forever by a weird non-building philosophy. While you may not want to have the City frozen in time, your efforts will accomplish that to the detriment of many thousands more than were killed on 9/11.

I agree that we must not live in fear, but slapping up towers so you can build a middle finger in the sky to Bin Laden is narrow minded and begs for this tragedy to happen again.

I'm glad to hear that you don't think we should live in fear. But your actions nonetheless pander to fear. Sure some would like to give the finger to Bin Laden. I don't happen to be one of them. I simply see no point in that. On the other hand, if we don't gain real, not symbolic, vengeance, he will have succeeded in his mission to shut us down as a nation and as the American people that we are.

Your use of the phrase "slapping up towers" gives a false tone to what we're all about. We don't believe in slapping up new towers. We're for building new, bold and exciting towers where people will be proud and feel safe to work.

Would they be a target for a new terrorist attack? Why would they be more of a target than existing buildings? Should we tear down the Empire State Building or the Sears Tower in Chicago because they are potential targets? What was targeted by the terrorists were not tall buildings, but symbols of America qua America. The Pentagon is not a tall building. If the Capitol Building was indeed the target of the hijacked plane that went down in Pennsylvania, that's not a tall building either.

What was attacked is our system of freedom, individual rights and civilized life. The attack was against us as a unique nation, a nation of people dedicated for the most part to enjoying life on earth in spite of the otherworldly wishes of the religious. Even the most devout believers in a heaven beyond the clouds have a good time now and then and are probably grateful for the offerings that life on earth provides.

The terrorists were attacking the very spirit and soul of America and all that we hold dear. The World Trade Center Towers, the Pentagon and if it was a target, the Capitol Building are symbols of that spirit, of that soul. That is the only reason they were attacked.

So, it is totally false to say that new towers would be a target because they are tall and that a shorter WTC would not be a target. In fact, think about this: What would be an even greater target than a new, stunted WTC than your grand sixteen acre memorial? If you can put yourself in the mind of a terrorist, wouldn't it be just great to drop a bomb on your little memorial park thus striking at something you value more than a new tall or taller Trade Center? Talk about demoralization!

As I said, the terrorists struck at symbols. Considering this, your memorial would be a perfect target for a new attack.

After September 11th, the world changed and the only thing that buoyed my broken spirit is that the world stood strong and united.

Quite frankly, I'm tired of hearing the phrase that 9/11 changed the world. Events every day change the world. It's meaningless and fruitless to sit and contemplate your navel while trying to find out what exactly has changed. Nothing has changed. The spirit that moves America hasn't changed, hasn't surrendered, hasn't given up. Sure, we all have suffered, you all as victims' families certainly more so. But have you really changed? I certainly hope not. Fundamentally, I haven't changed. I grow in experience and knowledge every day, but my sense of life hasn't changed. It remains as pure and strong as it was when I was a kid. It simply expresses itself in new ways as horizons broaden and new things are experienced.

Tall buildings and business did not create this resilience, the triumph of the human spirit did and what is built on that site must reflect that.

Of course tall buildings did not create this resilience. Neither would short towers. Resilience is of the spirit, of the soul, of your sense of life. Paraphrasing Jonathan Hakala who had offices on the seventy-seventh floor of the North Tower, standing next to a tall building doesn't make you any bigger or better or more resilient a person.

However, seeing and experiencing what man can do in building skyscrapers does inspire and bring excitement to life. I, for one, don't buy into the naturalist idea where I'm inspired by looking at the Grand Canyon or a field of grass. I'm inspired by creation at the hands of man. Nature just is. But man creates and builds and thereby overcomes the limits of nature, rising above nature and the universe itself.

Though I have a severe case of vertigo, so severe that even seeing a person on television standing at the edge of a tall building can generate the feeling, I love working on the highest floors, staying on the highest floors in hotels, living on the highest floors in an apartment building, and visiting the top of the Empire State Building. I'd be one of the first to visit a new observation deck atop a new World Trade Center tower built as tall as or taller than the original towers. I'd be one of the first to eat in a rebuilt Windows on the World. And, if I could afford it, I'd be one of the first to rent office space on the highest floor available. Unfortunately on this last point, I have had offices in Lower Manhattan and don't happen to like the neighborhood. But that's beside the point.

So, I say, speak for yourself here. Don't stand in the way of millions of other people who want to live their lives without being dictated to by your organizations or the LMDC.

> *Creating something poignant and everlasting takes time. The families, businesses, residents and the LMDC are working hard to do just that. To rebuild what was there before is shortsighted and insensitive to the thousands of families still grieving and a sad legacy to leave the thousands of children left without a parent.*

If you haven't grasped it by now, you should know that I'm opposed to any memorial as such, especially a mega-memorial occupying sixteen acres or any significant amount of that space. I am one who believes that new twin towers built as tall or taller would be the greatest memorial to victims of 9/11. I know others have said this and phrased it as worshipping life, not focusing on death, but that's exactly the way I look at it.

I'm writing a book about my father's work in show business, not as an actor, mind you, but as a showman, who from the 1930s ran tent shows, indoor theaters and ultimately a drive-in movie theater in Western Kentucky until the 1960s when he died. The only thing in the book about his death is the obituary notice that was printed in the local newspaper. The rest of the book is about his life and what he did. His death is important only in the sense that it ended his life and my enjoyment of shared experiences. The book is about life, not death.

To build the world's largest tombstone on the site of the WTC would be an incredibly insensitive way to honor the victims of 9/11. I don't visit my father's grave. Why? Because he's not there. What I do visit are places where he worked, operated theaters, visited friends and relatives, had a drink, ate barbecue sandwiches, etc. I retrace the paths he took in life and I celebrate those and experience the great memories of those days so long ago when I would travel with him. And that's not to say that all was sweetness and light. We certainly disagreed on some things, but they, in the overall scheme of things, were unimportant. I delight in telling the stories of conflict as much as those of wonder and discovery.

I'm just consistently so focused on living and enjoying life that I won't let death dictate anything to me. I give it no great presence in my life and accord it no power.

You on the other hand are setting yourself up for agony forever. And you want to concretize your agony and your grief in the form of a memorial that will be with you forever. I can't imagine a more anti-life thing to do.

Again, I say it is not insensitive to build a new WTC. It is insensitive *not to rebuild* and it is senseless not to rebuild on the very footprints of the original towers. Saying that the ground is sacred or hallowed is nothing more than a feeling. It is not a fact of nature. It's a relationship that you feel to a scene.

But you can't let that feeling stand in the way of or replace living your life. Your grief will disappear over time, but not if you persist in thinking you're doing something great by building gigantic memorials and places to go and grieve. And as I said above, you have no right to inflict your grief on others and destroy their lives with your thoughtless and insensitive construction of a cemetery in the midst of Lower Manhattan.

As I said at the beginning, I have no intention of adding you to any of my email lists. You don't have to ask to be taken off because you are not on any list. I didn't start the conversation, you wrote directly to Louis Epstein and me. So, I have the right to reply. And that I have done. If anyone else whose address is on this email continues to attack us, I will, if I choose, answer those attacks.

We have a strong case for rebuilding the WTC as tall or taller. There are over a thousand members of our ad hoc group known as the World Trade Center Restoration Movement (WTCRM). Few have seen one another, communicating primarily with each other via email and the web. We have almost 2,000 signatures on petitions signed by people walking on the streets around Ground Zero, many of them visitors from outside New York City, many from outside the USA. The petition asks simply if they believe that the World Trade Center twin towers should be rebuilt as tall or taller. Other rebuilding advocacy groups have experienced the same response. One group solicited signatures on the anniversary of 9/11 and collected over 2,000 signatures. Another group has collected over 10,000 signatures on an online poll. Additionally, general polls on TV and the web have shown that an overwhelming majority of those who participated want the towers rebuilt at least as tall if not taller.

Finally, contrary to the spin from the LMDC, the participants in the various LTTC (Listening to the City) meetings did not reject tall towers nor did they reject rebuilding all eleven million square feet of office space. What they and I among them rejected was the pathetic collection of stunted little buildings proposed as a replacement for the soaring twin towers. What they and I rejected was the clumping of these disgraceful buildings in such a way that no room was left on the site and that the plaza concept was completely destroyed.

Accepting for a minute that there should be a memorial on the site, the best way to ensure its stature would be to rebuild two tall towers which would occupy the least amount of area at their bases, less than the LMDC clumped buildings. I'm amazed that the memorialists don't see this.

Monica Iken (head of September Mission), who lost her husband on 9/11, is perhaps an exception. In a recent email from a member of her organization, it has suddenly dawned on them that extending Greenwich Street through the site will virtually destroy the possibility of a memorial. Though a tiny point, September Mission and we agree on the issue of keeping the site free and clear. Of course, we disagree for what purpose the site should be free and clear of obstructions. She and all of you are apparently for a memorial and we are for new trade center towers proudly reaching into the clouds.

As a final point, I question the very existence of the LMDC and argue that it should be dismantled. Who in their right mind would grant total power over the economy of Lower Manhattan and arguably the entire city to a bunch of political appointees equipped with the power of eminent domain, with which they could run roughshod over the entire city searching for places to build replacement office space that they are so adamant will not be built in the only logical place available: an empty lot of some sixteen acres in size.

We have fought wars against regimes that have these kinds of autocratic powers. The LMDC is a rogue operation that should be shut down. They are obstructions to progress.

The fate of Lower Manhattan and the WTC site in particular should be left exclusively to the owners and leaseholders.

Just as sincerely as you, saying in closing, if asked, "Should we rebuild the WTC as tall or taller?" I reply, without a doubt and the quicker we get started, the better for one and for all even everyone of you on this email.

The Dead Are Gone. What about the Living?

By Joe Wright

I'm well known for advocating rebuilding the twin towers on the footprints, i.e. restoring what was destroyed by the terrorists.

And I'm also well known for opposing the memorialization and destruction of Lower Manhattan as the financial capital of the world. They are one and the same thing. Memorials = destruction.

Where did this idea, that if you die on someone else's property, you become the owner or have gained the power to dictate how that property is used, come from? It's totally disrespectful of property rights and totally un-American.

Museums to tell the story of 9/11? Who in the world doesn't know this story? Who wants to be reminded on a daily basis of this horrible event? Who wants Lower Manhattan turned into a 24/7 cemetery? Who wants the circus of grief that would result?

Not to rebuild the WTC is a capitulation to the terrorists, as many have said. To build anything less than a new twin-tower WTC (as tall or taller with all commercial and retail space restored) — and on the footprints — is accepting Mohammed Atta and his fellow terrorists as the urban planners of Lower Manhattan.

Sure, something modest and in proportion would be acceptable as a memorial. Nearly 60,000 people died in the Vietnam War. Look at the size of that memorial. Now explain how sixteen acres or even one acre should be devoted to the victims of 9/11. Absurd.

Look at Hiroshima, totally destroyed by an atomic bomb with over 100,000 killed. It's now rebuilt as a thriving city, not a cemetery.

While victim spokespersons rant about memorials and sacred ground, let's admit it: They don't know and no one else knows what the victims would want. The victims' lives were not a sacrifice. A sacrifice implies that you have a choice. The victims had no choice. They went to work that day expecting to do the things that they did on every workday: pursue their happiness and financial betterment for themselves and their families. They weren't sacrificed and didn't commit a sacrifice. They were murdered.

It is also false to assume that victims' family members speak with a unified voice on the issue of rebuilding, even on rebuilding on the footprints, and on the subject of memorials. Even amongst the self-appointed spokespersons there is no unity on every issue. As would be expected. So, it is a gigantic mistake to take the words of one speaker and assume it represents all victim families and then, like the LMDC, cater to that view to the exclusion of all others. Further, to assume that what a victim family member desires is what the victim would desire is an act of faith (the belief in something for which there is no evidence).

As brutal as it may sound to say it, the victims are gone. There's nothing that can be done to bring them back. But tens of thousands of living people have their lives disrupted to this day because their jobs and/or businesses were destroyed on 9/11. We can do something to benefit the living: We can start rebuilding the WTC NOW! That means dismantling the LMDC and recognizing the rights of the Port Authority, Larry Silverstein and Westfield Properties to rebuild. The LMDC doesn't own anything and should be told to butt out.

Why should the entire city and indeed the nation be victimized by the victims' families? Why should we suffer because they suffer? Grief is a private matter. No one has the right to impose their grief on another person. Less than 3,000 people died on 9/11. Tens of thousands survived and have lives to live. To say that what they lost should not be restored would be sacrificing the living to the dead. Even the victim's families have lives to live. Grieving is a process that everyone who suffers a loss goes through, but it must be allowed to dissipate and it will dissipate over time. Living will and must reassert itself as the primary focus.

The Pentagon has been rebuilt. Construction started immediately. What do we have ten years after 9/11? A hole in the ground and a sorry excuse for a WTC Tower, Zero World Trade Center. And if it's left up to the autocratic rule of the LMDC and their bizarre architectural plans and the mega-memorialists, we may as well leave it that way.

Not rebuilding honors the terrorists. Rebuilding honors the victims, the survivors and the spirit of America.

An Autopsy of the WTC Rebuilding Process

By Joe Wright

Steve Cuozzo of the *New York Post* wrote an article about *The New York Times* July 14, 2003, editorial entitled "Ground Zero Developments." I'd like to present a different analysis, an autopsy I call it, of the *Times* position on rebuilding the World Trade Center.

The *Times*, in that July editorial, remarks that Larry Silverstein has been "…designated as the man who will bring to life the conceptual vision of the architect Daniel Libeskind, whose design for ground zero was chosen at the end of a very public process."

There are three errors in that statement.

Larry Silverstein has not been designated. As the exclusive leaseholder on the World Trade Center, he does not need to be designated. The lease obligates him and grants him the sole right to rebuild the World Trade Center.

Error two is the implication that Silverstein is obligated to rebuild according to the Libeskind plan. Since that plan didn't exist prior to or at the time the lease agreement between the Port Authority and Larry Silverstein was signed, there can be no contractual obligation.

Silverstein is obligated to restore the World Trade Center. The Libeskind plan decidedly does not restore the World Trade Center. On the contrary, the Libeskind plan completes the goal of the terrorists to destroy it forever.

The third error is the claim that the Libeskind plan was chosen in "a very public process." Anyone who attended knows that all the public hearings were irrelevant to the decision.

The choice of the LMDC committee charged with making the decision was not the Libeskind plan. It was the THINK Team's plan called the World Cultural Center.

Far from being a public process, even this decision was made behind closed doors in discussions from which everyone was excluded except the committee members themselves.

So, how did the Libeskind plan become the "winner?" Blame then Governor George E. Pataki for this mistake. He designated the Libeskind plan as the winner, probably in cahoots with Mayor Michael Bloomberg, overriding the choice of his own appointees on the LMDC committee.

Three errors in a single sentence. Is this a record for the *Times*?

With the LMDC committee discussion secreted behind closed doors and Governor George E. Pataki's unexplained imposition of the Libeskind plan, which the *Times* characterizes as an open, public process, it's hard to fathom why they say that "...the public does not have an adequate way of seeing and assessing [Larry Silverstein's] proposed changes to the Libeskind concept since much of the planning process is taking place in private."

Larry Silverstein is under no obligation to reveal any of his plans though, from a public relations standpoint, he might be well advised to do so. What the *Times* chooses to ignore is that, unlike the government construct, the LMDC, that is funded by taxpayer money and is required by law to conduct open meetings, a private developer is not.

(As an aside, it could be argued that the LMDC meetings were and are in violation of the New York open meetings law.)

The *Times* worries that Silverstein may change the Libeskind plan "...into something that falls far short of its original promise." I for one hope he does!

As an example, the *Times* cites the possibility that Libeskind's 1776 tower might be relocated on the site and that this "...could undermine its impact on New York's skyline."

Libeskind's vaunted 1776 tower is nothing more than a skyline element, an ornament. Mostly unoccupied by human life, it is not a replacement for massive, monumental twin towers. At best it is nothing more than a base for the proposed antenna farm.

If it is built, it will forever symbolize not American Revolutionary Freedom, but the success of the terrorists who destroyed the World Trade Center.

In this July 14 editorial, the *Times* also complains that Silverstein is moving too fast to rebuild too much space. Steve Cuozzo accurately points out in his article that the *Times* and its developer Forest City Ratner is itself building a new building that lacks tenants except for the *Times* itself. Somehow, that's okay.

But, unlike Silverstein, the *Times* and its developer are building its new headquarters at the expense of the taxpayers and are stealing the property on which it will be built.

Even worse, Forest City Ratner announced that it is seeking

money from the Liberty Bond program, a program that was intended exclusively to be used to rebuild Lower Manhattan, not a new headquarters for the *Times*. The *Times* and Forest City Ratner's approach to building is quite different than Larry Silverstein's.

The *Times* and Forest City Ratner built on property stolen from its rightful owners, by the coercive power of eminent domain exercised by the Empire State Development Corporation, for the exclusive benefit of the *Times* and Forest City Ratner. This is in violation of the Fifth Amendment to the US Constitution, which limits such takings to those for a "public use," not for the benefit of private businesses. If this is not bad enough, they also sought and gained a tax abatement amounting to over twenty-nine million dollars — some say more. And there is no guarantee that the *Times* or Forest City Ratner will ever pay this back. In the meantime, you and I will be making up for the budget gap caused by the tax break given to the *Times* and Forest City Ratner.

Who can lay claim to the high moral ground? The man who builds with his own money on property he has a legal right to build on or an organization that takes property by legalized theft and sticks taxpayers with paying part of the bill?

In spite of its complaints about Silverstein making changes to the Libeskind plan, the *Times* itself, in the spirit of its socialist ideology, urges that more residential (read affordable, read government subsidized) housing be built in lieu of commercial buildings. This would, of course, indirectly help the *Times* increase the occupancy of its own building, which at the moment will be empty except for the *Times* itself.

Saying that the building at Ground Zero "…cannot ever be treated as a normal real estate development," the *Times* claims that the World Trade Center was public property and that Silverstein's lease "…cannot prevail over the public's interest in this land."

Excuse me, but this implies that the *Times* doesn't believe in the sanctity of contracts, instead that individual rights are subordinate to "public interests."

Let me tell you that that's exactly what the *Times* anti-capitalistic ideological position is and not just with respect to rebuilding the World Trade Center. Witness their own actions in taking property from its rightful owners.

At least the *Times* is ideologically consistent.

The *Times* decries the possibility that Silverstein "…might make an obscene profit as a result of this tragedy."

What is more obscene: making a profit on an honest investment under the terms of a voluntarily negotiated contract or stealing property and, in spite of being a multi-million dollar operation, pleading for tax exemptions and money from a fund intended solely to be used to rebuild what was destroyed in "this tragedy?"

Prior to the July 14 editorial, on June 30 the *Times* editorialized about "…the thrilling structures planned by Studio Daniel Libeskind."

The *Times* said, "…the greatest memorial to all the victims will be a grand, vibrant, diverse community of residences, businesses, cultural institutions and parks."

Oh really? Have the seers at the *Times* been channeling the victims? Or are they just pushing their own socialist view of what they think Lower Manhattan should look like? Are they embracing Mayor Bloomberg's hallucination for Lower Manhattan?

The fact is, there is no great public support for any of this in Lower Manhattan and to impose these programs on the Financial District will complete the destruction that started with the terrorists attack on 9/11.

The opera on Wall Street? Preposterous! Residences? There are more appropriate places in the City to build apartment buildings. Cultural institutions? The culture of Lower Manhattan is finance. Parks? Is the *Times* unaware of Battery Park?

"Ground Zero has now become the most public of all America's public places and the decision on what to do with it must be made by public bodies for the public good," says the *Times*, which goes on to say "…this site now belongs to all of its survivors, not one group."

Apparently, the *Times* has never heard of private property rights, allowing for ownership by one group or another with power over what is done with the property determined by which group is the largest or the one that has the greatest political pull. To the *Times*, might makes right and to hell with anyone who gets in the way of the power of the public and its fascist bulldozer.

The fact is, the *Times* is ignorant of reality. There is no such entity as "the public." Since it doesn't exist, it can have no rights. All that can be said about "the public" is that it is a collection of individuals and that "public interest" is a consensus of the interests of individuals in the collection. Theoretically. In actuality, socialism devolves into rule by the group that has the most power. In other words, gang warfare.

From this it is clear that only individuals possess rights and that these rights are neither enhanced nor diminished by joining a group.

The idea of the "public interest" being superior to the interests of individuals always has and always will lead to dictatorship. My group is bigger than your group. My group has the power. Submit to our rule, relinquish your freedom or die!

Or in the *Times*' present argument, submit to the Libeskind imposed plan or Ground Zero will be taken away from its owners and those who have the exclusive right to build on it.

Believe it or not, the *Times* actually said that. In the June editorial, they said, on the chance that private developers fail to build the Libeskind plan, "…the public representatives should not hesitate to consider condemning the property and taking control on behalf of the people." *Sieg Heil!*

Am I the only one who is outraged by such a bold disregard of individual rights and freedom? Who the hell do they think they are? Well, we know who they are, no matter what they say.

It is ironic that, urging the powers-that-be to take property by force of law from its rightful owners, nonetheless, the *Times* in its next breath says, "All of ground zero, from the memorial to the 1,776-foot tower, must express the concept of freedom." A concept apparently the *Times* itself has yet to discover, a concept rendered null and void by their statement that Ground Zero should be condemned and control given to "the people." The people, of course, doesn't mean you, me or any particular individual. It means fascist government regulation and thereby control.

What about the freedom to peacefully own, use and enjoy one's own property without being threatened by the *Times* and others who believe their purposes are of a superior caliber than the underlings like us that stand in their way?

The *Times* condemns Larry Silverstein and other leaseholders for failing to recognize that "...the site now belongs to a bruised public that has already resoundingly rejected plans that call for massive blocks of office buildings and stores." The *Times* would very much like for you to believe that. Unfortunately, it simply is not true.

The fact is, at none of the public forums did the idea of rebuilding two tall twin towers get rejected. One reason was that we were denied the opportunity to discuss and vote on this alternative. Instead we have been offered pabulum and the hideous Libeskind death pit. As Andrew Oliff has said, in none of the polls did the Libeskind plan win. In most, it was defeated by the powerful choice, "none of the above." What does that tell you about where the public interest is?

I am confident that, in spite of the massive propaganda operation being conducted by *The New York Times*, if given a choice of Libeskind (or any of the other nine LMDC plans) and rebuilding two new twin towers as tall as or taller than the original World Trade Center, there would be tremendous support for the latter and no substantial support for Libeskind. Even the *Times*' own architecture critic rejected the Libeskind plan.

And so do I. Even ten years after 9/11, we urge you to write to the *Times*. Tell them you want the World Trade Center restored with two dramatic new twin towers.

Looks Worse than Albany

By Joe Wright

At the Javits Center public hearing on rebuilding the World Trade Center, a series of plans was submitted and was resoundingly rejected. One comment, with which many of the some 5,000 people in attendance agreed, was that the plans "Look like Albany," the implication being that they were incredibly bland. This was Crap Design One.

Then the LMDC presented the famous nine plans. Because they disallowed rebuilding the twin towers as an alternative, call them Crap Design Two.

On Friday, December 19, 2003, the first building of the Final Plan was presented with great hoopla by the powers-that-be to the public at large. My immediate response was: "Looks worse than Albany." Call the final plan Crap Design Three.

At least in Albany, they have real buildings occupied by real people, not stunted little sixty- or seventy-story buildings pretending to be the tallest in the world.

From Daniel Libeskind and David Childs, we have form over function, ornament over design, symbol over substance.

And... IT IS NOT A 1776-FOOT BUILDING!

It's a seventy-story building, originally planned to be topped off with a void, windmills and that goofy Libeskind spire all of which was eventually deleted. We don't need any reference to the Statue of Liberty. She stands on her own as the sole symbol of liberty. Why would anyone dare to diminish her stature by sticking a needle on top of a building? And who in the future would even make the connection?

Windmills? Give me a break! Who's going to pick up the remains of birds chopped up by the windmills?

I've had enough of this garbage about unoccupiable, uneconomical tall buildings. If these hooples, Pataki, Bloomberg, Silverstein, Childs, Libeskind and the LMDC can't build in the spirit of New York City, get out of the way and open the field to the inspired, the ambitious, the heroic. Let's put a real New York builder in charge. (Where is "the Donald?" Well, he was actually involved for a short time supporting and displaying a model of Ken Gardner's design. But he dropped out for some unknown reason.)

The announcement of the "final" design was just another shameful day in the history of the failure to rebuild the WTC.

Did you observe that all of the buildings spiraling upwards toward the 1776 tower will, by the nature of an upward spiral, have to be even shorter? What is this, design by and for the dwarfs of stature as well as intellect? Of course this spiraling upward is yet another dumb idea from the Libeskind "blaster plan."

More than any other, Libeskind's plan grants the terrorists what they wanted: to demoralize and humiliate America by destroying her symbols. The terrorists cut us down to size. The Libeskind plan and all of its supporters appear content with us remaining in that state. The Leave Manhattan Destroyed Corporation certainly isn't going to help.

What we have is not Freedom Tower, but Surrender Tower, as so accurately designated by my colleague Andrew Oliff.

The powers-that-be don't have the courage, the insight, the foresight or the ambition to do anything but the mediocre. We are, after all, dealing with politicians and their appointees who always hew to the pragmatic, and the "dead" middle with emphasis on "dead." They love to rush to the front of a charging crowd, claiming to be its leader. They seek the banality of consensus.

They pander to all interests in a hopeless attempt to please them all. The windmills were a sop to the environmentalists. The latticework is a sop to the artsy-fartsy crowd. Allowing Greenwich Street to slash through the property, destroying the whole plaza concept, is a sop to the vaunted urban planners who always hated the WTC.

But they dare not challenge the merchants of grief! To the self-appointed lobbyists for the victims, there is total capitulation. They want a death pit and so they get a death pit. The Libeskind plan was imposed because it offered the greatest space for memorializing death and the least space for celebrating life. Interestingly, some victim family members have courageously spoken out in favor of rebuilding the twin towers. But their voices are silenced and ignored.

Had the twin towers of the World Trade Center never been built, the Libeskind-Childs "building" might have been praised

214

for its inventiveness, for its spectacular design and for being the tallest structure in the world. But since the twin towers were built, replacing them with anything of less stature, of less grandness, with less functionality as office and commercial space can only be regarded as an utter disgrace. An insult to all Americans. An even grosser insult to New Yorkers who deserve better and even grander buildings on the site.

So, we have Crap Design One, Crap Design Two and Crap Design Three. To paraphrase Johnny Paycheck, "Take this crap and shovel it!"

And I haven't yet said a word about the memorial! Needless to say, the plans are atrocious. The idea of turning the site into a cemetery is grossly repugnant. I don't want the WTC site to become Tombstone City. Neither do residents in the area.

The most magnificent way to honor those murdered by terrorists on 9/11 is to rebuild what was destroyed. We can't bring back the dead, but we can rebuild what was important in their lives, what they worked for and where they worked, visited and enjoyed themselves and where others risked their lives to save those who were horribly entombed by the fires started by the terrorists.

My memorial would consist of elements of the destroyed towers placed on a new plaza between two new twin towers, built as tall or taller and exactly on the footprints of the original towers. Pieces of the steel beams, of the unique facade, the damaged Fritz Koenig *Sphere* (not repaired) and a proportionally sized monument on which names of the murdered would be inscribed.

As to an explanation of the meaning of the memorial, it would simply be that "On 9/11/01 these people were murdered by fanatical Islamic religious terrorists who hate America for everything that makes it and us great. We are not defeated and we submit these grand new twin towers as proof."

The Mayor's Gaff: The WTC Tombstone

By Joe Wright

In his address before the Republican Convention, August 30, 2004, Mayor Michael R. Bloomberg said, "And our city is also where, on Independence Day, Governor Pataki and I laid the *tombstone* for the Freedom Tower at the site of the World Trade Center." (Emphasis added.)

Let us hope that he meant what he said, but not what he meant.

Afterword

By Joe Wright

So, where do we stand after ten years? As Gary Taustine said, ten years gone meaning ten years wasted.

Where is the dramatic reconstruction of a landmark known worldwide where people came from every nation, not only to visit the observation deck, but to work in these two remarkable buildings?

Where are they working now? In some stunted little Midtown office building of no significance? Well, maybe also in 7 WTC. And the tourists? They still have the Empire State Building, but they've "been there, seen that."

What we have "under construction" is a sorry substitute that is shamefully being called 1 World Trade Center. It may be tall, but it falls short of matching either of the original Twin Towers. It's not that great to look at either. It's not unique and resembles other twisted towers. Aside from 7 WTC, that's it. No other building is even near beginning to rise from the ashes of the 9/11 attack on the World Trade Center.

But the site is not without elements under construction. After all, we have the Wading Pools of Grief, which cost a fortune and which apparently have no funding for maintenance. These wading pools, of course, occupy the footprints of the original Twin Towers. Since those towers should have been rebuilt, these wading pools are yet another insult, another defamation of the site. I can't wait until someone falls into the water and drowns or jumps in to commit suicide. The real consequence of this appalling construct will then be revealed: to worship death, not life.

Oh, and we have the Flightless Bird replacing the PATH terminal. Apparently because of cost, its wings have been clipped, so to speak. They will no longer move. Why should they have ever moved? Was this intended to be part of an amusement park?

Steve Cuozzo remarked in the August 11, 2011, issue of the *New York Post*:

> If he's [New Jersey Governor Chris Christie] serious

about curbing cost overruns at the WTC, he might try scratching the site's biggest bloodsucker: the vast PATH terminal dolled up as a "Transportation Hub." [8]

Before 9/11, there were seven WTC towers, five of which were nowhere equal in height or grandeur to 1 WTC and 2 WTC. Are they being rebuilt? Of course not.

One of those destroyed towers was 3 WTC, the Marriott Hotel. Is it not worth rebuilding? It served thousands of people who visited the WTC and the surrounding sites of historical interest. And, yes, those who shopped in the area.

The powers-that-be are not into restoring the WTC, they are into destroying it. Any office building, other than Zero WTC (aka Freedom Tower) now under construction, may be delayed for years. There's no demand for office space say the naysayers of negativism. The best that is going to happen is that a series of stunted little buildings will be constructed with the possibility that sometime in the unknown future, they might heighten them by, in essence, building an additional building atop them. I have one immediate question: Who the hell is going to work in a building on top of which another forty- or fifty-story building is being constructed? I'm not a fear monger, but you wouldn't get me into that stunted building with the risk that the building atop it might collapse. If it did, you could call it the Mohammad Atta Effect. In other words, he'd still be bringing down the WTC because we have let him dictate what gets done on the site.

Apparently we're also getting a memorial of some description on the site, yet another desecration. As I stated in another essay herein, the memorial will certainly be out of proportion. I reminded you that at one time, there were those in and out of power who argued for the entire site to be a memorial. That would be the ultimate insult to the Twin Towers and those who loved the site either for pleasure in touring or making money in working on the site.

But really, any memorial is a desecration, a celebration, not of life, but of death. See my comments in my essay "Reply to a Victim Family Group."

It defies logic, reason and morality that someone would argue that the site become a cemetery. Yet, to a large extent that is what is happening. The focus is not even on Zero World Trade Center.

The focus is on the Wading Pools of Grief, the memorial, the so-called museum and the absurd steel cross that the powers-that-be who rule over the site actually think contributes something to the site. It is yet another defamation. And probably a violation of the separation of church and state.

Many think the site is holy and sacred in a religious sense and should not be touched by anything but the spiritual. Nothing should be built over the graves of those killed on 9/11. Yet, of all things, an entertainment center is contemplated. The grave advocates don't even want you walking on the site, on the graves.

But dancing and singing atop the graves is okay? Clogging and rapping are okay? What, no hymns, no solemn prayer, no church on site where one can go immediately after having had grief inflicted on them, where the sorrowful visitors can go and kneel and pray to whatever god they worship? Will atheists like me and tens of thousands of others be evicted? You won't have to evict me. I won't put a foot on the site.

Maybe there should be a mausoleum? Maybe we should name the site the WTC Mausoleum and let Zero World Trade Center be the tombstone. After all, it is being constructed more in line with death than with life.

Take two elements of the site. First though, let me remind you that there has always been fear that another truck bomb might be used to attack any new buildings. How would that happen if there was no pathway onto the site on which the truck could drive? Element one is therefore, why extend Greenwich Street through the site if there is a fear of another truck bombing? Element two is the stupid response to this danger which is created by the powers-that-be themselves. That response is to sit Zero World Trade Center atop a pedestal, which should be named after New York City Police Commissioner Raymond Kelly. It should be Kelly's Memorial Pedestal.

The intention is for Kelly's Pedestal to absorb the blast from a truck bomb. Let me ask a simple question. If there was no way to drive a truck onto the site, would that not obviate the building of Kelly's Pedestal? Wouldn't that allow Zero World Trade Center to actually rest on the ground? Wouldn't this whole problem of truck bombing be resolved by not allowing Greenwich Street to enter onto and cross the site?

And one comment of lesser importance than the threat of truck bombs: Isn't running Greenwich and Fulton Streets through the site detracting from Plaza space, space where people can go and talk, smoke, grab some lunch, sun themselves, converse with friends and business associates, etc? Many people took advantage of the WTC Plaza for those purposes. Why should it be destroyed or reduced in size and accessibility by unnecessarily running streets through it? Plus, a pedestrian crossing problem arises that would not exist if the streets did not enter the site.

It's odd that Mayor Bloomberg supports running Greenwich and Fulton Streets through the site. After all, he is well known as an "open space" fanatic who, along with his cohort and intellectual brain sister Janette Sadik-Khan, takes every space they can find in the City and turns it into a plaza with resulting traffic congestion that both of them allegedly claim to abhor. What? Bloomberg has tried to reduce traffic congestion, but his actions have actually increased congestion. Sadik-Khan's bike lanes alone have been a major cause of congestion.

Greenwich and Fulton Streets clearly *should not* be allowed to traverse the WTC site. There would be two immediate benefits. One, it would not be necessary, assuming it is considered a necessity anywhere but in Kelly's and Mayor Bloomberg's head, to build it. Look at the money that could be saved. Look at the spacious lobby that could be built that would be open to the light of day and the light of night. Wouldn't this be better than the dung heap that the Port Authority, at the behest of Commissioner Kelly and Mayor Bloomberg, is placing beneath Zero World Trade Center?

The latest faux pas is the failed attempt to make the sides of Kelly's Pedestal look like glass, fake though it be. Unfortunately (or in my mind, fortunately), when an attempt was made to mount the glass, it cracked and fell apart. This is what should happen to Kelly's Dung Heap Pedestal, it should crack and fall apart. Then it would be forbidden to exist and the fraud exposed.

In the beginning, there were seven World Trade Center buildings, two of which were of course the famous Twin Towers, 1 WTC and 2 WTC, aka the North Tower and the South Tower, respectively.

In a way, one other building should be counted as having been part of the complex. That would be the Deutsche Bank Building because the LMDC bought it and is now treating it or at least the property it was built on as part of its domain.

On 9/11, Mohammad Atta and his terrorist cohorts destroyed the two Twin Towers. The Deutsche Bank Building was destroyed by the LMDC. (I maintain it could have been repaired and made usable once again. But such ideas are foreign to the destroyers at the LMDC.)

One building was rebuilt, 7 WTC, by Larry Silverstein, who leased the WTC site from the Port Authority. In ten years, 7 WTC is the only building, the only business that has been restored. Although there are negotiations in play with Westfield, none of the retail property has been restored, none of the hundreds of businesses have been reopened. Westfield Properties, who operated the underground mall where these small businesses were located, was in effect booted from the project. I hasten to say that it is encouraging to see Westfield back at work, so to speak, and planning to reopen the mall. I welcome this element of commerce and capitalism far more than all the elements of officially sponsored grief.

But this is only a small item in the overall WTC operation as it was. Ambition has been at its lowest level ever in NYC. There is no "USA, USA" being shouted at the WTC site.

Had the powers-that-now-be been in power in the early years of NYC, there would have been no Empire State Building, no Rockefeller Center, no George Washington Bridge, no Fifth Avenue, no Lincoln Center, etc. NYC would never have been regarded as Capital of the World.

The City would have been ruled by the likes of a person who came to one of the WTCRM rallies where we were soliciting signatures on a petition to rebuild the Twin Towers. He commented that he was opposed to the towers because they cast a shadow over the neighborhood. I asked, "At what height should buildings in NYC be restricted? The height of a tepee when the City was occupied by Indians?" He expressed disgust that I would ask something like this. But, after all, even an ant casts a shadow.

To add insult to injury, is it, can it be true that the powers-that-be are not going to return the Koenig *Sphere* to the WTC site? Even after having gotten over 7,000 signatures from 9/11 victim's family members requesting that?

Well, as per usual with the powers-that-be, they know better about such things than we mere mortals. In a Wikipedia article on *The Sphere*, it is said that:

> Officials from the 9/11 Memorial have stated that they do not want any 9/11 artifacts cluttering the 8-acre memorial plaza. There are no plans to place *The Sphere* on the 9/11 Memorial site. Liberty Park, which is south of the 9/11 Memorial, is not part of or on the site of the 9/11 Memorial.

Yet there is apparently a large constituency advocating that the steel cross be put on the site, under the pretense that anything that is cross-shaped must be from or must contain a message from God. These so-called officials are perfectly content to disallow the return of one of the true surviving and widely admired elements of the WTC site. Yet they will allow the construction of the Wading Pools of Grief and all kinds of other sadly mournful trash to be installed there. Will photos be allowed in the Memorial Space?

Against what artifact would you expect most people would want their photo taken upon visiting the WTC? The Wading Pools of Grief or the Koenig *Sphere*? As a clue, consider the fact that more photos are taken of the Bull on Broadway than of the front of the New York Stock Exchange.

No one would expect that the WTC would be restored exactly as it was. After all, there are new building techniques and materials and even new and exciting designs such as those offered by Ken Gardner. See them at www.triroc.com/wtc.

What we rebuilders seek is simple and achievable at far less cost than what the powers-that-be and the Port Authority are doing. We want two new twin towers built stronger and taller than the originals and on the footprints of the original towers.

Money wasted on Wading Pools of Grief, the garish mausoleum aka the memorial, Kelly's Memorial Pedestal, extending Greenwich and Fulton Streets through the site and other monstrous things being constructed in a mystical hodgepodge on the WTC site could be saved or put toward building two new towers. Like those proposed by Ken Gardner.

The WTC was not the only thing attacked on 9/11, though other attacks were of far less consequence. What happened to those other things and to the sites of other attacks?

222

The Pentagon was restored and a modest memorial built. In Oklahoma City, the building destroyed by Timothy McVeigh was rebuilt. The USS *Arizona* was not left destroyed, but was turned into a museum. Hiroshima, Nagasaki, Berlin and other cities destroyed in war were rebuilt. (I hasten to add that the situation with Flight 93 crashing in Pennsylvania is not so admirable. The disreputable memorialists have tried to steal acres and acres of land from its owner for their own garish memorial. Our freedom loving government offered to help by invoking its power of eminent domain. The last I heard, a purchase agreeable to the owner of the property and the memorialists had been achieved, under threats from the government.)

But what is the one thing that has not been restored? The Twin Towers of the WTC. Obstructed by Governors of New Jersey and New York, especially George Pataki, then governor of New York, the Port Authority, the LMDC, Mayors Rudolph Giuliani and Michael Bloomberg and other members of the team of destroyers, the towers remain, after ten years, still destroyed. What's being built in their place is a big zero illustrated by Zero World Trade Center itself. Just this first week of August 2011, the Port Authority announced that there would be huge (my word, not theirs) increases in tolls on the bridges and tunnels into and out of NYC. Part of the reason for increasing the tolls is reportedly to help pay for construction of the WTC, the fake one, not the real one.

The Port Authority is a government owned and operated transportation system that, as expected, doesn't know from one day to another whether it has any money in its bank account or not and doesn't know if it can complete a project or not. Its budget is always out of balance and it is always panhandling before local, state and the federal government for funding, Why this operation exists is beyond me. It should, like the equally nefarious MTA (Metropolitan Transportation Authority), be sold to the highest bidder and privatized. The MTA has announced an equally onerous increase in fares with zero increase in service. Some say that MTA said backwards is ATM. In both cases, the MTA and the Port Authority are connected to the ATM that is every citizen's wallet. Yes, friends in Kentucky, you are funding both the MTA and the Port of Lack of Authority via the benevolent federal government whether you ever ride the subways or cross a bridge or drive through a tunnel. But apparently you're not paying enough. Otherwise, why would tolls and fares be heading up by almost 100%? Why is there "sudden" doubt that the funding to build the new WTC, fake though it be, is not there?

Not only is the Port of Lack of Authority short of money, so is the annual Tribute in Light. According to press reports, they have no money for next year's event. Maybe they should have saved all the money spent on this foolish gesture and instead spent it on building two new twin towers.

A friend of mine, Roxanne Albertoli, made a remark that I found telling and pertinent to the subject:

> What is important to me is that the lack of a proper response leaving the US population feeling almost deserving of the attack is a big part of why it hasn't been rebuilt. It is the intellectuals who've deserted the common man who are most responsible for this travesty of an un-rebuilt WTC.
>
> The not rebuilding of the WTC is a travesty in and of itself, but it's also a symptom of how self-effacing, self-sacrificing our society has become. To rebuild it is too gutsy, too self-assertive, too pro-living for those who own the parcel and what used to be the WTC.

I couldn't agree more.

How about you? Do you want two new twin World Trade Center towers and the rest of what was the grand WTC site rebuilt? Or are you content with what the powers-that-be is foisting upon us?

I hope that the essays herein help you to decide for the former instead of the latter.

Notes

1 Adapted from Kevin Traynor's skyscraper speech in *Phantom Train*, pp. 170.

2 Conversation between Gail Wynand and Dominique Francon in Ayn Rand, *The Fountainhead*. New York: Signet, 1996 (50th Anniversary Edition), p. 446.

3 Abraham Lincoln, Gettysburg Address.

4 Philip Nobel, *Sixteen Acres: Architecture and the Outrageous Struggle for the Future of Ground Zero*. New York: Metropolitan Books, 2005, p. 184.

5 The CBS/*New York Times* poll was conducted from August 25 to 29, 2002.

6 Philip Nobel, *Sixteen Acres: Architecture and the Outrageous Struggle for the Future of Ground Zero*. New York: Metropolitan Books, 2005, p. 184.

7 Did you know that Mohamed Atta was an architect and worked in urban planning?
From Wikipedia, "As one of the highest-scoring students, Atta was admitted into the very selective architecture program during his senior year." He graduated with a degree in architecture.
"Atta worked at the Urban Development Center in Cairo, where he worked on architectural, planning, and building design."
Was the destruction of the World Trade Center his greatest urban planning project?
Follow this link for more information: http://en.wikipedia.org/wiki/Mohamed_Atta

8 Steve Cuozzo, "Christie's Power Play," *New York Post*, August 11, 2011.
nypost.com/p/news/opinion/opedcolumnists/christie_power_pl ay_atWbZ9vvArztmic2ky6kqM

Authors' Biographies

In alphabetical order, here is biographical information on the essayists writing herein.

Tal Barzilai

Tal Barzilai's involvement in wanting the Twin Towers rebuilt began when he heard about them being destroyed. He was on the Throgs Neck Bridge when the attacks happened. He took this stance, because as a native of Israel, he felt that it would be wrong to accept something less when something of such importance to the world was taken away by just a few terrorists.

Although he has been active from the beginning in getting the Twin Towers rebuilt, he says his biggest moment came on the one year anniversary of 9/11 when an essay he wrote was selected for PBS's *America Rebuilds* in 2002.

Another big moment was at the Aftershock Event at Pace University. He became known as the guy whose microphone was cut off just for telling the truth about what was really happening and why rebuilding the Twin Towers should be an option.

At the ceremony held at The Winter Garden, at which Daniel Libeskind was announced the winner of the WTC design contest, he held out a copy of the official poll that said Libeskind was not a winner with the people. Then Governor George E. Pataki refused to acknowledge that the architect he was awarding was never liked at all.

Later, he did manage to meet Amanda Burden, Director of the New York City Department of City Planning, and tried to talk to her about why the Twin Towers should be rebuilt. She just kept indicating that not only did she support the official plan, but she denied that there was anything wrong with the process.

Even with what is going on, he continues to fight to have the Twin Towers rebuilt no matter what it takes.

Robert Begley

Robert Begley is a lifelong New Yorker with a profound passion for the city. He is the Founder and President of the NY Heroes Society (nyheroes.org) and Director of Marketing for

InterMarket Forecasting, Inc., a financial forecasting firm (intermarketforecasting.com). He was the producer and host of the Manhattan Cable Television program *The Voice of Reason*. He is now devoting his time to investing.

Alexander Butziger

Alexander Butziger is the author of the Kevin Traynor novels, *Torch in the Night*, *Phantom Train*, and *Mysterious Boat*. The next novel in the series, *Mystic Triangle*, deals with the history and triumph of capitalism. Currently, he is writing the most comprehensive account to date on the Bermuda Triangle phenomenon, serialized at bermudatrianglecentral.blogspot.com. He translated the forthcoming *Laughter under Tears*, Stefan Frey's biography of Ayn Rand's favorite operetta composer, Emmerich Kálmán, from German into English. Even before he ever heard of Ayn Rand, he was an advocate of reason and liberty, and an admirer of skyscrapers and other wonders of man.

The World Trade Center Twin Towers were his favorite place in New York. He has supported rebuilding them taller, stronger, and safer since September 11, 2001. He is a member of the WTCRM planning committee and of Team Twin Towers.

Edward Cline

Edward Cline is the author of the Sparrowhawk novels set in pre-Revolutionary America, and of detective and suspense novels — *First Prize*, *Presence of Mind*, *Honors Due*, *Whisper the Guns*, *We Three Kings*, *Run from Judgment*, *China Basin*, and *The Head of Athena*. He is working on *The Daedàlus Conspiracy*, his third Roaring Twenties detective novel. He has written numerous published articles, book and movie reviews, and essays for the *Colonial Williamsburg Journal*, Marine Corps League, the *Encyclopedia of Library and Information Sciences*, and McGraw-Hill's *Western Civilization*. You can find him blogging at ruleofreason.blogspot.com.

Fred Cookinham

Frederick Cookinham is a student of history who works as a legal proofreader for a Wall Street law firm half a mile from Ground Zero. He is also the owner and operator of In Depth Walking Tours (InDepthWalkingTours.com), featuring the "Ayn Rand's New York" and the "Revolutionary Manhattan" series of tours. His essay is written from the perspective of a tour guide with many years experience working for several tour operators in NYC. He provided a custom tour for attendees at the 2002 Celebrate Capitalism rally on an extremely cold day at City Hall Park. He holds a Masters degree in American History from Brooklyn College.

Margaret Donovan

Margaret Donovan was raised in a small town sandwiched between the country's original twin towers of Lexington and Concord. She and Richard Hughes started the Rebuild-The-Towers.org website in 2005 and The Twin Towers Alliance (twintowersalliance.com) in 2006. She is President of the Twin Towers Alliance Foundation, a non-profit organization with a dual mission — to promote the return of the Twin Towers to America's Skyline and to advance the practice of muscular citizenship. She believes that the struggle to rebuild the Towers is central to our nation's character and success.

Louis Epstein

Louis Epstein is the Founder and Director of the World Trade Center Restoration Movement (WTCRM). He owns and operates an ISP in Putnam County, New York. He hosts the official WTCRM website at put.com/wtc.

Stuart Mark Feldman

Stuart Mark Feldman is a sculptor currently living and working in Philadelphia, PA. He holds a Masters Degree in Art from Rowan University in New Jersey, studied at the Frudakis Academy in Philadelphia, and was an apprentice for the renowned sculptor and educator, Dr. Boris Blai. Dr. Blai, a Russian born artist, was a student of the French sculptor Auguste Rodin.

Feldman also taught for many years at the Pennsylvania Academy of the Fine Arts in Philadelphia, until he and his partners opened the Schuylkill Academy of Fine Art, in Philadelphia. He has given courses at three previous summer conferences.

He works in bronze, stone and wood, creating sculptures of the human figure that express man's most noble and inspiring qualities. He has created a number of commissioned sculptures including a fountain sculpture consisting of eight, life-size bronze figures for Reservoir Park in Harrisburg, PA.

His sculptures are in numerous private collections, and he is available for commissions, both public and private. Contact Feldman directly at his home at 610-931-2169 or via email at aisapa@verizon.net.

Cherie L. Fernandez

Cherie L. Fernandez lives in Linden, NJ. She has always been an admirer of the Twin Towers and ultra tall buildings in general. The events of 9/11 have permanently changed her life. She went from being merely a railroad signal maintainer, artificial intelligence/robotics hobbyist and recreational science fiction writer to a civil/structural engineering student and founder of a startup artificial intelligence/building automation firm Project AVATAR. Among the groups she has contributed to in her new specialties are the Council on Tall Buildings and Urban Habitat, the Continental Automated Buildings Association, Team Twin Towers, the Skyscraper Museum and the World Trade Center Restoration Movement. She is known on the web as Rayden Tron.

Joy Goldberg

Joy Goldberg has been a resident of Brooklyn since 1992. She is employed by the US Postal Service as a station clerk and is a columnist for their union newspaper, *The Brooklyn Bridge*. In her spare time, she has written three screenplays and two books and she is halfway through a new novel. The first book is a collection of short stories entitled: *Songs to New York*, in which she has not so much sought to capture in black and white the love she holds for the city; rather, that it is the city who holds her captive in her grand, exhilarating manner.

A staunch advocate for rebuilding the Twin Towers and raising up an honorable, aesthetic memorial befitting the World Trade Center site, she is a member of the Twin Towers Alliance and the World Trade Center Restoration Movement and belongs to all people everywhere who seek the same.

Jonathan Hakala

Jonathan Hakala served as Chair and Chief Executive Officer of Threshold Capital Management, which had its offices on the seventy-seventh floor of One World Trade Center.

Richard Hughes

Richard Hughes was born in Philadelphia, but moved to New York City after college. The Twin Towers had been completed, but were not yet fully occupied. He and a friend visited the Towers repeatedly in those days and would sneak up to an unoccupied floor near the top of one of the Towers and look down on the city and the harbor. They would have the whole floor to themselves and would walk the perimeter, entranced. He never got over the magic of those visits. The Towers were always New York to him. He is a cofounder of Rebuild-the-Towers.org and The Twin Towers Alliance (twintowersalliance.com).

Deroy Murdock

New York commentator Deroy Murdock is a syndicated columnist with the Scripps Howard News Service and a Senior Fellow with the Atlas Economic Research Foundation. He has written and spoken extensively on September 11, its aftermath, and the ongoing effort to restore the Twin Towers to their former glory. Read his articles in your local newspaper and also at NationalReview.com.

Robert Murphy

Robert Murphy resides in Richmond, VA. He is the web master of 4commonsense.net and publishes *This Week on the Web*, a free weekly email newsletter with links to news and commentary. His hobbies include writing about current events as well as working in live theater as an actor and technician. In his spare time, he enjoys listening to eighties music and playing with his Golden Retriever, Harker.

Andrew Oliff

Dr. Andrew Oliff is a surgical pathologist with specialty training in brain and nervous system diseases who practices in Brooklyn, New York. A portion of his fellowship training was spent in the NYC Medical Examiner's office while the remains of the victims of 9/11 were being identified. While in college, he minored in urban studies and maintains a strong interest in the history and development of American cities, as well as an enthusiasm for American history in general. He is a member of the College of American Pathologists and is a former member of the WTCRM planning committee.

Ilene Skeen

Ilene Skeen is the founder and CEO of the international art calendar contest, Nudes-of-the-Month, online since 2006. Hundreds of artists participate worldwide. After "retiring" from a career of business systems design, she obtained a graduate degree in anthropology and started the contest website as her "retirement project."

She has an undergraduate degree in art and an MBA in management and operations research. She is a resident artist and former board member of the Salmagundi Club of New York, founded in 1871 as "A Center for American Art."

Her principal oeuvre had been the "Bare Brush" series of watercolor sketches. Currently, her painting series has expanded to include acrylics. She lives "in the shadow of the Empire State Building." Visit her website at Barebrush.com.

Gary Taustine

Gary Taustine is a software developer, writer and photographer who lives in Manhattan. He was the official photographer for all of the WTCRM rallies.

Jennifer Thorpe-Moscon

Jennifer Thorpe-Moscon, Ph.D., is a lifelong resident of New York City. She was born in Brooklyn and attended Stuyvesant High School, located four blocks from the Twin Towers, as well as Columbia University for her undergraduate education and New York University for her graduate education. She is a former member of the WTCRM planning committee and former President and cofounder of Students United for America, a Columbia University campus organization dedicated to supporting the fight against terrorism. Currently she is Vice-President of Marketing and Research at Body Care by Emylee.

Joe Wright

Joe Wright designs, sells, installs and maintains voice processing systems, from telephones to very sophisticated IVR (Interactive Voice Response) systems. He had three customers in 1 WTC, including the Port Authority of NY and NJ who used one of his IVR systems. That system provided bridge and tunnel information via telephone to thousands of drivers heading into and out from the City. All systems were destroyed on 9/11.

This was not his first encounter with terrorism at the WTC. He was almost in 1 WTC when it was bombed in 1993. He was on his way to a meeting with Port Authority customer service representatives to discuss a new version of the IVR and was 15 minutes late. Had he been on time, he would have suffered the effects of that attack.

He is also a telecommunications and reservations systems consultant specializing in airlines. He was behind the startup of New York Air and Virgin Atlantic Airways and was involved, to one degree or another, with almost all airlines that arose from deregulation back in the 1980s. His career in the airline industry began at Icelandic Airlines in 1969 where he was eventually

Director of Telecommunications and Assistant Manager Reservations for North America.

So, it was not surprising that his first reaction to hearing on the radio that a plane had flown into the WTC was, "That's not an accident."

He has written widely on the subject of individual rights, particularly property rights, the draft, antitrust and eminent domain. He has spoken on the steps of City Hall in NYC and before the City Council, development authorities and community groups fighting against eminent domain.

As a member of the planning committee of the WTCRM (World Trade Center Restoration Movement) he was the organizer of and the public relations manager for rallies sponsored by the WTCRM.

The first ever Celebrate Capitalism (aka Walk for Capitalism) rally held in NYC was coordinated by him on behalf of Prodos.com.

You'll find him blogging on *Crain's New York Business*, NY1 and *The Washington Post*.

In addition to editing this book, he is writing a book on the history of his father and mother's traveling tent show, aka road show, and drive-in theater in Western Kentucky.

Check out some of his writings at TheNewIntellectual.com.

Resources for Further Exploration

Ken Gardner / Make NY NY Again

http://www.triroc.com/wtc/

Team Twin Towers

http://teamtwintowers.org/

Twin Towers Alliance

http://www.twintowersalliance.com/

World Trade Center Restoration Movement

http://www.put.com/wtc/

The End of the Essays

Will the Twin Towers return?